CAMBRIDGE TE
HISTORY OF P

CW00969675

SEXTUS EI
Against the Logicians

CAMBRIDGE TEXTS IN THE HISTORY OF PHILOSOPHY

Series editors

KARL AMERIKS
Professor of Philosophy at the University of Notre Dame

DESMOND M. CLARKE
Professor of Philosophy at University College Cork

The main objective of Cambridge Texts in the History of Philosophy is to expand the range, variety and quality of texts in the history of philosophy which are available in English. The series includes texts by familiar names (such as Descartes and Kant) and also by less well-known authors. Wherever possible, texts are published in complete and unabridged form, and translations are specially commissioned for the series. Each volume contains a critical introduction together with a guide to further reading and any necessary glossaries and textual apparatus. The volumes are designed for student use at undergraduate and postgraduate level and will be of interest not only to students of philosophy, but also to a wider audience of readers in the history of science, the history of theology and the history of ideas.

For a list of titles published in the series, please see end of book.

SEXTUS EMPIRICUS

Against the Logicians

TRANSLATED AND EDITED BY

RICHARD BETT

Johns Hopkins University

CAMBRIDGE
UNIVERSITY PRESS

CAMBRIDGE
UNIVERSITY PRESS

University Printing House, Cambridge CB2 8BS, United Kingdom

Cambridge University Press is part of the University of Cambridge.

It furthers the University's mission by disseminating knowledge in the pursuit of
education, learning and research at the highest international levels of excellence.

www.cambridge.org
Information on this title: www.cambridge.org/9780521531955

First published 2005

A catalogue record for this publication is available from the British Library

ISBN 978-0-521-82497-2 Hardback
ISBN 978-0-521-53195-5 Paperback

Contents

Acknowledgments

Completion of this volume was greatly facilitated by a semester of paid leave granted me in the spring of 2004; I thank the Philosophy Department, as well as the School of Arts and Sciences, of Johns Hopkins University for making this possible. I also thank the series editor, Desmond Clarke, for valuable comments on a draft of the translation. Finally, I thank Paul Woodruff for forcefully reminding me of the true meaning of *aporia*.

Abbreviations

DK   H. Diels and W. Kranz, *Die Fragmente der Vorsokratiker* (Berlin: Weidmann, 1951)

LS   A. Long and D. Sedley, *The Hellenistic Philosophers* (Cambridge: Cambridge University Press, 1987)

M   Sextus Empiricus, *Adversus Mathematicos* (see Introduction, pp. IX–XXX)

PH   Sextus Empiricus, *Outlines of Pyrrhonism*

SVF   H. von Arnim, *Stoicorum Veterum Fragmenta* (Leipzig: Teubner, 1903–1905)

Introduction

Sextus' life and works

The two books *Against the Logicians* are part of a larger work by Sextus Empiricus, the best known ancient Greek skeptic and the only one from whom we possess complete texts, as opposed to fragments or second-hand summaries. About Sextus Empiricus himself we know virtually nothing. He identifies himself as a member of the Pyrrhonist skeptical tradition, on which more in the next section. He occasionally refers to himself in the first person as a medical practitioner (*PH* 2.238, *M* 1.260, cf. *M* 11.47). His title would suggest that he was a member of the Empiricist school of medicine. This is confirmed by Diogenes Laertius (9.116), who refers to him as "Sextus the Empiricist"; it would anyway not be surprising, given that we know the names of several other Pyrrhonists who were also Empiricists. Sextus at one point addresses the question whether medical Empiricism is the same as Pyrrhonist skepticism (*PH* 1.236–241), and unexpectedly replies that another school, the Methodist school, has closer affinities with skepticism. However, it is possible to read this passage as expressing suspicion towards a certain specific form of Empiricism, rather than towards the school as a whole.[1]

Such indications as there are concerning where Sextus was born, or where he worked in his maturity, are too slender to bear any significant weight. The evidence suggests that he lived in the second century CE, but

---

[1] On the major approaches to medicine in later antiquity see Galen, *On the Sects for Beginners*, translated in Galen, *Three Treatises on the Nature of Science*, tr. R. Walzer and M. Frede (Hackett Publishing, 1985), with Frede's introduction.

it is not clear that we can fix his dates with any more precision than that.[2] In any case he appears to be curiously isolated from the philosophical currents of his own day. In the second century there were flourishing Aristotelian and Platonist movements, yet Sextus shows no awareness of them whatever; his focus is invariably on the Hellenistic period (that is, roughly, the last three centuries BCE) and earlier. His immediate influence appears to have been virtually non-existent; we hear of a student of his, Saturninus, but for the rest of antiquity interest in skepticism seems to have been extremely limited. It is a very different story when Sextus' works were rediscovered in the early modern period; and this belated influence makes his writings of interest to students not only of ancient but also of modern philosophy.

Sextus' voluminous surviving oeuvre comprises three distinct works. The best known is *Outlines of Pyrrhonism* (commonly referred to by *PH*, the abbreviated form of the title in Greek), which survives complete in three books. Of these the first is a general summary of the Pyrrhonist outlook, and the other two deal with the theories of non-skeptical philosophers in each of the three standardly recognized areas of philosophy in the post-Aristotelian period, namely logic, physics, and ethics; the discussion of logic occupies the whole of Book 2, while Book 3 is shared between physics and ethics.[3] Another work, *Against the Learned* (*Pros Mathēmatikous* – also referred to by the Latinized title *Adversus Mathematicos*, or by the abbreviation *M*), is complete in six books, and is quite different in subject-matter. It addresses a variety of specialized sciences (one per book); in order, the subjects are grammar, rhetoric, geometry, arithmetic, astrology, and musical theory.[4] This work

---

[2] On the paucity of our evidence for Sextus' life, see D. K. House, "The Life of Sextus Empiricus," *Classical Quarterly* 30 (1980), 227–238.

[3] This division of philosophy into three major fields, and the relations thought to obtain between them, are discussed in (among other places) the opening pages of *Against the Logicians*, Bk. 1.

[4] It will be noticed that this list corresponds with the seven "liberal arts" that made up the standard medieval curriculum, with just two exceptions. First, Sextus explicitly excludes astronomy and concentrates solely on astrology (5.1–2). Second, and more importantly for our purposes, the list omits logic, which in the medieval period belonged with grammar and rhetoric to form the *trivium* (the other four being the *quadrivium*). Since logic is included in both of Sextus' other works, it would have been superfluous to address it here. But given the place of logic in the threefold division of philosophy just mentioned, the list of "liberal arts" may in any case not yet have taken its eventual medieval form. Sextus suggests (1.7) that his list of six subjects was standard in his day, but he says nothing about logic belonging on the list as well. The matter is further complicated by the fact that logic itself was conceived, at least in some quarters, as including grammar and rhetoric; see pp. xv–xvi below.

is of interest for many reasons, but of only marginal relevance to this volume.

It is the third work to which the books translated in this volume belonged. Surviving from this work, in addition to the two books *Against the Logicians* (and in this order), are two books *Against the Physicists* and one book *Against the Ethicists*.[5] But it is all but certain that there was originally more. The final sentence of *Against the Ethicists* clearly signals that the entire work has come to an end. But the opening sentence of *Against the Logicians* refers back to a just-completed general treatment of Pyrrhonism. This was long thought to be a reference to *PH*. But that cannot be correct, since *PH* is *not*, as a whole, a general treatment of Pyrrhonism; the reference must rather be to a lost portion that discussed Pyrrhonism in general terms, as does Book 1 of *PH*. It appears, then, that this work as a whole covered the same broad subjects, in the same order, as *PH*, but at considerably greater length. Sextus himself calls this entire work *Skeptical Treatises* (*Skeptika Hupomnēmata*); he makes several references, using this title, to what are clearly passages from *Against the Logicians* and *Against the Physicists* (*M* 1.29 [26], 2.106, 6.52). That this is not the title by which the work is now generally known is due to an egregious error committed at some point in the manuscript tradition. The manuscripts represent the five surviving books as a continuation of the six books of *M*; as a result, *Against the Logicians*, *Against the Physicists*, and *Against the Ethicists* are generally referred to collectively as *M* 7–11.[6] There is reason to believe that the complete work was ten books long – that is, that the lost general portion occupied five books.[7] In the manuscripts, the two books of *Against the Physicists* and the single book *Against the Ethicists* are labeled (either at the beginning or the end) as the eighth, ninth, and tenth books respectively of Sextus' *Skeptika*, or of his *Hupomnēmata*, both

---

[5] These titles are largely an artifice of modern editors. In the manuscripts the first book of *Against the Logicians* opens with the heading "The first of Sextus' two books against the logicians," but none of the other books has any analogous heading. (On what appears in the manuscripts before or after the other books, more in a moment.) Sextus does, however, regularly refer in the text to his arguments against the logicians, the physicists, or the ethicists. It is not at all clear that *he* means these words as titles, as opposed to descriptions; but they clearly function well as titles, and are the names by which the respective portions of the work are generally known today.

[6] I shall follow this conventional but misleading terminology in the rare cases where I cite passages from *Against the Physicists* and *Against the Ethicists* (so, *M* 9–10 for the former and *M* 11 for the latter). For *Against the Logicians* I shall simply refer to the two books by the numbers 1 and 2.

[7] This was first spotted by J. Blomqvist, "Die Skeptika des Sextus Empiricus," *Grazer Beiträge* 2 (1974), 7–14.

clearly abbreviations of *Skeptika Hupomnēmata*; and Diogenes Laertius (9.116) refers approvingly to a ten-book work of Sextus entitled *Skeptika*, which is presumably the same work. If this is not all the product of some other, now inexplicable, error, the entire original work must have been very extensive indeed. Even in its current, incomplete form, it is roughly twice as long as either of the other two complete works.

Ancient Greek skepticism before Sextus

Contemporary scholarship recognizes two traditions of Greek skepticism, Academic and Pyrrhonist. It was only the Pyrrhonists who actually called themselves skeptics. But already in antiquity the two traditions were widely seen as having certain crucial features in common, so that the term "skepticism" is readily applied to the Academics as well. The word *skeptikos* literally means "inquirer." As Sextus explains it at the beginning of *PH* 1, the skeptic is someone who is still searching for the truth, as opposed to believing either that he has found it or that it is undiscoverable. Sextus regularly refers to members of the first non-skeptical group as dogmatists; by analogy, members of the second group are today sometimes called negative dogmatists. It is important to note, then, that skepticism as understood in the ancient Greek world did not consist in a denial of the possibility of knowledge (or, for that matter, a denial of anything else). In modern philosophy this is precisely what skepticism has generally been taken to be; but from the ancient skeptical perspective this position is just as much anathema as are dogmatic positions that claim to be in possession of the truth. The skeptic's attitude is rather one of open-mindedness, of not thinking that one has discovered the truth, but not ruling out the possibility of its discovery either; the skeptic neither affirms nor denies, but suspends judgment. Suspension of judgment (*epochē*) is, then, a key term in the self-description of both the Academic and Pyrrhonist skeptical traditions.

Pyrrhonism takes its name from Pyrrho of Elis, a little-known figure from the late fourth and early third centuries BCE. Pyrrho attracted an immediate following, notably including his biographer Timon of Phlius, who is undoubtedly the most important source of our meager evidence about him. But it looks as if this early Pyrrhonism died out after a generation or two. Meanwhile, in the early to mid-third century the Academy, the school founded by Plato, was taken in a skeptical direction – a direction apparently encouraged by elements in Plato's portrait of Socrates – under the leadership of Arcesilaus. The skeptical Academy persisted until the early first century BCE, when the skepticism softened and the school itself fragmented. But around the same time, in part as a reaction against the softening of the Academy's skepticism, a new skeptical movement, claiming inspiration from Pyrrho, was started by another little-known figure, Aenesidemus of Cnossos, himself apparently an Academic at first. It is this revived Pyrrhonist movement to which Sextus later belonged. We know the names of several other Pyrrhonists, but virtually nothing about their thought.

I spoke of suspension of judgment as the hallmark of ancient Greek skepticism, both Academic and Pyrrhonist. But it should not be thought that skepticism in the period was entirely uniform, either between the two traditions or within each of them. The most obvious difference between the two traditions is that the Pyrrhonists consider suspension of judgment to have a very significant practical effect. According to them, suspension of judgment frees one from the tremendous turmoil, both intellectual and emotional, that is associated with the holding of definite beliefs about how things really are. The result of suspension of judgment is therefore *ataraxia*, freedom from worry. This theme does not appear in *Against the Logicians*; it is concerned with the marshaling of arguments designed to generate suspension of judgment, not with the further outcome for someone in that condition. However, *ataraxia* does receive considerable attention in *PH*, and also in *Against the Ethicists*. The Academic skeptics, on the other hand, give no indication of holding that suspension of judgment has any particular practical benefit. Both Arcesilaus and Carneades, his greatest successor, took pains to show that choice and action were *possible* in the absence of definite beliefs; a passage from Book I of *Against the Logicians* (150–189) is our most substantial evidence of this. But there is no suggestion that one is *better off* withdrawing from definite beliefs, other than in terms of intellectual respectability.

Quite apart from this major difference, Sextus does not consider the Academics to be genuine skeptics. That is, he does not consider the position they have adopted to be genuine suspension of judgment. This could perhaps be gathered from the passage of *Against the Logicians* just referred to. Arcesilaus and Carneades are examined in the course of Sextus' review of thinkers who accepted the existence of a criterion of truth – a central tenet in any dogmatist philosophy. Now, this may seem to be unfair of

Sextus. For the criteria that he attributes to Arcesilaus and Carneades are criteria to be used in practical decisions; yet he himself has earlier distinguished a criterion of truth (on the existence of which he will suspend judgment) from a criterion of action, which even the skeptic inevitably employs (1.29–30). However, it is clear from a passage of *PH* 1, where Sextus emphasizes the distinction between Pyrrhonism and Academic thinking, that he takes the *specific character* of the Academics' practical criteria, as well as other features of their thought, to commit them to dogmatism, both positive and negative (*PH* 1.226–234). He allows that the Academics (especially Arcesilaus) say many things that sound like Pyrrhonism. But in their mouths, unlike those of the Pyrrhonists, these things are in his view delivered in the guise of definite beliefs, and therefore disqualify them from the title of skeptics. It is open to serious question whether Sextus is right about this – which is why the notion of Academic skepticism can be upheld in modern scholarship. But the fact remains that Sextus does not regard Arcesilaus and Carneades as kindred spirits; for him, Pyrrhonism is something quite different, and not only because of the place it assigns to *ataraxia*.

Ataraxia as the ultimate product of one's intellectual activity appears to be a constant in the history of Pyrrhonism, from Pyrrho himself through Aenesidemus to Sextus. But it is by no means so clear that the precise nature of that intellectual activity, or of the suspension of judgment that results from it, was the same at every stage of the tradition. It is questionable whether Pyrrho practiced any full-scale suspension of judgment at all. While he is reported as recommending that we not trust our sensations and opinions as guides to the nature of things, the basis for that recommendation appears to be either a metaphysical thesis that things are inherently indefinite (which would make him a dogmatist) or an epistemological thesis that the nature of things is unknowable (which would make him a negative dogmatist).[8] Certainly Sextus does not appeal to Pyrrho's thought in any detail; he simply says that Pyrrho seems to have been closer to skepticism than any of his predecessors (*PH* 1.7). Indeed, he rarely even mentions him (never, in *Against the Logicians*). Aenesidemus is reported as claiming to "philosophize in the manner of Pyrrho" (Photius, *Bibl.* 169b26–27 = LS 71C3), but this too can be understood as implying

[8] For a summary of these two possible interpretations of Pyrrho's thought, see my "Pyrrho," *Stanford Encyclopedia of Philosophy*, http://plato.stanford.edu/entries/pyrrho/. I have argued for the metaphysical reading in *Pyrrho, his Antecedents, and his Legacy* (Oxford University Press, 2000).

a general similarity of approach rather than a detailed correspondence of doctrine. So Pyrrho may well have served more as an inspiring prototype than as a source of specific arguments or ideas. Uniquely in Greek philosophy (before the later Pyrrhonists), he claimed to have arrived at tranquillity by way of a certain kind of mistrust or withdrawal of belief – rather than by gaining an understanding of the detailed workings of the universe; this may have been enough to make Aenesidemus adopt him as a kind of founding father.

Leaving aside Pyrrho himself, it also appears that the Pyrrhonism of Aenesidemus was in important respects different from the version to be found in most of Sextus, including *Against the Logicians*. But since this difference is not unconnected with the way we read *Against the Logicians* itself, it will be convenient to touch on it later (see pp. xix–xxiv).

The general character of *Against the Logicians*

The status of logic as one of the three major parts of philosophy has already been mentioned. But it is important to note that logic, in this context, covers considerably more than what we would normally understand by this term. The Greek word *logos* can mean both "speech" and "reason" (among other things), and the scope of logic, as conceived in the Hellenistic period, reflects this duality. For the Stoics, whose philosophical taxonomy was by far the most complete and systematic of any at the time, logic included rhetoric and the study of language, as well as the study of the means for determining what is true and what is false (and what is neither). And under the latter heading came not only the study of the components, structure, and validity of arguments – that is, material that we would call logic – but also the study of whether and how we can tell the way the things really are – in other words, material that for us would fall under epistemology.[9] The Epicureans rejected many of these topics as useless, including the study of argument forms for its own sake, and this led some to claim that they rejected logic itself. But they were certainly interested in methods for determining what is true, and this, as both Sextus (*Against the Logicians* 1.22, cf. 14–15) and Seneca (*Letter* 89.11) point out, means that

---

[9] There appears to have been some dispute among the Stoics about how precisely these various sub-fields were to be classified (Diogenes Laertius 7.41–42). But it is clear that, wherever exactly they were placed in the scheme, they all belonged to logic.

they did in fact make contributions to logic as understood in antiquity, whatever label they or others might give to it.

Sextus' *Against the Logicians* does not cover all the areas included in the Stoics' conception of logic. The more purely linguistic aspects of the subject, as they conceived it, are addressed in *Against the Grammarians* and *Against the Rhetoricians* (*M* 1–2).[10] But *Against the Logicians* certainly discusses epistemological matters in addition to – in fact, far more than – logical ones in our narrower sense. The whole of the first book is occupied with the question whether there is a criterion of truth. The second book then tackles the topics of truth itself, sign, and demonstration.[11] With the partial exception of truth, all of these topics have to do with methods for settling what is the case. In the second book there is a fair amount of discussion of logical matters, in our sense, along the way; but much, if not most, of the time this is ancillary to the broadly epistemological themes that constitute the basic outline. Both sign and demonstration, for example, are defined in terms that require reference to logical notions such as premises, consequences, and conditionals (2.244–256, 300–315); but both of them are means for discovering truths about unobservable things, and Sextus' overriding question is whether *there are* any reliable means for doing this. The first book, by contrast, contains virtually no discussion of what we would call logic. This is because Sextus (most of the time, at any rate)[12] understands a criterion of truth as a means for grasping immediately observable truths, rather than for inferring to unobservable ones; see 1.25 for the initial distinction in these terms between criteria on the one hand, and signs and demonstrations on the other. Hence in the discussion of the criterion, questions about the reliability of inferences, or more generally about the logical relations between distinct propositions in an argument, remain in the background.

---

[10] This may reflect the influence of competing curricula from different periods and sources; cf. n. 4.

[11] For a detailed summary of the contents of the work, see "Outline of argument."

[12] But not always. Most egregiously, 1.33 introduces a notion of criterion as a means of apprehending *unclear* (i.e., *not* immediately observable) objects. It is clear that there were competing conceptions of what a criterion of truth was supposed to be or to do; see G. Striker, "Κριτήριον τῆς Ἀληθείας" and "The Problem of the Criterion," both in G. Striker, *Essays in Hellenistic Epistemology and Ethics* (Cambridge University Press, 1996 – originally published 1974 and 1990 respectively). It is also clear that Sextus does not fully succeed in keeping these competing conceptions disentangled; see J. Brunschwig, "Sextus Empiricus on the *Kritērion*: The Skeptic as Conceptual Legatee," in J. Brunschwig, *Papers in Hellenistic Philosophy* (Cambridge University Press, 1994 – originally published 1988).

Described in outline, Sextus' method is simply to subject to scrutiny the views of the dogmatists in these areas. This means that, in addition to his own criticisms and counter-arguments, *Against the Logicians* (like most of Sextus' works) contains a considerable amount of summary of other people's views. The most extensive case of this is the long historical survey that makes up roughly the first half of the discussion of the criterion of truth (1.46–260). Sextus describes all the earlier views that might be thought to bear on this subject (even though the Hellenistic *term* "criterion of truth" postdates most of the thinkers in question). As a result, this passage is a mine of information about ideas that in many cases are otherwise poorly recorded. But there are numerous other passages of the same kind throughout both books. Outside the first half of Book 1, it is the Stoics, always for Sextus the preeminent dogmatists, whose views receive the most scrutiny, and therefore the most summary. This is particularly true on technical logical matters, where the Stoics are almost the only school represented; the most obvious exception is the views on the truth-conditions for conditionals held by Philo and Diodorus (2.113–117, cf. 265) – but even these are closely associated with the Stoics, since the founder of Stoicism, Zeno of Citium, studied logic with them (Diogenes Laertius 7.16, 25). It is striking that Aristotle and the Peripatetics, whose formal logic was the main rival to that of the Stoics (and was far more influential beyond antiquity), are never mentioned in this context in *Against the Logicians*. Nor, for that matter, does Aristotle's theory of demonstration, elaborated in the *Posterior Analytics*, receive any attention in the section of Book 2 devoted to that subject. But these are just extreme cases of a general phenomenon – namely, Sextus' comparative lack of interest in Aristotle's philosophy and his heavy concentration on Stoicism. Again, one fortunate by-product of this preference is that Sextus supplies many details about Stoic philosophy that we would not otherwise have.

A cursory reading of *Against the Logicians* might leave one with the impression that Sextus' goal is to show that the dogmatists are *wrong* about the issues addressed: for example, that there is *no such thing* as a criterion of truth. But this would be a mistake. It is true that a great deal of the argumentation takes the form of undermining the dogmatists' pretensions to knowing the answers in these areas. But Sextus several times takes the trouble to make clear that his aim is something other than this might suggest (1.443, 2.2, 159–160, 298, 476–477). In keeping with what was explained in the previous section, he intends to bring us to a position of suspension of judgment on the topics in question, such as whether or not there is a criterion of truth. This is to be accomplished by juxtaposing the positive arguments of the dogmatists with the critical arguments supplied by himself, resulting in a situation of "equal strength" (*isostheneia*) between the opposing arguments. "Equal strength" is best understood as a psychological notion; it is not that both or all of the opposing positions are rationally justified to an equal degree (which would require endorsement of theoretical notions that would themselves be objectionably dogmatic), but simply that one is supposed to find them equally persuasive – in which case, according to Sextus, suspension of judgment inevitably results. Sextus does not, then, *identify* with the critical arguments, even though we may presume them to have been largely devised by the skeptics; they are offered as a counter-weight to the dogmatists' arguments, the eventual outcome being that one identifies with *no* particular set of arguments.[13]

This strategy is a further reason, besides clarification of what is to be attacked, for the lengthy summaries of dogmatic views. As Sextus says (2.476–477, cf. 160), it actually suits his purpose for the dogmatists' arguments to be presented as strong ones – strong enough, that is, to balance his own counter-arguments, but no stronger; equally, then, it suits his purpose to present these arguments fully and sympathetically. Another, similar argumentative purpose may perhaps be discerned in the way he structures the opening review of positions on the criterion of truth; this begins by listing those he takes to have denied the existence of such a criterion, and continues with the believers in a criterion – who in turn differ among themselves in significant ways. The effect is to balance a great many dogmatic arguments against each other; from a skeptic's perspective this is ideal, since, if the arguments are of comparable strength, it may be calculated to generate suspension of judgment without the skeptic himself having to lift a finger. Sextus does not actually say that this is what he is doing, but his mention, at the close of this section, of having just laid out the "disagreement" about the criterion (1.261) may suggest such an agenda. Regardless of Sextus' own purposes, it is plausible that

---

[13] The care and forethought with which Sextus constructs these juxtapositions of arguments may make one question his self-description as *skeptikos*. Both in *Against the Logicians* and elsewhere, such argumentative constructions are not obviously consistent with the picture of an open-minded inquirer still looking for the truth. They seem, rather, to be the product of someone who has already decided on *ataraxia* as the goal and suspension of judgment as the necessary means to it, and who is therefore focused on finding the most effective route to suspension of judgment. On the skeptic's goal, see *PH* 1.25–30.

this was the intention of whoever originally compiled the material in this way.

Earlier sources and an earlier phase of Pyrrhonism

The last comment raises the question of Sextus' relation to the Pyrrhonist tradition that preceded him. It has long been understood that Sextus draws to a very considerable extent on earlier sources in the Pyrrhonist tradition and probably elsewhere. As noted earlier, there are no other Pyrrhonists besides Sextus whose work has survived intact. But there are correspondences between passages of Sextus and passages of Diogenes Laertius' summary of Pyrrhonism (9.74–108) that are too close for coincidence; they extend beyond similarities of subject-matter to parallels in argumentative structure, and even detailed correspondences in vocabulary and sentence-structure. They also occur at numerous different places in Sextus' work, as opposed to being confined to a single book. (There are occasional parallels between Sextus and other authors as well, but I shall ignore these; the parallels with Diogenes are by far the most wide-ranging.) Since Diogenes mentions Sextus, and also Sextus' pupil Saturninus (of whom nothing more is known), he is clearly the later of the two, and one might suppose that he is simply copying his material from Sextus. But there are also sufficiently many differences between the two authors to make this highly unlikely. In addition to some stylistic differences, Diogenes very often treats material in a different order from Sextus, and some of his material does not correspond to anything in Sextus (but this is interspersed with material that does). Diogenes is quite explicit about using earlier sources, and he could hardly have made up this non-corresponding material. The conclusion therefore seems inevitable that Sextus and Diogenes are both drawing on the same earlier (but now lost) source or sources, either directly or at one or more removes.[14]

There is room for debate as to how much Sextus modified the material that he took from these unknown predecessors. Many scholars have seen him, like Diogenes, as little more than a copyist of previous material. But this seems unduly patronising. For one thing, as noted earlier, *Against the Logicians*, *Against the Physicists*, and *Against the Ethicists* cover roughly

---

[14] For further discussion of this topic, see J. Barnes, "Diogenes Laertius IX 61–116: The Philosophy of Pyrrhonism," *Aufstieg und Niedergang der Römischen Welt* II.36.6 (1992), 4241–4301.

the same ground as *PH* 2–3. Here again there are a great many parallel passages in the two works, and in some of these cases, too, there is a very close similarity of thought and language. Clearly one of these works is a revised version of the other; either Sextus wrote *PH* first and then expanded it into the work of which *M* 7–11 is the surviving portion, or he wrote the latter work first and then condensed it into *PH*. I shall return in the next section to the question of which work came first. But either way, it must be allowed that Sextus shows some initiative in the way he organizes and reworks his material. For despite the many close parallels, there are also significant differences; entire topics are treated in one work and ignored in the other, and the language and approach do sometimes differ considerably. Besides, it is fair to say that a consistent authorial personality comes through in Sextus' works; however little we know of Sextus the man, his writing has a characteristic voice (the precise tone of which I will leave it to readers to discover for themselves). His extensive use of preexisting material is not to be doubted. However, it looks as if he does not just passively appropriate this material, but molds it into a product that is distinctively his own.

One likely source of material for Sextus, either directly or indirectly, is Aenesidemus. We know from Sextus himself and from others that Aenesidemus wrote a work in eight books called *Pyrrhonist Discourses* (*Purrōneioi Logoi*); given Aenesidemus' position as the originator of the later Pyrrhonist tradition, we may plausibly assume that this work was treated as seminal by at least some in that tradition. In *Against the Logicians* (1.345) Sextus refers in passing to the Ten Modes, one of the several sets of standardized forms of skeptical argumentation (summarized in *PH* 1), as the Ten Modes of Aenesidemus. But it would hardly be surprising if much more of what Sextus borrows from the tradition derived ultimately from Aenesidemus, even though he mentions him only relatively infrequently. But if this is so, then Sextus is apparently using material that originally belonged to a version of Pyrrhonism somewhat different from the version his own works mostly espouse. For there is good reason to believe that, at some point between Aenesidemus and Sextus, Pyrrhonism underwent a change.

For Sextus, as we have seen, suspension of judgment is reached by the juxtaposition of opposing arguments of "equal strength," so that one withdraws assent from either (or any) of these arguments. The dogmatists are thereby exposed as misguided for trusting in the truth of their arguments. But the goal is not to show that the items in which they believe, such as criteria of truth, signs, and demonstrations, do not exist, or that their beliefs about the nature of these items are false; rather, it is to generate equally powerful arguments on either side, thus relieving one of the burden of beliefs on these topics either way.[15] But there is evidence of an earlier form of Pyrrhonism, associated with Aenesidemus, in which endorsement of conclusions to the effect that certain things (in which the dogmatists believe) do not exist was quite acceptable skeptical procedure.

Our most substantial piece of evidence on Aenesidemus' thought is a summary of his *Pyrrhonist Discourses* by Photius, the ninth-century patriarch of Constantinople (*Bibl.* 169b18–170b35 = LS 71C + 72L). It appears that the first book expounded the Pyrrhonist outlook in general terms. The other seven books then dealt with particular topics addressed by the dogmatists; Photius only gives us a sentence about each, but his report is nonetheless striking. Among the topics included was that of signs, and on this topic Photius tells us, "In the fourth book he asserts that signs (in the sense that we call things that are clear signs of things that are unclear) do not exist at all, and that those who think they do exist are deceived by a vain attraction" (170b12–14). Contrary to Sextus' careful preface to his arguments against the sign (2.159–161), where he makes clear that these arguments are not to be endorsed but to be balanced against the dogmatists' positive arguments, Aenesidemus apparently did endorse such arguments, and in no uncertain terms. Photius reports the same kind of conclusion, delivered with similar degrees of outspokenness, in the case of Aenesidemus' discussions of causes (170b17–22) and of the ethical end (170b30–35).

Photius might, of course, be accused of misunderstanding Aenesidemus. No doubt Aenesidemus' discussion of signs (and of the other topics) did *include* arguments against their existence. Indeed, Sextus reports an argument from Aenesidemus' fourth book, an argument to the conclusion

---

[15] There is a long-standing controversy about the *extent* of the beliefs from which Sextus means us to withdraw. Is one supposed to suspend judgment only about theoretical beliefs such as the dogmatists put forward, or is suspension of judgment meant to apply also to everyday beliefs such as anyone might hold? It is not clear that Sextus gives us an unambiguous answer to that question. But the answer clearly affects one's view of the feasibility and the attractiveness of this form of skepticism. A collection of important essays on this question is M. Burnyeat and M. Frede, eds., *The Original Skeptics: A Controversy* (Hackett Publishing, 1997). Fortunately, we need not attempt to settle the question here, since the beliefs subjected to scrutiny in *Against the Logicians* are clearly theoretical beliefs of the dogmatists. (It is a different matter when one is dealing with, say, ethical beliefs.)

that signs are not apparent things (2.215, 234). Since the very concept of a sign is of something observable that licenses an inference to something unobservable, this is essentially equivalent to concluding that signs do not exist. But Sextus has no trouble using this argument as part of a strategy of generating suspension of judgment about the existence of signs; and Aenesidemus himself, one might say, could just as well have done the same thing. The impression Photius gives of vigorous denial might be explained as simply the product of an unsympathetic reading; it is clear from the largely dismissive criticisms following his summary (170b36–171a4) that he does not take Aenesidemus particularly seriously.

But this reaction would be a mistake. For, leaving aside the question of Photius' own credibility, Photius is not the only author to describe Pyrrhonists as denying the existence of things. Diogenes Laertius' summary of Pyrrhonism also includes numerous reports of Pyrrhonists arguing to conclusions of the form "there is no such thing as X" – signs are just one example (9.96) – and also reports of Pyrrhonists "doing away with" (*anairein*) various things believed in by dogmatists, which appears to amount to the same thing. And, if Diogenes too might be impugned as a philosophically naive reporter, the same phenomenon can be observed in one book of Sextus himself, namely *Against the Ethicists*. Here Sextus argues for the conclusion that nothing is good or bad by nature. And here it is not open to us to claim that he means these arguments to function as one side of an opposition, with the dogmatists supplying the other side. Not only does he not say that this is what he is doing (as he does in *Against the Logicians*). He also tells us several times that it is the skeptic's *acceptance* of the conclusion that nothing is by nature good or bad that produces the desired state of tranquillity (*M* 11.118, 130, 140).

There was, then, a phase of Pyrrhonism – a phase that, given Photius' report, it is plausible to trace to Aenesidemus – in which arguing that the dogmatists were mistaken, and that the entities in which they believed did not exist, *without* any juxtaposition of those arguments against the dogmatists' own positive arguments, was normal and accepted Pyrrhonist procedure. This, of course, raises the question how such a procedure could be considered compatible with any form of suspension of judgment. The issue is somewhat complicated,[16] and not really germane to

---

[16] I have discussed this question, and the nature of Aenesidemus' Pyrrhonism in general, in *Pyrrho, his Antecedents, and his Legacy* (cf. n. 8), ch. 4.

our present concerns. But very briefly, one possible answer centers around a certain conception of what it is for something to be *by nature* a certain way. According to this conception, the nature of something is fixed and invariable. Hence, to take two examples already mentioned, to say that something is by nature good, or by nature a sign, is to say that it is invariably and in all circumstances good, or a sign. And to *deny* that anything is by nature good, or by nature a sign, is to deny that anything is invariably and in all circumstances good, or a sign. Now, a denial of this kind does not offer any positive characterization of the nature of anything; to say that nothing is invariably good, or invariably a sign, is not to assert that anything *is* invariably (and therefore by nature) of any particular character. And this suggests a way in which such denials could be understood as compatible with a certain form of suspension of judgment: a suspension of judgment, that is, that consisted in refusing any attempt to specify the nature of anything.[17]

But let us leave this issue aside. The important point for our purposes is simply that a version of Pyrrhonism that seems to precede Sextus himself (but that survives intact in one of his books) allowed a method of argumentation that, by Sextus' usual standards, would qualify as negative dogmatism. Now, given this state of affairs, as well as Sextus' undoubted reliance on earlier sources, it is natural to wonder whether *Against the Logicians* contains any traces of this earlier phase of Pyrrhonism. One obvious possibility is that the long stretches of argument against the dogmatists – stretches of argument that, as I said, look on superficial inspection as if Sextus intends them to show that the dogmatists are wrong – derive from this earlier phase, in which that was precisely the intention. As we saw, Sextus does explicitly appeal to Aenesidemus in one part of the discussion of signs; and the debt may well be more extensive.[18] Again, it is not that Sextus does not make clear his own intentions in employing these destructive arguments. But one may well wonder whether, had he approached these topics with a clean slate instead of adapting already

---

[17] This depends on understanding statements such as "the sign does not exist," as reported by Photius and Diogenes, as equivalent to "nothing is such as to be *by nature* a sign." *Against the Logicians* provides some evidence that, at least in the case of signs, the Pyrrhonists did conceive the matter this way; Sextus says that the indicative sign, the kind of sign that is the focus of his discussion, "is said to signify that of which it is indicative simply by means of its own nature and constitution" (2.154, cf. *PH* 2.101).

[18] He also enlists him at 2.40ff., in the discussion on truth.

existing materials, he might have structured his discussion differently, so as not to give even an impression of negative dogmatism.

Another possible indication of the same thing is Sextus' periodic use, in *Against the Logicians*, of the word *anairein*, "do away with," to describe the skeptic's activity. As we saw, this word occurs a number of times in Diogenes Laertius' summary of Pyrrhonism, where it is interchangeable with "argue for the non-existence of." For the Pyrrhonists to "do away with" things, in this sense, was normal in the earlier phase of Pyrrhonism.[19] But in *Against the Logicians* Sextus' strategy, as he several times reminds us, is different from and indeed incompatible with this. Nevertheless, in numerous places (1.299, 371, 2.1, 142, 157–158, 290, 338) he describes himself as "doing away with" certain kinds of objects posited by the dogmatists. In one place (1.26) he even uses the term "do away with" in the same context as "suspend judgment"; to "do away with" a set of objects posited by the dogmatists is, according to this passage, sufficient for putting us into a state of suspension of judgment about them. Now again, this is far from conclusive. One can perhaps understand "do away with X" as shorthand for "offer arguments against the existence of X, which will then be juxtaposed with arguments for the opposite conclusion." But even if this is correct, the possibility remains that the repeated occurrence of this word is due to Sextus' use of material that had its original home in a version of Pyrrhonism where the Pyrrhonist could quite straightforwardly, and without any resort to shorthand, claim to "do away with" the entities that he discussed. Once again, *Against the Logicians*, unlike *Against the Ethicists*, is not an *instance* of the earlier variety of Pyrrhonism.[20] But it would hardly be surprising, given Sextus' use of preexisting sources, if it contained traces of that earlier variety.

Against the Logicians compared with *PH* 2

The question of similarities and differences between *PH* 2–3 and *Against the Logicians*, *Physicists*, and *Ethicists* was introduced in the last section.

---

[19] That is (to head off a possible misunderstanding), the earlier phase of the Pyrrhonist tradition initiated by Aenesidemus. The views of Pyrrho himself have nothing to do with the issues in this section.

[20] It is a puzzle how Sextus could have thought it acceptable to place *Against the Logicians* and *Against the Ethicists*, which represent incompatible versions of Pyrrhonism, in the *same* larger work. For some speculation on this, see Introduction, sect. V of Sextus Empiricus, *Against the Ethicists*, tr. with an introduction and commentary by Richard Bett (Oxford University Press, 1997).

A comparison between *Against the Logicians* and its counterpart *PH* 2 reveals some notable differences; each contains a considerable amount of material that the other omits. The largest and most obvious portion of text in *Against the Logicians* having no parallel in *PH* 2 is the long survey of previous positions for and against the criterion of truth (1.46–260). Since *PH* is designed as an outline account, it is not surprising that Sextus would have decided not to include this material in any form in *PH* 2; although, as we saw (pp. xvii–xix), it plays a valuable role in *Against the Logicians*, it is not strictly necessary for a skeptical treatment of the criterion of truth, and is easily detachable from the rest of Sextus' account. What is more surprising is that *PH* 2, although it is less than a third the length of *Against the Logicians*, discusses a number of topics that are not explicitly dealt with at all in the longer work. After the end of the section on demonstration (134–192), which corresponds to the final portion of *Against the Logicians*, there are chapters on deduction, induction, definition, division, "division of a name into things signified" (214), whole and part, genus and species, common attributes, and sophisms, none of which has any counterpart in *Against the Logicians*. Thus, despite being much shorter, *PH* 2 is in a certain sense more comprehensive than *Against the Logicians*. And while, as we saw, *Against the Logicians* is devoted (at least if one looks at its broad structure) largely to epistemological topics, with logic in our narrower sense being treated most of the time as ancillary to these, *PH* 2 focuses explicitly on a number of subjects that are clearly (in our sense) logical in nature. There is even a hint in these chapters of some of the linguistic concerns that the Stoics also classified under logic.

This just underscores the extent to which, when it comes to the topics that both works do include, *Against the Logicians* is lengthier in its treatment than *PH* 2. The former contains numerous arguments that the latter omits, and, even where both works have versions of what is recognizably the same argument, *Against the Logicians* regularly develops the argument in a much more leisurely, and frequently more rambling, fashion. "Lengthier" in this context, therefore, does not necessarily mean "better." Indeed, there is a diffuse, everything-but-the-kitchen-sink quality to much of *Against the Logicians*, which often makes it hard to keep track of the main thread of the discussion. I have tried to compensate for this by including an outline of the argument, both as a complete whole immediately before the translation and in the form of headings within it.

It will be noticed that the outline of the second book is considerably longer than that of the first, even though the two books themselves are not very different in length; this is because the general structure, and the place of each passage within it, takes even more effort to grasp in the second book than in the first.

So the greater extent of *Against the Logicians* compared with *PH* 2 does not obviously work to its advantage. *PH* 2 is more concise and therefore easier to follow, and this is generally not at the expense of any cogency in argument – often the reverse. In addition, even in the areas covered by both works, there are some cases where *Against the Logicians* does not include material that it might profitably have included, and that *PH* 2 does include. Both works mention a series of "indemonstrable" arguments – that is, basic argument-forms not admitting of justification in still more basic terms – that play an important role in Stoic logic. The Stoics held that there were five such forms of argument; but while *PH* 2 mentions all five (157–158), *Against the Logicians* mentions only three (2.223–226). This is partly due to the different roles these summaries play in the two works. In *PH* 2 the indemonstrable arguments are introduced as examples of redundancy in argument. If all five such arguments can be shown up as redundant, then, it is claimed, "all of dialectic is overturned" (156); so it clearly suits Sextus to introduce all five. In *Against the Logicians*, on the other hand, the indemonstrables are introduced as part of a lengthy digression analyzing Aenesidemus' argument about signs, and for this purpose only the first three need to be mentioned. But this is just another example of *PH* 2's generally more adroit handling of its material. For the digression in *Against the Logicians* is really not necessary for the purpose at hand; the validity of Aenesidemus' argument is obvious without any excursus on indemonstrable arguments – as, indeed, Sextus has already made clear before the excursus begins (2.217–222). Yet a more complete treatment of indemonstrable arguments might well have been useful in some other place.

Again, *PH* 2 gives a more complete summary of the variety of views about the truth-conditions for conditionals. Both works include the views of Philo and Diodorus (*Against the Logicians* 2.113–117, *PH* 2.110–111). But *PH* 2 then adds a view centered around a notion of "connectedness" (*sunartēsis*) between the antecedent and the consequent of the conditional – mentioned in *Against the Logicians* only in a later and wholly unexplained reference $(2.265)^{21}$ – and a further view as well (*PH* 2.111–112). Finally, *PH* 2 includes at least some passing mention of Peripatetic logic (*PH* 2.163–166, 193–198), of which, as I noted earlier, *Against the Logicians* appears to be wholly unaware.

PH 2 seems, then, to be in various respects superior to *Against the Logicians*. Another glaring organizational example is this. Both works include discussions of the Stoic distinction between the truth (*hē alētheia*) and what is true (*to alēthes*). But whereas the discussion in *PH* 2 belongs where one would expect, in the course of the discussion of truth (81–83), in *Against the Logicians* it is placed very awkwardly between an introductory section on the criterion and the review of historical positions on the criterion (1.38–45). The effect is to interrupt the discussion of the criterion and to insert material that has no connection with anything else in the first book. Scholars have also pointed to Sextus' treatments of the criterion and of the sign as cases where *Against the Logicians* is inferior, in respect of structure, cogency of argumentation, or both, to *PH* 2.[22] Moreover, it must be admitted that in some places in *Against the Logicians* the writing, or the transition of thought, is just very ungainly (and that *PH* 2 is not comparable in this respect); I have indicated the most extreme cases in my notes. These defects do not by any means render *Against the Logicians* valueless or uninteresting. But they do make it in some ways difficult reading, which I hope my notes and outline will do something to mitigate.

They also put into sharp focus the question which of the two works came first. The traditional view has been that *PH* was Sextus' first work, and that *Against the Logicians* and the larger work to which it belongs are the result of his revising and expanding the material that went into *PH*. But this view was based on comparisons of style and vocabulary in the two works that, while of considerable interest for various reasons, are worthless for establishing their chronology.[23] The question therefore needs to be considered afresh.

---

[21] Cf. Book 2, n. 84.

[22] See Brunschwig, "Sextus Empiricus on the *kritērion*" (cf. n. 12); T. Ebert, "The Origin of the Stoic Theory of Signs in Sextus Empiricus," *Oxford Studies in Ancient Philosophy* 5 (1987), 83–126.

[23] These comparisons were the work of the Czech scholar Karel Janáček; see especially his *Sextus Empiricus' Skeptical Methods* (Charles University, Prague, 1972). On the uselessness of these studies for chronological purposes, *pace* Janáček, see Appendix C to my commentary on *Against the Ethicists* (cf. n. 20). For more on Janáček's work, see "Further reading."

I have mentioned the existence of a large number of parallels between *PH* 2–3 and the larger work. The specific case of *PH* 2 and *Against the Logicians* is no exception. These parallel passages are listed in a special section at the end of the volume.[24] A glance at this list reveals that in both works, the discussion of the topics in logic that they share unfolds in roughly the same order; inspection of the passages themselves shows that there are a great many instances of the same specific arguments in both, and even some close verbal similarities. My impression is that there are fewer of the latter than in the case of *Against the Ethicists* and the corresponding ethical section of *PH* 3.[25] Nonetheless, the nature and extent of the common material makes it evident that one of these treatments of logic is a revised version of the other, just as in the case of ethics (and, for that matter, physics). But now, if this is the case, the superiority of *PH* 2 over *Against the Logicians*, in the numerous respects just mentioned, would seem to favor the view that *Against the Logicians* came first, and that *PH* 2 is a later, cleaned-up version of roughly the same material; one normally expects revision to result in improvement, not deterioration. Of course, this is no more than a general rule. It is not inherently impossible that Sextus became more inept in his style of composition and more sloppy in his argumentation as he got older, or that he had more trouble with works on a larger scale. But it is difficult to imagine why anyone would have made some of the *specific* changes that we would have to suppose he made, if *PH* 2 was the earlier work. Why, for example, would one remove the discussion of the Stoic distinction between the truth and what is true from its natural place in the section on truth (where it belongs in *PH* 2), and put it in the section on the criterion, where it does nothing but interrupt the flow? Or why, in a discussion designed to emphasize disagreement about the truth-conditions for conditionals (*Against the Logicians* 2.112–117), would one limit oneself to just two views on this issue, suppressing any mention of two other views that the earlier, shorter work had already included? It is much more natural in such cases

---

[24] A list of this kind cannot hope to be definitive. Whether or not two passages count as parallel is a matter of degree; some may find the similarities in a few of the cases I list to be too slender to qualify, while others may feel that additional pairs of passages could have been included. In the great majority of cases, however, there is no doubt about the presence of common material.

[25] I have analyzed the ethical parallels in my commentary on *Against the Ethicists* (cf. n. 20); see especially Appendix A.

to suppose that the shorter and more neatly composed work is the later one.[26]

Another consideration points in the same direction. I mentioned that *Against the Logicians* sometimes uses the word *anairein*, "do away with," to describe what the skeptic does with the dogmatists' views, and that this seemed to be a relic of an earlier version of Pyrrhonism distinct from Sextus' own. But it is striking that *PH never* uses the word *anairein* to describe the skeptic's own procedure. In *PH* the word is sometimes used to refer, as one might expect, to the demolishing of someone's view. But it is never suggested that this is something the skeptic does; on the contrary, it is several times stated that this is precisely what the skeptic does *not* do (1.193, 196, 197). It would be very surprising if Sextus *first* used the word in a way appropriate to his version of Pyrrhonism and *then*, in revising the work, started using it in a way that conformed to an earlier version incompatible with his own. It is far more likely that he uncritically reproduced this earlier usage in his first work, which stuck more closely to its sources, and then, in revising this material, adjusted his vocabulary so as to make it conform better to his own position.

These brief remarks certainly do not settle the question. But if they are on track, they point to the conclusion that *Against the Logicians* was Sextus' first attempt at the subject-matter of logic, and that many of the awkwardnesses of that first attempt were ironed out in the subsequent revisions and improvements that led to *PH* 2. I have argued elsewhere that *Against the Ethicists* was composed before the ethical section of *PH* 3; the evidence in that case is similar in kind to that appealed to just now, but much more extensive.[27] If we assume that each work was written in its entirety at separate periods of Sextus' life, then the priority of *Against the Ethicists* would lead us to infer the priority of *Against the Logicians* as well. Unfortunately, that assumption is clearly not beyond question. Differences of style and vocabulary between the two works, considered in

[26] For other examples of the same kind of thing, see again the two studies cited in n. 22. According to both, detailed comparison of the two discussions (of the criterion and the sign respectively) suggests that *PH* 2 contains later, reworked material. Ebert ("The Origin of the Stoic Theory of Signs," 100) speaks of Sextus' *source* for *PH* 2 being a later revision of his *source* for *Against the Logicians*, rather than of *PH* 2 being a revision of *Against the Logicians*. But the only reason for this cumbersome hypothesis seems to be the assumption that Sextus was never anything other than a compiler of other people's material. Yet, as was mentioned earlier, there is no basis for this assumption.

[27] See my Introduction to and Commentary on *Against the Ethicists* (cf. n. 20).

their entirety, may perhaps support it. But stylistic considerations are a notoriously shaky basis on which to construct arguments about order of composition; the last century or more of scholarship on Plato has made this all too clear. What we can say, though, is that the idea that *Against the Logicians* is a revised and expanded version of *PH* 2, representing his mature thinking on the subject, is at least open to serious question. Once again, to think of *Against the Logicians* as Sextus' first attempt in this area, rather than as his final word, does nothing to deprive it of historical and philosophical interest. But it may result in our regarding it, flaws included, in a somewhat different light.

Chronological table

600	500	400	300	200	100	BCE CE	100	200

Thales

Other Early Physicists

Democritus

Plato

Aristotle

Pyrrho

Timon

Arcesilaus

Epicurus

Zeno of Citium

Alexander the Great

Chrysippus

Carneades

Antiochus

Cicero

Jesus

Aenesidemus

Plutarch

Sextus

Galen

Diogenes L.

M. Aurelius

Names of Pyrrhonian skeptics are printed in **bold**; names of other philosophers are *italicized*; other names are in roman. (The distinction between philosophers and non-philosophers has in some cases been arbitrarily made.) Many of the dates indicated by the horizontal lines are at best approximate; and some of them are mere guesswork.

Further reading

The standard Greek text for all of Sextus Empiricus is the three-volume Teubner edition by H. Mutschmann and J. Mau (vol. 1, 1958; vol. 2, 1914; vol. 3, 1961). Supplementing this is a fourth volume containing indices of words and names by K. Janáček (1962); even in the age of electronic word searches, this is still very useful for anyone approaching Sextus in the original. Another vital resource on the original text is W. Heintz, ed. R. Harder, *Studien zu Sextus Empiricus* (Max Niemeyer Verlag, 1932).

There is a translation of the whole of Sextus (with facing Greek text) by R. G. Bury in four volumes of the Loeb series (Harvard University Press, 1933–1949). Unfortunately this is archaic and often philosophically unhelpful, but for a number of books of Sextus it remains the only version in English. There is a fine recent translation of *PH*, with notes, by J. Annas and J. Barnes in the same series as this volume (originally published 1994; incorporated into the series, with a new introduction, 2000). Translations, with extensive commentary, in Oxford's Clarendon Later Ancient Philosophers series exist for *Against the Ethicists* (R. Bett, 1997) and *Against the Grammarians* (D. Blank, 1998). There is a translation of *Against the Musicians*, with notes and a newly edited Greek text, by D. D. Greaves (University of Nebraska Press, 1986). A translation of selected texts, including small portions of *Against the Logicians* and *Against the Physicists*, with an idiosyncratic introduction and notes, is *Sextus Empiricus: Selections from the Major Writings on Skepticism, Man, and God*, ed. P. P. Hallie, tr. S. G. Etheridge (Hackett, 1985, originally published 1968).

Any serious student of Sextus must confront the prolific work of K. Janáček. Much of this involves detailed study of Sextus' language;

the two major works in this vein are *Prolegomena to Sextus Empiricus* (Nákladem Palackého University, Olomouc, 1948) and *Sextus Empiricus' Skeptical Methods* (Charles University, Prague, 1972). Also important is "Die Hauptschrift des Sextus Empiricus als Torso erhalten?" *Philologus* 107 (1963), 271–277, which established that *Against the Logicians* was preceded by a lost general treatment of Pyrrhonism. A complete list of Janáček's works on Sextus and Pyrrhonism (most of them in English or German) can be found in the bibliography to J. Barnes, "Diogenes Laertius IX 61–116: The Philosophy of Pyrrhonism," *Aufstieg und Niedergang der Römischen Welt* II.36.6 (1992), 4241–4301.

A good short book on Hellenistic philosophy (the period most important for understanding Sextus) is R. W. Sharples, *Stoics, Epicureans and Skeptics: An Introduction to Hellenistic Philosophy* (Routledge, 1996). Much more extensive, but still accessible, is K. Algra, J. Barnes, J. Mansfeld, and M. Schofield, eds., *The Cambridge History of Hellenistic Philosophy* (Cambridge University Press, 1999). The parts on logic and epistemology are particularly relevant to *Against the Logicians*; especially to be recommended are the sections by Suzanne Bobzien on the logic of the Stoics and of the "Megarics." (A shorter version of the Stoic material appears in Bobzien's contribution to B. Inwood, ed., *The Cambridge Companion to the Stoics* [Cambridge University Press, 2003].) Significant collections containing relevant essays are M. Schofield, M. Burnyeat, and J. Barnes, eds., *Doubt and Dogmatism: Studies in Hellenistic Epistemology* (Oxford University Press, 1980); M. Frede, *Essays in Ancient Philosophy* (University of Minnesota Press, 1987); S. Everson, ed., *Epistemology* (Cambridge University Press, 1990); J. Brunschwig, *Papers in Hellenistic Philosophy* (Cambridge University Press, 1994); and G. Striker, *Essays on Hellenistic Epistemology and Ethics* (Cambridge University Press, 1996). On sign theory, in Sextus and elsewhere, J. Allen, *Inference from Signs: Ancient Debates about the Nature of Evidence* (Oxford University Press, 2001) is difficult but rewarding.

Good collections of original texts in translation from, or about, the Hellenistic period are A. A. Long and D. N. Sedley, *The Hellenistic Philosophers* (2 vols., Cambridge University Press, 1987) and B. Inwood and L. Gerson, *Hellenistic Philosophy: Introductory Readings* (2nd edn., Hackett, 1997). Long and Sedley contains translations with philosophical commentary in vol. 1, the Greek and Latin texts with philological notes in vol. 2. Inwood and Gerson has only translations and no commentary, but has the advantage of presenting more continuous texts. Diogenes Laertius' summary of Stoic logic, for example, can be read from beginning to end (111–124), whereas in Long and Sedley portions of this material appear as twenty-six different passages in numerous different sections.

On Greek skepticism specifically, the best book-length survey is R. J. Hankinson, *The Sceptics* (Routledge, 1995). Still worth consulting is V. Brochard, *Les sceptiques grecs* (originally published 1887, reissued by Le Livre de Poche, 2002). The origins and development of the Pyrrhonist tradition are examined in R. Bett, *Pyrrho, his Antecedents, and his Legacy* (Oxford University Press, 2000). Two highly readable studies of the Pyrrhonist modes, or standardized forms of argumentation (especially as they occur in Sextus), are J. Annas and J. Barnes, *The Modes of Scepticism* (Cambridge University Press, 1985) and J. Barnes, *The Toils of Scepticism* (Cambridge University Press, 1990). Valuable collections of essays touching on both the Academic and Pyrrhonist traditions are M. Burnyeat, ed., *The Skeptical Tradition* (University of California Press, 1983) and M. Burnyeat and M. Frede, eds., *The Original Sceptics: A Controversy* (Hackett, 1997). The first of these contains numerous essays on skepticism in the modern period and the influence of ancient Greek skepticism upon it. This has also been a major theme of the work of R. Popkin; see in particular his *The History of Scepticism from Erasmus to Spinoza* (University of California Press, 1979) and (ed. R. A Watson and J. E. Force) *The High Road to Pyrrhonism* (Austin Hill Press, 1980).

Note on the text and translation

The translation follows the text of H. Mutschmann (Teubner, 1914), except where indicated in the notes. The bold numerals inserted in parentheses in the translation give the section numbers that are standard in editions of Sextus. Headings in bold are the chapter titles present in the manuscripts (and generally thought to originate with Sextus himself); other headings are my own, and correspond with the outline of the argument that appears before the translation. When I deviate from the text of Mutschmann, I often follow the textual proposal of some other scholar; in all such cases, that scholar is named in the note specifying the change. The proposals of these other scholars are listed in Mutschmann's apparatus criticus, with a partial exception in the case of W. Heintz; most of the suggestions that I adopt from him are instead to be found in his *Studien zu Sextus Empiricus* (see "Further reading").

Cross-references in the notes (i.e., references to other passages of *Against the Logicians*) are given by section number if the reference is to a passage in the same book, and by book number (1 or 2) plus section number if the reference is to a passage in the other book.

Very occasionally, a word appears in the translation in square brackets [ ]. This is where some addition is needed to make the text intelligible – for example, a word from the original Greek, where Sextus is engaging in wordplay not reproducible in English. Diagonal brackets < > appear somewhat more often, and indicate difficulties with the Greek text. If there is no word inside them <...>, a lacuna (that is, a gap in the original Greek text) is indicated; if there are words inside them, this indicates a supplement to the text (that is, words required to complete the sense but not present in any manuscript, and conjectured to have been lost during manuscript transmission). However, only supplements not recognized by Mutschmann are indicated in this way; I do not mark Mutschmann's own supplements, in cases where I have no quarrel with them. All cases of either square or diagonal brackets receive explanation in the notes. Material inside ordinary parentheses ( ) is simply part of the translation.

Like most translators, I have attempted as far as possible to render philosophically significant terms with the same English words throughout; again like most translators, I have abandoned this policy when the result would have been misleading or intolerable English. Choices of translation are occasionally mentioned in the notes, but are more often confined to the Glossary. The Glossary also indicates cases where I translate a certain word differently from Julia Annas and Jonathan Barnes' translation (in the same series as this volume) of *PH*; such cases are indicated by "A/B," followed by their translation of the word, in parentheses.

Translation from Greek to English always involves a difficult balance between the competing demands of natural English expression and fidelity to the original Greek. I found this difficulty particularly acute when it came to the translation of technical terms in logic. Many such terms have obvious equivalents, or near-equivalents, in modern logical terminology; yet these modern equivalents often fail to reflect the original meanings of the Greek words (many of which began as non-technical words in ordinary language). Thus, for example, I have rendered *hēgoumenon* and *lēgon*, which are the terms for what we call the antecedent and the consequent of conditionals, not by "antecedent" and "consequent," but by "leader" and "finisher." They are participle forms of ordinary Greek verbs meaning "lead" and "finish," and this link seemed worth preserving – especially since the verbs themselves regularly occur in logical contexts as well, and the connection with *hēgoumenon* and *lēgon* would have been natural and obvious to an ancient Greek reader. On the other hand, the term for a complete conditional, *sunēmmenon*, is translated by "conditional," even though it literally means "connected." In an early version I tried rendering it by "connected proposition." But the need to add "proposition," for which there was usually no word in the original, made for some very cumbersome sentences. In addition, unlike in the case of *hēgoumenon* and *lēgon*, there was no etymological connection with other terms in the translation lost by using "conditional." And finally, while it is easy to get the point of "leader" and "finisher," used to refer to components of a conditional, it would have taken somewhat more effort for the reader to remember that a "connected proposition" is what we call a conditional. These are the sorts of trade-offs that routinely need to be negotiated in a work of this kind.

The translation freely uses the generic "he." The ancient Greek language exhibits a bias toward the masculine (grammatical) gender in referring to human beings in general, and the generic "he" naturally reproduces this. Ancient Greek does, however, have separate words for "man" (*anēr*) and "human being" (*anthrōpos*) – as Sextus himself points out, in fact, in this very work (1.50) – and I translate accordingly. This leads to the rather extensive use of the term "the human being" in the second half of Book 1, where *ho anthrōpos* repeatedly occurs as a universal or kind term. An older tradition of translation would effortlessly have used "man" in this context; but we can no longer hear "man" as equivalent to "human being." An alternative, adopted by Annas and Barnes in the corresponding passage of *PH* 2, is to use the plural "humans" or "human beings." But this, despite an undeniable gain in naturalness of expression, also seems to me to misrepresent the original; so I decided it was preferable to hold on to the literal, if slightly awkward, term "the human being" (understood by analogy with "the cow," "the horse," etc., which are perfectly normal in English).

Some will be outraged at the almost ubiquitous use of transliteration for Greek words, even in footnotes discussing textual matters. (The only exception is where differences of accent are at issue.) But this volume is designed to be as user-friendly as possible to readers who have no knowledge of ancient (or modern) Greek, and who are not likely ever to learn it. Those who do have such knowledge often wildly underestimate the intimidation caused by the presence of an alien alphabet. No doubt it would be better, for a number of reasons, if people would overcome this reaction. But that is not part of the educational mission of this book.

Outline of argument

Note. This outline takes no account of the chapter headings, which in *Against the Logicians* (unlike some other works of Sextus) are sporadic and often unhelpful.

Book 1
A. Introduction (1–24)
   1. The parts of philosophy (2–23)
   2. Decision to begin with logic (24)
B. The Criterion (25–445)
   1. Introductory remarks (25–45)
      a. Methodological comments (25–28)
      b. Different types of criterion (29–37)
      c. Stoic distinction between the truth and what is true (38–45)
   2. Review of previous positions on the criterion (46–260)
      a. Deniers of the criterion (48–88): Xenophanes (49–52), Xeniades (53–54), Anacharsis (55–59), Protagoras (60–64), Euthydemus and Dionysodorus (64), Gorgias (65–87), Metrodorus, Anaxarchus, and Monimus (88)
      b. Adherents of a criterion (89–260)
         i. Early physicists (89–140): Anaxagoras (90–91), Pythagoreans (92–109), Xenophanes (110), Parmenides (111–114), Empedocles (115–125 – digression on like knowing like, 116–119), Heraclitus (126–134), Democritus (135–140)
         ii. Post-physicists (141–260): Plato (141–144), Speusippus (145–146), Xenocrates (147–149), Arcesilaus (150–158),

Against the Logicians

Book I

A. Introduction (1–24)

(1) The general character of the skeptical ability has been indicated with the appropriate treatment, sketched out in part directly and in part by means of a division of the philosophies close to it.[1] What is left is to explain, next, how it is applied to the particulars,[2] with a view to avoiding a reckless haste either when inquiring about things on our own or when rebutting the dogmatists. (2) But since philosophy is a many-faceted sort of thing, it will be necessary, for the sake of an orderly and systematic search, to draw a few distinctions concerning its parts.

1. The parts of philosophy (2–23)

For, to begin with, some people seem to have supposed that it has one part, some two parts, and some three parts; and of those who have posited one part some have posited the physical part, some the ethical part, and some the logical part, (3) and similarly of those who divide it into two some have divided it into the physical and the logical parts, some into the physical and the ethical, and some into the logical and the ethical; (4) whereas those who divide it into three have agreed in dividing it into the physical, the logical, and the ethical parts.

(5) The ones who maintained that it has just the physical part are Thales, Anaximenes and Anaximander, Empedocles, Parmenides, and Heraclitus – Thales, Anaximenes, and Anaximander according to

---

[1] See Introduction (p. xi) for the significance of this back-reference.
[2] I.e., the various specific parts of philosophy.

3

everyone and without dispute, but Empedocles and Parmenides and also Heraclitus not according to everyone. (6) For Aristotle says that Empedocles got rhetoric started, of which dialectic is a "counterpart" [*antistrophon*]³ – that is, correlated with it [*isostrophon*], because of being related to the same material, just as the poet called Odysseus "godlike" [*antitheon*],⁴ that is, equal to god [*isotheon*]. (7) And Parmenides would seem to be not inexperienced in dialectic, since again Aristotle took his companion Zeno to be the originator of dialectic. And in Heraclitus' case as well, there was an issue as to whether he was not only a physical philosopher but also an ethical one.

(8) Well, the people who were prominent in the physical part are these; but Socrates was concerned, at least according to his other companions,⁵ with only the ethical part, seeing that Xenophon in his *Memoirs* explicitly says that he rejected the physical part as being beyond us, and studied the ethical part alone as being our business.⁶ And Timon too knows that he was like this, when he says

From them the stone-chiseler,⁷ blatherer on the lawful, turned away⁸

– that is, away from physical matters to reflection on ethics; that is why he added "blatherer on the lawful," seeing that discussion about laws belongs to the ethical part. (9) Plato, though, has him contributing to every part of philosophy, the logical in so far as he is brought in as a searcher after definitions and divisions and etymology (which are logical matters), the ethical because he inquires about virtue and government and laws, (10) and the physical because he also did some thinking about the universe, and about the generation of animals and the soul. Hence Timon blames Plato for embellishing Socrates in this way with multiple disciplines: "Indeed," he says, "the one who was not willing for him

³ *Rhetoric* 1354a1 (the first sentence of the work) says that rhetoric is the "counterpart" of dialectic. But the claim about Empedocles (and Zeno, cf. 7) occurred in Aristotle's lost work *Sophist*; see Diogenes Laertius 8.57.
⁴ A common epithet in Homer (and applied to others besides Odysseus). The wordplay in this sentence is impossible to reproduce in English; the words beginning *anti-* are from Sextus' point of view archaic – at least in these senses – needing an explanation in terms of the words beginning *iso-*.
⁵ I.e., other than Plato; see 9.   ⁶ See Xenophon, *Memorabilia* 1.1.11ff.
⁷ Socrates is reputed to have started as a stonemason (following in the family business). The Greek word (*laxoos*) may also suggest the meaning "people-chiseler" (from *laos*, "people"); see A. A. Long, "Socrates in Hellenistic Philosophy," *Classical Quarterly* 38 (1988), 150–171, at 150.
⁸ From Timon's poem *Silloi* (*Lampoons*), as attested by Diogenes Laertius (2.19) and Clement (1.14.63.3), both of whom give slightly more extensive quotations.

to remain a character-depicter."⁹ (11) The Cyrenaics also seem to some people to embrace the ethical part only, and to put aside the physical and logical parts as contributing nothing to living happily. Yet some have thought that these people are turned about,¹⁰ given that they divide the ethical part into the topic of things to be chosen and to be avoided, and that of effects on us, and then into that of actions and in addition that of causes, and finally into that of proofs. For among these the topic of causes, they say, comes from the physical part, and that of proofs from the logical part. (12) Ariston of Chios, too, they say, not only used to dismiss physical and logical reflection on account of their being useless and detrimental to those who investigate them, but even used to circumscribe some topics in the ethical part, namely the topic of exhortation and that of advice. For he thought these belonged to nurses and children's attendants, while it was enough for the purpose of living happily to have reasoning that oriented one towards virtue, alienated one from vice, and disparaged the things between these, over which the masses get excited and are unhappy. (13) And Panthoides and Alexinus and Eubulides and Bryson, as well as Dionysodorus and Euthydemus, were inclined toward the logical part.

(14) Of those who maintained that philosophy has two parts, Xenophanes, as some people say, pursued the physical and the logical parts together, whereas Archelaus of Athens pursued the physical and the ethical parts; with him some people also classify Epicurus as rejecting logical reflection. (15) But there were others who say that he did not excuse himself from logic in general, but only from that of the Stoics, so that in effect he left philosophy intact with three parts. And there is a view attributed by some to the Cyrenaics – indeed, Sotion has given evidence of this – namely, that they say there is an ethical and a logical part of philosophy.

(16) Well, these people seem to have been deficient in their approach; by comparison, the approach of those who say that one part of philosophy is physics, another ethics, and another logic seems to have been more complete. Of this group Plato is in effect the founder, since he engaged in discussion on many matters in physics, many in ethics, and not a few in logic. But the most explicit adherents of this division are Xenocrates,

---

⁹ Timon's original words were also probably from his *Silloi*. But in this case either Sextus or his copyists have mangled the quotation; the words as they stand do not scan. *Ethologon*, translated "character-depicter," normally refers to a mime; but Timon is clearly playing with the etymology so as to suggest someone who engages in discourse (*logos*) *about* character (*ēthos*).

¹⁰ I.e., convicted of self-refutation; this term is common in Sextus.

the Peripatetics, and the Stoics. (17) Hence they implausibly[11] compare philosophy with a garden covered in fruit, so that the physical part can be likened to the height of the plants, the ethical part to the succulence of the fruits, and the logical part to the strength of the walls. (18) Others say that it is like an egg; for ethics is like the yolk, which some people say is the chick, physics is like the white, which is food for the yolk, and logic is like the outside shell. (19) But since the parts of philosophy are inseparable from one another, whereas plants are considered distinct from their fruit and walls are separate from plants, Posidonius thought it more appropriate to liken philosophy to an animal, the physical part being likened to blood and flesh, the logical part to bones and sinews, and the ethical part to soul.

(20) Now, given that philosophy has three parts, some rank physics as the first part, since the business of physical inquiry has precedence both in time (so that even up to now the first who engaged in philosophy are called physicists), and in order, because it makes sense first to make determinations about the universe and then to inquire about the specifics and about the human being. (21) Others began with ethical matters, on the grounds that they are more necessary and draw us towards happiness; for example, Socrates instructed us to examine nothing else except

Whatever good and bad is wrought within the halls.[12]

(22) And the Epicureans begin with logical matters; for they look first at questions to do with rules,[13] and do their survey on things that are plain and unclear and matters related to these. The Stoics, too, say that logical matters lead, that ethical matters take second place, and that physical matters come last in order. (23) For they hold that the intellect must first be fortified, with a view to making its guard of the tradition hard to shake off, and that the area of dialectic tends to strengthen one's thinking; that, second, one must add ethical reflection with a view to the improvement of character traits (for the acquisition of this on top of the already present logical ability holds no danger); and that one must bring in physical reflection last (for it is more divine and needs deeper attention).

---

[11] I retain the mss. reading *enthende(n) apithanōs*.

[12] *Odyssey* 4.392; Sextus also quotes this line in the context of Socrates' ethical thinking at *M* 11.2, as does Diogenes Laertius (2.21).

[13] I.e., rules relating to correct inference. Epicurus' work on this topic was actually called *Rule* (*Kanōn*).

2. *Decision to begin with logic (24)*

(**24**) This is what these people say. We, on the other hand, are not right now looking into the exact state of the matter. We do, however, say this: that if in every part of philosophy what is to be sought is the truth, one must above all have starting-points and processes for discerning this that are reliable. But *logic* is the area that contains reflection about criteria and demonstrations; so this is where we should make our start.[14]

B. The Criterion (25–445)

1. *Introductory remarks (25–45)*

a. Methodological comments (25–28)

(**25**) And we can get our investigation against the dogmatists well under-way as follows. Since plain things are thought to become known all by themselves through some criterion, while unclear things are thought to be tracked down through signs and demonstrations, by way of a transition from plain things, let us inquire in the first place into whether there is any criterion of the things that strike us all by themselves via sense-perception or thought, and then after that into whether there is a process capable of signifying or of demonstrating unclear things.[15] (**26**) For I think that once these have been done away with, there will be nothing left to investigate about our needing to suspend judgment, seeing that nothing true is found either in things in plain view or in things that are obscured. So let the discussion of the criterion be our starting-point, since it is actually thought to include all the processes of apprehension.

Whether there is a criterion of truth

(**27**) The investigation of the criterion is universally contentious, not only because the human being is by nature a truth-loving animal, but also because the highest-level schools of philosophy are here making judgments about the most important matters. For either the dogmatists' big solemn boast will need to be completely done away with, if no standard is found for the true reality of things, or, on the contrary, the skeptics will

---

[14] See Introduction (pp. x–xii) for the place of *Against the Logicians* in the entire work to which it belonged.

[15] A reference to the sections on sign and demonstration in Book 2 (141ff.).

need to be convicted as rash and dismissive of common belief, if something comes to light which is capable of leading our way to the apprehension of the truth. For it will be too bad if we expend extreme effort in investigating the external criteria, such as rulers and compasses, weights and balances, while we leave aside the one that is in us, and that is thought to be able to test those very things. (28) Let us therefore take up the matter in order, as befits the fact that our inquiry is about the whole subject. Since the issue contains two parts, the criterion and the truth, let us discuss each of these in turn, sometimes indicating by way of explanation the multiple ways in which the criterion and the truth are spoken of, and what on earth their nature is according to the dogmatists, and at other times inquiring in more of a spirit of impasse into whether any of these things can be real.

b. Different types of criterion (29–37)

On the criterion

(29) To begin with, then, the criterion (for we should start with this) is spoken of in two ways: in one way it is that to which we attend when we do some things and not others, while in another way it is that to which we attend when we say that some things are real and others are not real, and that these things are true and those things are false. The first of these we have laid out earlier in "On the skeptical method".[16] (30) For inevitably the person who does philosophy in a spirit of impasse – so as not to be completely inactive and without any part in the affairs of life – must have some criterion of choice as well as avoidance, namely what appears, as Timon has also attested in saying

But what appears is powerful everywhere, wherever it comes.[17]

(31) The other one (I mean the one to do with reality, about which we are currently inquiring) seems to be spoken of in three ways, generally and specifically and most specifically. Generally, it is every measure of

---

[16] Editors have seen this as a reference to the chapter on the skeptic's method of acting in *PH* (1.21–24). But the title of that chapter is "On the skeptic's criterion." Rather, the reference is probably to a discussion in the lost portion of the larger work of which *Against the Logicians* is a part.

[17] Also quoted by Diogenes Laertius (9.105), who says that it came from Timon's poem *Indalmoi* (*Images*), and by Galen (8.781 Kühn).

apprehension, and in this signification even the natural criteria, such as sight, hearing, and taste, qualify for this label. (32) Specifically, it is every technical measure of apprehension – as one would call a cubit and a pair of scales and a ruler and a compass criteria, in so far as they are technical, but not by any means sight and hearing and in general the remaining common sense-organs, which are constituted naturally. (33) More specifically[18] it is every measure of apprehension of an unclear object, in terms of which the everyday ones are no longer called criteria; it is only the logical ones that are so called – namely, those that the dogmatists bring in for the discovery of the truth.[19]

(34) So, since the criterion is spoken of in many ways, the task before us is again to inquire primarily into the logical one that the philosophers go on about, but, as a subordinate matter, into each of the everyday ones as well. (35) It is, however, possible to subdivide this logical one, too, saying that one is a criterion in the manner of "by which," one in the manner of "through which," and one in the manner of "impact and state": "By which" – namely, a human being; "through which" – namely, sense-perception; the third one – namely, the impact of the appearance. (36) Compare the testing of heavy and light objects, in which there are three criteria, the weigher, the pair of scales, and the position of the scales, and of these the weigher is the criterion "by which," the scales are the criterion "through which," and the position of the scales is the criterion as "state." Or again, for the determination of straight and crooked objects there is a need for the craftsman and the ruler and the application[20] of this. In just the same way, in philosophy, too, we need the three aforementioned criteria for distinguishing true and false things, (37) and the human being, "by whom" the judgment occurs, is like the weigher or carpenter; sense-perception and thought, "through which" the judgment occurs, are like the scales and ruler; and the impact of the appearance, in virtue of which the human being undertakes to judge, is like the state of the aforementioned tools. This much was necessary, for the present, by way of preface on the criterion.

---

[18] I retain the mss. reading *idiaiteron*.

[19] This classification is not well adapted to Sextus' subsequent discussion, since at least some philosophers considered the senses to be a criterion in the "logical" sense just introduced (as is immediately stated, in fact, at 35) – despite Sextus' labeling them as criteria in only the "general" sense. See also Introduction, n. 12.

[20] *Prosbolē*, translated "impact" elsewhere in this passage.

c. Stoic distinction between the truth and what is true (38–45)

On truth

(38) As for the truth, some people, and especially the Stoics, think that it differs from what is true in three ways, in being, in composition, and in power. In being, in so far as the truth is a body, while what is true is incorporeal. And reasonably so, they say; for the latter is a proposition, and the proposition is a sayable, and the sayable is an incorporeal.[21] The truth, by contrast, is a body in so far as it is thought to be knowledge that is capable of asserting everything that is true, (39) and all knowledge is the leading part[22] in a certain state (just as the hand in a certain state is thought of as a fist). But the leading part, according to these people, is a body; therefore the truth too is bodily in kind. (40) In composition, in so far as what is true is thought of as something uniform and simple in nature, such as (at present) "It is day" and "I am having a discussion," while the truth, on the contrary, is supposed (on the assumption that it consists in knowledge) to be composite and an aggregation of many things. (41) Thus, just as the populace is one thing and the citizen another, and the populace is the aggregation of many citizens while the citizen is the single one, by the same reasoning the truth differs from what is true, and the truth resembles the populace and what is true resembles the citizen, because the former is composite, the latter simple. (42) And they are separate from one another in power since what is true is not entirely connected with knowledge (for the inferior and the stupid and the insane sometimes say something true, but do not have *knowledge* of what is true), while the truth is regarded as related to knowledge. Hence the person who has this is wise (for he has knowledge of things that are true), and he never lies, even if he speaks a falsehood, owing to the fact that it is uttered not from a bad but from a sophisticated disposition. (43) The doctor says something false about the health of the sick person, and promises to give him something but does not give it. He says something false but does not lie; for it is with a view to the health of the person in his care that he takes such a recourse. And the best military leaders often fabricate letters from allied states to cheer up the soldiers under their command; they say something false, but do not lie, because they do not do this with a bad

---

[21] On "sayables" (*lekta*), see 2.70ff. and LS sect. 33.

[22] I.e., the leading part of the soul. Cf. 232ff. for this Stoic term. On the Stoic view of the soul see also LS sect. 53.

purpose. (44) And the grammarian, in offering an example of misuse of language, cites a misuse of language but does not misuse language; for it is not by way of ignorance of correct speech that this happens. Just like them, the wise person too – that is, the person who has knowledge of what is true – will sometimes speak a falsehood, but will never lie, because of not having a mind-set that assents to what is false. (45) For, they say, one can learn that the liar is to be judged from his disposition, and not from the simple utterance, by means of the examples that are about to be offered. Someone is called a grave-digger both when he does this with the goal of stripping the corpses and when he digs graves for the corpses. But the first person is punished as doing this from a bad disposition, while the second actually gets payment for his service for the opposite reason. It is clear, therefore, that speaking a falsehood indeed differs a great deal from lying, in that the one comes about from a sophisticated mind-set, but lying comes about from a bad one.

2. Review of previous positions on the criterion (46–260)

(46) Having first laid out these points about the truth (according to some), let us next look at the disagreement that has occurred among the dogmatic philosophers about the criterion; while investigating the reality of this, we also have to consider at the same time what it is. (47) Many varied divisions are produced on this topic; but for now it is enough for us to say that some people have done away with the criterion, while others have held on to it. And of those who have held on to it, three positions are uppermost; some have held on to it in reason, others in non-rational plain experience, and others in both.

a. Deniers of the criterion (48–88)
(48) And Xenophanes of Colophon, Xeniades of Corinth, Anacharsis of Scythia, Protagoras, and Dionysodorus have in fact done away with it, as well as Gorgias of Leontini, Metrodorus of Chios, "Mr. Happiness" Anaxarchus, and Monimus the Cynic.

Xenophanes (49–52)   (49) Of these Xenophanes occupied this position, according to some, in saying that everything is inapprehensible, when he writes

And as for what is clear, no man has seen it, nor will there be anyone
Who knows about the gods and what I say about all things;
For even if one should happen to say what has absolutely come to pass
Nonetheless one does not oneself know; but opinion has been constructed
    in all cases.[23]

(50) For by "clear", in this context, he seems to mean what is true, i.e.,
what is familiar, just as in the saying

Straightforward is the word of truth.[24]

And by "man" he seems to mean "human being," using the specific term
instead of the generic; for man is a form of human being. The use of
this mode of speech is common also in Hippocrates, as when he says
"A woman is not born rightwards"[25] – that is, a *female* does not come
together in the right-hand parts of the womb. He says "about the gods"
by way of example, talking about any unclear matters, and he uses *dokos*
["opinion"] for *dokēsis* or *doxa*.[26] **(51)** So what he is saying, in an expanded
version, is something like this: "What is true or familiar no human being
knows, at least in unclear matters; for even if one hits upon this by chance,
nonetheless one does not know that one has hit upon it, but one believes
and opines." **(52)** For if we were to imagine some people looking for
gold in a dark room containing many valuables, it will happen that each
of them, upon seizing one of the objects lying in the room, will believe
that he has taken hold of the gold, yet none of them will be sure that
he has encountered the gold – even if it turns out that he absolutely has
encountered it. And so, too, into this universe, as into a large house, a
crowd of philosophers has passed on the search for the truth, and the
person who seizes it probably does not trust that he was on target.

He, then, says that there is no criterion of truth, on account of there
being nothing apprehensible in the nature of the things being investigated.

Xeniades (53–54) **(53)** But Xeniades of Corinth, whom Democritus
mentions, says that everything is false, and that every appearance and
opinion lies, and that all that comes to be comes to be out of what is not, and

---

[23] Also quoted at 110, 2.326, and (whole or in part) by other authors. For interpretation see J. H. Lesher, *Xenophanes of Colophon* (University of Toronto Press, 1992), 155–169.

[24] Euripides, *Phoenician Women* 469.

[25] *Amphidexios* – which usually means "ambidextrous," but must here refer to the right-hand side.

[26] All words for "opinion"; but *dokos* is rare and from Sextus' point of view archaic.

all that perishes perishes into what is not. In doing so he in effect adheres to the same position as Xenophanes. (54) For if there is not anything true, as distinct from false, but everything is false and for this reason inapprehensible, neither will there be any criterion capable of discerning these things. That everything is false and for this reason inapprehensible is shown by vilifying the senses; for if the ultimate criterion of all things is false, then necessarily everything is false. But the ultimate criterion of all things is the senses, and they are shown to be false; therefore all things are false.

Anacharsis (55–59) (55) And Anacharsis the Scythian, they say, does away with the apprehension that is capable of judging every skill, and strenuously criticizes the Greeks for holding on to it. For who, he says, is the person who judges something skillfully? Is it the ordinary person or the skilled person? We would not say it is the ordinary person. For he is defective in his knowledge of the peculiarities of skills. The blind person does not grasp the workings of sight, nor the deaf person those of hearing. And so, too, the unskilled person does not have a sharp eye when it comes to the apprehension of what has been achieved through skill, since if we actually back this person in his judgment on some matter of skill, there will be no difference between skill and lack of skill, which is absurd. So the ordinary person is not a judge of the peculiarities of skills. (56) It remains, then, to say that it is the skilled person – which is again unbelievable. For one judges either a person with the same pursuits as oneself, or a person with different pursuits. But one is not capable of judging someone with different pursuits; for one is familiar with one's own skill, (57) but as far as someone else's skill is concerned one's status is that of an ordinary person. Yet neither can one certify a person with the same pursuits as oneself. For this was the very issue we were examining: who is to be the judge of these people, who are of identical ability as regards the same skill. Besides, if one person judges the other, the same thing will become both judging and judged, trustworthy and untrustworthy. (58) For in so far as the other person has the same pursuits as the one being judged, he will be untrustworthy since he too is being judged, while in so far as he is judging he will be trustworthy. But it is not possible for the same thing to be both judging and judged, trustworthy and untrustworthy; therefore there is no one who judges skillfully. For this reason there is not a criterion either. (59) For some criteria are skilled and some are ordinary; but neither do the ordinary ones judge (just as the ordinary person does not), nor do the skilled ones (just as the skilled person does not), for the reasons stated earlier. Therefore nothing is a criterion.

Protagoras (60–64) **(60)** Some people have also included Protagoras of Abdera in the chorus of philosophers who do away with the criterion, since he says that all appearances and opinions are true, and that truth is among the things in relation to something,[27] given the fact that everything that has appeared to or been opined by someone is immediately the case in relation to that person. At any rate, at the beginning of his *Downthrowers* he announced "A human being is measure of all things, of the things that are that they are, and of the things that are not that they are not."[28] **(61)** And the opposing argument appears to testify in favor of this. For if someone says to you[29] that the human being is not the criterion of all things, he will confirm that the human being *is* the criterion of all things. For the very person saying this is a human being, and in positing that which appears in relation to himself,[30] he agrees that this very point is among the things that appear in relation to himself. Hence, too, the insane person is a reliable criterion of the things that appear in insanity, and the sleeping person of the things that strike us in sleep, the child of the things that strike us in childhood, and the old person of the things that strike us in old age. **(62)** And it is not appropriate to reject one set of circumstances on the basis of a different set of circumstances – that is, to reject the things that appear when one is insane on the basis of the things that happen when one is of sound mind, or those in sleep on the basis of those in wakefulness, or those in childhood on the basis of those in old age. For just as the latter ones do not appear to the former people, so too on the contrary the things that appear to the former do not strike the latter. **(63)** For this reason, if the insane person or the sleeping person is not a solid judge of the things that appear to him because he is observed to be in a certain kind of condition, then since the person of sound mind and the waking person are also in a certain kind of condition, they too will not be reliable as regards the discernment of the things that happen to

---

[27] I.e., a relative thing. For explanation of this term and its counterpart "in virtue of a difference" (i.e., absolute), see 2.161–162.

[28] A famous fragment quoted by many ancient authors (though never in any fuller form than this), and subjected to lengthy interpretation and criticism in Plato, *Theaetetus* 152a–183c. See also *PH* 1.216–219.

[29] I retain the mss. *soi*.   [30] I do not accept the addition of the word *kritērion*.

them. So, since nothing is apprehended independently of circumstances, we have to trust each person <about>[31] the things that are grasped in his own circumstances. **(64)** And some people have supposed that this man removed[32] the criterion, since this claims to be capable of scrutinizing the underlying things in themselves, and to be capable of distinguishing the true and the false, but the man previously mentioned has left in place neither anything that is in itself real nor falsehood.

Euthydemus and Dionysodorus (64)   Euthydemus and Dionysodorus are also said to have been like this; for they too assign what is so, and what is true, to the things in relation to something.[33]

Gorgias (65–87)   **(65)** Gorgias of Leontini belonged to the same troop as those who did away with the criterion, but not by way of the same approach as Protagoras. For in the work entitled *On What Is Not* or *On Nature* he sets up three main points one after the other: first, that there is nothing; second, that even if there is [something],[34] it is not apprehensible by a human being; third, that even if it is apprehensible, it is still not expressible or explainable to the next person.[35] **(66)** That there is nothing, then, he reckons in the following way. If there is anything, either there is what is or what is not, or there is both what is and what is not. But neither is there what is, as he will establish, nor what is not, as he will explain, nor what is *and* what is not, as he will also teach. Therefore there is not anything. **(67)** Now, there is not what is not. For if there is what is not, it will both be and not be at the same time; in so far as it is considered as not being, it will not be, but in so far as what is not[36] is, it will on the other hand be.

---

[31] I adopt Bury's supplement *peri*.

[32] With Heintz I retain the mss. *kinein* and alter *toutōi* to *touton*.   [33] Cf. n. 27.

[34] The word "something" does not appear in the Greek; in (philosophical) Greek "is" (*esti*) often stands alone, but in this context this is scarcely tolerable in English. That this is what Sextus intends is shown by 77, where "something" (*ti*) does appear in the text.

[35] The meaning and intent of Gorgias' treatise is the subject of much controversy. For one standard account see G. B. Kerferd, *The Sophistic Movement* (Cambridge University Press, 1981), 93–100. In particular, there is controversy over what Gorgias means by "is," "being," etc. (*esti* and cognate forms). Although I lean somewhat toward an existential reading in my periodic use of the phrase "there is," I never actually translate *esti* by "exists" (here or anywhere else); "exist," in this passage and elsewhere, renders *hupokeimai*, a term that (in this philosophical usage) postdates Gorgias. Another summary of Gorgias' treatise, widely regarded as closer to Gorgias' actual intentions but afflicted with many textual problems, occurs in the pseudo-Aristotelian *On Melissus, Xenophanes, Gorgias*; for a good recent translation see M. Gagarin and P. Woodruff, eds., *Early Greek Political Thought from Homer to the Sophists* (Cambridge University Press, 1995), 206–209.

[36] I insert *to* before *mē on*, as recorded in the oldest manuscript.

But it is completely absurd that something should both be and not be at the same time; therefore there is not what is not. And besides, if there is what is not, there will not be what is; for these are the opposites of one another, and if being is an attribute of what is not, not being will be an attribute of what is. But it is *not* the case that there is not what is; neither[37] will there be what is not.

(68) Then again, neither is there what is. For if there is what is, it is either eternal or generated or eternal and at the same time generated. But it is neither eternal nor generated nor both, as we will show; therefore there is not what is. For if what is is eternal (that is where we should start from), it does not have any beginning. (69) For everything that undergoes generation has some beginning, but the eternal, being ungenerated, did not have a beginning. But not having a beginning, it is unlimited. But if it is unlimited it is nowhere. For if it is anywhere, that in which it is is distinct from itself, and thus what is will no longer be unlimited since it is enclosed by something. For what encloses is bigger than what is enclosed, but there is nothing bigger than the unlimited, so that the unlimited is not anywhere. (70) Then again, nor is it enclosed within itself. For the thing in which it is and the thing in that thing will be the same, and what is will become double, both place and body (for the thing in which it is is place, and the thing in that thing is body). But this is absurd; therefore what is is not within itself. So that if what is is eternal, it is unlimited, and if it is unlimited, it is nowhere, and if it is nowhere, it is not. Therefore if what is is eternal, it is not a being in the first place. (71) Then again, nor can what is be generated. For if it has been generated, it has been generated either out of a being or out of a non-being. But it has not been generated out of what is; for if it is a being, it has not been generated but it already is. But neither has it been generated out of what is not; for what is not cannot generate anything, on account of the fact that what is capable of generating something is bound necessarily to share in reality. Therefore what is is not generated either. (72) In the same way, neither is it the combination, both eternal and generated. For these are destructive of one another, and if what is is eternal, it has not been generated, and if it has been generated, it is not eternal. Therefore if it is neither eternal nor generated nor the combination, what is cannot be. (73) Besides, if it is, it is either one or many. But it is neither one nor many, as will be

---

[37] I do not accept the addition *toinun*.

shown; therefore there is not what is. For if it is one, it is either of a certain quantity or continuous or a magnitude or a body. But whichever of these it is, it is not one. If it is of a certain magnitude it will be divided, while if it is continuous it will be cut. Similarly, if it is thought of as a magnitude it will not be indivisible, and if it turns out to be a body it will be triple; for it will have length and breadth and depth. But it is absurd to say that what is is none of these; therefore what is is not one. **(74)** Then again, neither is it many. For if it is not one, it is not many; for the many is a combination of things taken individually, which means that if the one is done away with, the many are also done away with at the same time.

Now, it is evident from these points that neither is there what is nor is there what is not; **(75)** and that there is not both (what is *and* what is not) either, is easily argued. For if there is what is not and there is what is, what is not will be the same as what is as far as being is concerned; and for this reason there is neither of them. For that there is not what is not is agreed. But what is has been shown to be the same as this; therefore it too will not be. **(76)** And again, if what is is the same as what is not, it cannot be that both of them are; for if both are, they are not the same thing, and if they are the same thing, it is not the case that both are. From which it follows that there is nothing. For if there is neither what is nor what is not nor both, and nothing is conceived besides these, there is nothing.

(77) Next it has to be shown that even if there is something, this is unknowable and inconceivable by a human being. For, says Gorgias, if things that are thought are not beings, what is is not thought. And reasonably so. For just as, if things that are thought had as an attribute that they are white, white things would also have as an attribute that they are thought, so if things that are thought have as an attribute that they are not beings, then necessarily beings will have as an attribute that they are not thought. **(78)** So the statement "if things that are thought are not beings, what is is not thought" is sound and preserves consistency. But (to anticipate) things that are thought are *not* beings, as we will show; therefore what is is not thought. And that things that are thought are not beings is evident. **(79)** For if things that are thought are beings, all things that are thought are, however anyone thinks them – which does not seem right. For it is not the case that if someone thinks of a human flying or chariots speeding over the ocean, a human *is* right away flying or chariots *are* speeding over the ocean. So it is not the case that things that are thought are beings. **(80)** In addition, if things that are thought are beings, non-beings will not be thought. For opposite things have opposite attributes, and what is not is opposite to what is; and for this reason, if being thought is an attribute of what is, not being thought will definitely be an attribute of what is not. But this is absurd; for Scylla and Chimaera and many non-beings are thought. Therefore it is not the case that what is is thought. (81) Again, things that are seen are called visible for this reason – because they are seen – and audible things are called audible for this reason – because they are heard. We do not reject visible things because they are not heard, or put aside audible things because they are not seen; each one ought to be judged by its own sense, not by another. In just the same way, things that are thought will be, even if they are not seen by sight or heard by hearing, because they are grasped by means of their own criterion. (82) So if someone thinks of chariots speeding over the ocean, even if he does not see them, he ought to believe that there *are* chariots speeding over the ocean. But this is absurd; therefore it is not the case that what is is thought and apprehended.

(83) And even if it were apprehended, it is not expressible to someone else. For if beings are visible and audible and generally perceptible things, which exist externally, and the visible ones are apprehended by sight and the audible ones by hearing and not vice versa, then how is it possible for these things to be communicated to someone else? (84) For what we communicate with is speech, but speech is not the existing beings; therefore it is not the beings that we communicate to our neighbors, but speech, which is different from the existing things. Just as the visible, then, could not become audible, and conversely, so what is, since it exists externally, could not become our speech. (85) And if it is not speech it cannot be disclosed to someone else. Again, speech, he says, is constituted from the external objects that strike us – that is, from perceptible things. For from the occurrence of flavor there is born in us the speech uttered concerning this quality, and from the impact of color that concerning color. And if this is so, it is not that speech is indicative of the external thing; rather, the external thing becomes revelatory of speech. (86) Then again, it is not possible to say that in the same way as visible and audible things exist, so does speech, so that existing beings can be communicated by means of something that is itself an existing being. For, he says, even if speech exists, it differs, however, from the rest of the things that exist, and visible bodies differ the most from words; for the visible is graspable through one organ and speech through another. Therefore speech does

not indicate the majority[38] of existing things, just as they do not disclose each other's nature. **(87)** Such, then, are the impasses created by Gorgias, and as far as they are concerned the criterion of truth is gone. For nothing could be a criterion of what neither is nor can be known nor is of a nature to be indicated to someone else.

Metrodorus, Anaxarchus, and Monimus (88) **(88)** There have been no small number, as I said before, who have said that Metrodorus and Anaxarchus and also Monimus did away with the criterion: Metrodorus because he said "We know nothing; we do not even know this very fact, that we know nothing," and Anaxarchus and Monimus because they likened the things that are to stage-painting and supposed them to be similar to the things that strike us while asleep or insane.

b. Adherents of a criterion (89–260)
i. *Early physicists (89–140)*
(89) These people, then, adhered to a position of this kind. But it is the physicists, from Thales on, who are thought to have first introduced the inquiry into the criterion. For having condemned sense-perception in many cases as unreliable, they established reason as judge of the truth in the things that there are; beginning from here they structured their ideas about principles and elements and the rest, the apprehension of which comes about through the power of reason.

Anaxagoras (90–91) **(90)** Hence the arch-physicist Anaxagoras, casting aspersions on the senses as weak, says "Because of their feebleness we are not able to judge the truth." And as grounds for trust in their untrustworthiness he cites incremental color change. For if we were to take two colors, black and white, and then pour from the one to the other drop by drop, sight will not be able to discern the incremental changes, even though, at the level of nature, they do exist. **(91)** Asclepiades, too, is found using this argument, in effect, in the first book of his *On Wine Dosage*, where he touches upon white and red: he says "For when these are mixed, sense-perception is unable to distinguish whether the underlying thing is one single color or not." So Anaxagoras said that reason in general is the criterion.

---

[38] I retain the mss. *polla*, instead of altering to *loipa*.

Pythagoreans (92–109) **(92)** But the Pythagoreans said it was reason, but not in general; rather, it is the reason that develops from the sciences. For example, Philolaus said that "Since it is capable of reflecting on the nature of the whole, it has a certain affinity with this, since like is naturally apprehended by like";

> For we see earth by earth, water by water,
> Heavenly air by air, and obliterating fire by fire,
> Love by love, and strife by dire strife.[39]

(93) And, as Posidonius says in expounding Plato's *Timaeus*, "Just as light is apprehended by sight, which is luminous, and sound by hearing, which is airy, so too the nature of the whole ought to be apprehended by something akin to it, namely reason." But the starting-point in the constitution of the whole is number. And this means that reason, the judge of all things, could also be called number, since it is not without a share in its power. **(94)** And in pointing this out the Pythagoreans are sometimes in the habit of saying

> Everything is like number

and at other times swearing the ultimate physicists' oath, as follows:

> No, by the man who handed down to us the tetractys,
> Spring holding the roots of everlasting nature.[40]

By "the man who handed down" they mean Pythagoras (for they made him a god), and by the "tetractys" they mean a certain number.[41] Since it is put together out of the first four numbers it produces the most perfect number, ten; for one and two and three and four make ten. And this number is the first tetractys, **(95)** and is called a "spring of everlasting nature" in so far as the entire universe, according to them, is administered in accordance with harmony. And harmony is a system of three musical intervals, the fourth, the fifth, and the octave; and the proportions of these three intervals are found in the four numbers mentioned before – one, two, three, and four. **(96)** For the interval of a fourth lies in a 4:3 ratio,

---

39 These lines are by Empedocles (cf. 121), whose thought has a Pythagorean dimension. They are also cited by Aristotle (*On the Soul* 404b13–15, *Metaphysics* 1000b6a–8).

40 Also cited as Pythagorean (but again without individual author) in Aetius 1.3, 8ff. (DK 58B15).

41 As Sextus implies, the word "tetractys" is a Pythagorean coinage; though based on the word for "four," it cannot really be translated, but only explained – as Sextus goes on to do.

that of a fifth in a 3:2 ratio, and that of an octave in a 2:1 ratio. Hence the number four, being a third more than three (since it is constituted out of three itself plus a third of three) contains the interval of a fourth; **(97)** three, being a half more than two (in as much it includes that number plus a half of it) reveals the interval of a fifth; and four, being double two, as well as two, being double one, are able to contain the octave. **(98)** Since, then, the tetractys furnishes the proportion of the intervals mentioned, and the intervals are such as to complete the perfect harmony, and everything is administered in accordance with perfect harmony, it is thanks to this that they have called it a "spring holding the roots of everlasting nature."

(99) Besides, both body and the incorporeal (from which everything derives) are conceived by way of the ratios of these four numbers. For we get the appearance of a line, which is length without breadth, from a running point, and we create breadth, which is a kind of surface without depth, from a running line, and from a running surface a solid body comes into being. **(100)** But corresponding to the point is the unit, which is indivisible (as is the point, too), and corresponding to the line is the number two;[42] for the line comes from somewhere,[43] that is from point to point and again from this one to another point. And corresponding to the solid body is four; for if over three points we hang a fourth point, a pyramid comes into being, which after all is the first form of solid body. It is reasonable, then, that the tetractys is the spring of the nature of the whole.

(101) Besides, everything that is apprehended by a human being, they say, is either body or incorporeal; but whether it is body or whether it is incorporeal, it is not apprehended separately from the conception of numbers. Body is not so apprehended, since being three-dimensional it implies the third number.[44] **(102)** And since some bodies are from things fastened together (like ships and chains and cabinets), others from unified things, which are held together by a single holding[45] (like plants and animals), and others from things standing apart (like choruses and armies and flocks) – but whether they are from things fastened together or from unified things or from things standing apart, they have numbers in so far as they consist of multiple things. **(103)** In addition, some bodies

---

[42] At this point Mutschmann (following Bekker) adds the words "and corresponding to the surface is the number three." It is true that one would expect a reference to this. But there is no indication of it in the transmitted text.

[43] I do not accept the addition *pou*.   [44] I retain the mss. *triton*, instead of altering to *tria*.

[45] *Hexis*. In Stoic theory (of which this point seems to be reminiscent) the *hexis* of something is what accounts for its unity; see LS sect. 47.

are possessed of single qualities, others of collections of qualities, such as the apple. For it has a certain kind of color (when it comes to sight) and flavor (when it comes to taste) and smell (when it comes to the sense of smell) and smoothness (when it comes to touch), and these of course are of the nature of numbers. (104) The same reasoning applies in the case of incorporeals, if in fact even time, which is incorporeal, is grasped by number, as is evident from years and months and days and hours. Similarly with the point and line and surface, and the other things we were talking about a little earlier, referring the concepts of them, too, to numbers.

(105) They say that the affairs of life are also in accord with what has been said, as well as the products of skills. For life judges each thing by criteria, which are numerical measures. After all, if we do away with number, the cubit will be done away with, since it consists of two half-cubits and six palms and twenty-four fingers, and the bushel and the talent and the other criteria[46] will be done away with. For all of these consist of a multiplicity, and are thereby forms of number. (106) Hence the rest, too, are involved with number – loans, testimonies, votes, times, periods. And generally it is impossible to find anything in life that has no part in number. And surely no skill was put together without proportion, and proportion depends on number; therefore every skill was put together through number. (107) The Rhodians, anyway (so they say), inquired of Chares the architect how much money it would cost to build the colossus. And when he had made a determination, they asked him again how much it would be if they wanted to build it twice the size. And when he demanded twice as much, they gave it, but he, after spending the amount given to him on the starting-points and the designs, did away with himself. (108) But when he had died, the craftsmen realized that he should have demanded not twice as much but eight times as much; for he needed to increase not only the length but every dimension of the work. So there is a certain proportion in sculpture, and similarly in painting, by means of which indistinguishable similarity is achieved. (109) And in general terms, every skill is a system made up of apprehensions, and system is number. Therefore

Everything is like number

---

[46] It seems odd to call these things criteria. But *kritērion* can also refer more generally to measures or standards. However, Sextus is clearly trying to relate these things to his main theme, and so I employ the English "criterion" as usual.

– that is, like reason, which judges and is similar in kind to the numbers that constitute everything.

Xenophanes (110) **(110)** This is what the Pythagoreans say. But Xenophanes, according to those who interpret him in another way,[47] when he says

> And as for what is clear, no man has seen it, nor will there be anyone
> Who knows about the gods and what I say about all things;
> For even if one should happen to say what has absolutely come to pass
> Nonetheless one does not oneself know; but opinion has been
>   constructed in all cases,

does not appear to do away with every apprehension, but the one that is knowledgeable and error-free, and to leave in place the opinion-based one. For this is conveyed by "but opinion has been constructed in all cases." So the criterion, according to him, becomes opinion-based reasoning, that is, the kind that has to do with the probable but not the certain.

Parmenides (111–114) **(111)** But his associate Parmenides condemned opinion-based reasoning – I mean the kind that contains weak suppositions – and proposed the knowledgeable, that is, the error-free, kind as the criterion, departing even from trust in the senses.[48] At any rate, at the beginning of *On Nature* he writes in this way:

> The mares that carry me as far as my spirit should reach
> Were transporting me, when they went and brought me to the famed road
> Of the goddess who carries a knowing mortal to all cities;
> On it I was being carried; the wise mares were carrying me on it
> Straining the chariot, and girls were leading the way.
> The axle in the center of the wheel sent forth the sound of a pipe,
> Burning bright, for it was being pressed forward by two rounded
> Wheels on either side, as the daughters of the Sun,
> Having left the house of Night, were hurrying to transport me
> Into the light, having pushed back the veils from their heads with
>   their hands.
> There are the gates of the paths of Night and Day
> And the lintel and the stone threshold hold them;
> High in the air they are filled with great doors

---

[47] I.e., differently from those who interpret him in the manner described in 49–52.
[48] I do not accept the addition *autos*.

To which much-punishing Justice holds the corresponding keys.
The girls, gently addressing her with soft words,
Cleverly persuaded her to push back for them the bolt with its iron peg
Swiftly from the gates. And they made a yawning chasm
Of the door-frame as they flew back, twisting around in turn
The bronze door posts, fitted with bolts and rivets,
In their sockets; straight through them
The girls held the chariot and horses along the highway.
And the goddess graciously received me, and took
My right hand in hers, and spoke these words and addressed me:
Welcome, boy, who have reached our house by the horses that carry you
In the company of immortal charioteers;
It was no bad destiny that sent you out to travel
This road (for indeed it is away from the beaten path of humans),
But right and justice. There is need for you to learn all things,
Both the stable heart of persuasive Truth
And the opinions of mortals, in which there is no true trust.[49]
But you, keep your thought away from this road of inquiry,
And do not let habit, product of much experience, force you along
    this road
To direct an unseeing eye and echoing ear
And tongue, but judge by reason the argument, product of much
    experience,
That is spoken by me. Only one spirit of a road
Is still left.

(112) In these words Parmenides is saying that the "mares" that carry him are the non-rational impulses and desires of the soul, and that it is reflection in line with philosophical reason that is conveyed along "the famed road of the goddess." This reason, like a divine escort, leads the way to the knowledge of all things. His "girls" that lead him forward are the senses. And of these, he hints at the ears in saying "for it was being pressed forward by two rounded wheels," that is the round part of the ears, through which they receive sound. (113) And he calls the eyes "daughters of Night," leaving the "house of Night," "pushed into the light" because there is no use for them without light. And coming upon

---

49 The lines so far make up almost all of the prologue of Parmenides' poem as we have it; Simplicius gives us two additional lines. As Simplicius' multiple quotations make clear, the remaining lines quoted by Sextus came from a different point in the poem (after two "roads of inquiry" have been introduced and one has been dismissed). Where Sextus has "spirit of a road" (*thumos hodoio*) Simplicius has "story of a road" (*muthos hodoio*).

"much-punishing" Justice that "holds the corresponding keys" is coming upon thought, which holds safe the apprehensions of objects. (114) And she receives him and then promises to teach the following two things: "both the stable heart of persuasive Truth," which is the immovable stage of knowledge, and also "the opinions of mortals, in which there is no true trust" – that is, everything that rests on opinion, because it is insecure. And at the end he explains further the necessity of not paying attention to the senses but to reason. For he says that you must not "let habit, product of much experience, force you along this road to direct an unseeing eye and echoing ear and tongue, but judge by reason the argument, product of much experience, that is spoken by me."

So he too, as is evident from what has been said, proclaimed knowledgeable reason as the standard of truth in the things that there are, and withdrew from attention to the senses.

Empedocles (115–125 – digression on like knowing like, 116–119) (115) But Empedocles of Acragas, according to those who seem to interpret him more simply,[50] delivers six criteria of truth. For having established two active principles of the universe, Love and Strife, and having at the same time mentioned the four – earth, water, air, and fire – as material principles, he said that these turn out to be criteria of all things. (116) For there is an old opinion, as I said before, circulating among the physicists from way back, about like things being capable of knowing like. Democritus seems to have contributed support for this opinion, while Plato too seems to have touched on it in the *Timaeus*. (117) Democritus bases his reasoning on both living and non-living things. For animals, he says, congregate with animals of the same kind, such as doves with doves and cranes with cranes, and this also applies to other non-rational animals. And the same applies to non-living things, as can be seen with seeds being sifted and pebbles at the beach. For in the one case, by way of the whirling of the sieve, lentils are arranged separately with lentils, barley with barley, and wheat with wheat, (118) while in the other case, by way of the motion of the waves, oblong pebbles are pushed into the same place as oblong ones, and round ones into the same place as round ones, as if similarity in these cases had a sort of uniting force over things.[51] So, then, Democritus;

---

[50] I.e., as compared with the interpretation at 122ff.

[51] Sections 117–118 are often taken as containing a quotation; see DK 68B164. Sextus' closing words "So, then, Democritus" certainly indicates that he takes himself to have accurately reported

(119) but Plato in the *Timaeus* uses the same type of demonstration for the purpose of demonstrating the fact that the soul is incorporeal. For, he says, if sight in apprehending light is right away luminous, and hearing, in discerning air being struck (which is sound), is right away observed to be airy, and smell in picking up vapors is definitely vaporous, and taste in picking up flavors is flavor-like, then necessarily the soul too, in grasping the incorporeal ideas, such as those in numbers and those in the limits of bodies, becomes an incorporeal sort of thing.[52]

(120) Such is the opinion among the earlier figures. Empedocles too seems to be swept along by this view, and to say that since the principles that constitute everything are six, the criteria are equal in number to these, so that he writes

> (121) For we see earth by earth, water by water,
> Heavenly air by air, and obliterating fire by fire,
> Love by love, and strife by dire strife,

making clear that we apprehend earth by the participation of earth, water by way of the participation of water, air by the participation of air, and similarly in the case of fire. (122) But there have been others saying that according to Empedocles the criterion of truth is not the senses but correct reason, and that of correct reason one sort is divine and the other human; and of these the divine one is inexpressible, while the human one is expressible. (123) On the fact that the judgment of what is true does not belong in the senses he speaks thus:

> Narrow are the devices scattered over our limbs,
> Many are the wretched sudden things that blunt our thoughts.
> Seeing a small part of their own life
> Lifted up like smoke they fly off to a swift fate
> Persuaded only of that which each has met with
> While being driven in all directions, but everyone boasts that he has found the whole.
> These things are not thus to be seen by men nor to be heard
> Nor to be grasped by the intellect.

Democritus' view. But it need not indicate that he has given Democritus' exact words; in fact, as is pointed out in DK itself, the language seems in places anachronistic for Democritus.

[52] See *Timaeus* 45b–c (the "like by like" principle applied to sight) and 37a–c (the same principle applied to soul). But Sextus' account is at best a creative paraphrase. In particular, the *Timaeus* never attempts to demonstrate the incorporeality of the soul – that is taken for granted.

(**124**) On the fact that the truth is not completely ungraspable, but is graspable as far as human reason reaches, he provides clarification when he adds to the preceding lines

> But you, since you have strayed hither,
> Will learn; mortal wit has not stirred itself further.[53]

And in the next lines, after criticizing those who profess to know more, he establishes that what is grasped through each sense is trustworthy when reason is in charge of them, despite earlier running down the assurance gained from them. (**125**) For he says

> But gods, turn away these people's madness from my tongue,
> And from holy mouths make flow a pure stream.
> And you, white-armed virgin Muse who remembers much,
> I entreat: what it is right for creatures of a day to hear,
> Send to me, driving your well-reined chariot from Piety's place.[54]
> Nor will the blooms of well-reputed honor from mortals
> Force you to take them up, on condition that you have the audacity
>   to say
> More than is holy, and then sit upon the heights of wisdom.
> But come, observe with every device, in the way each thing is clear,
> Not holding any sight in trust more than by way of hearing,
> Or loud-sounding hearing above the things made plain by the tongue,
> Nor by any means hold back trust from the other limbs,
> As many ways as there is a path for thinking, but think in the way
>   each thing is clear.

Heraclitus (126–134)   (**126**) Such are the things Empedocles said. But Heraclitus – since again the human being seemed to him to be equipped with two organs for knowledge of the truth, sense-perception and reason – thought (like the physicists mentioned before) that of these sense-perception was untrustworthy, and posits reason as the criterion. He convicts sense-perception saying in so many words "Bad witnesses for humans are the eyes and ears of those who have barbarian souls," which

---

[53] I retain the mss. *pleion ge*, instead of altering to *pleon ēe*.

[54] As commentators have noticed, these first five lines seem quite separate from those that follow; "you" up to this point refers to the Muse, but in the following lines to the addressee of the poem (Pausanias). Either some lines have dropped out of the text or Sextus is combining passages from different places (cf. 111).

amounts to "Trusting in the non-rational senses is the mark of barbarian souls." (127) But the reason that he proclaims to be judge of the truth is not just any kind of reason, but the common and divine one. What this is must be briefly indicated. This physicist adheres to the view that "What encompasses us is rational and endowed with mind."[55] (128) Homer points out this kind of thing much earlier, saying

> Such is the mind of earth-bound humans
> As is the day the father of men and gods brings on.[56]

And Archilochus says that humans think such things

> As is the day that Zeus brings on.

The same thing has also been said by Euripides:

> Whoever you are, hard to guess at or discern,
> Zeus, whether necessity of nature or mortal intellect,
> I pray to you.[57]

(129) By drawing in this divine reason through respiration, then, we become intelligent according to Heraclitus, and are forgetful in sleep, but come back to our senses on waking. For in sleep, when the passages of the senses have been closed, the intellect in us is separated from its natural connection with what encompasses us – only the natural connection by way of respiration being preserved, like a root, as it were – and being separated it loses the power of memory that it had before. (130) But in the waking state it emerges again through the passages of the senses (as if through windows, as it were), and on meeting with what encompasses us it puts on the power of reason. In the same way, then, as coals when near to fire undergo an alteration and become fiery, but are put out when taken away from it, so too the portion of what encompasses us that dwells like a foreigner in our bodies becomes virtually devoid of reason in the case of separation,[58] but in the case of natural connection through the multiple passages it becomes similar in kind to the whole.

(131) So it is this common and divine reason (by participation in which we become rational) that Heraclitus says is the criterion of truth. Hence

---

55 Cf. 2.286, where a similar thought with similar vocabulary is said to represent Heraclitus "in so many words." Despite Sextus' insistence, this is unlikely to be true; the word *logikos* ("rational") was probably not current in Heraclitus' day. But some of the vocabulary may be genuinely Heraclitean.
56 *Odyssey* 18.136–137.   57 *Trojan Women* 885–887.
58 I.e., when it is separated from the whole.

what appears in common to everyone is trustworthy (for it is grasped by the common and divine reason), whereas what strikes someone individually is untrustworthy on the opposite grounds. (132) At the beginning of *On Nature*, then,[59] indicating in a certain way what encompasses us, the man just mentioned says

> Of this reason,[60] which is,[61] humans are without understanding, both before hearing it and after first hearing it. For they are like people without experience of the things that happen[62] according to this reason when they try out such words and objects as I describe, dividing each thing according to its nature and saying how it is. Other humans fail to notice what they do when awake, just as they forget what they do when asleep.

(133) And having specifically established by these words that it is by way of participation in the divine reason that we do and think everything, after a little prior discussion he adds "Therefore it is necessary to follow what is[63] common" (for 'public' is 'common'). But though reason is public, most people live as if they had private insight." And this is none other than an explanation of the way all is administered. Therefore in so far as we share in the memory of it,[64] we speak truly, while whatever is private to us we speak falsely. (134) For now in these words he most specifically pronounces the common reason the criterion, and says that the things that appear in common are trustworthy on the grounds of being judged by the common reason, while those that appear in private to each person are false.

[59] I retain the mss. *oun*, instead of altering to *goun*.

[60] How to translate the word *logos* as Heraclitus originally intended it is a controversial question (and some prefer to leave it untranslated). However, it is clear from the surrounding context that Sextus understands it to mean "reason."

[61] Two other authors who quote part of this text confirm that it originally contained the word *aei*, "forever," at this point – Aristotle (*Rhetoric* 1407b17) and Hippolytus (9.9; see also the following note).

[62] Hippolytus' evidence (see the previous note) indicates that Sextus has omitted the word *pantōn*, "all," at this point; with this word in place, the sense becomes "For although all things happen according to this reason, they are like people without experience . . ."

[63] I translate the mss. as they stand. Mutschmann follows Bekker and Diels in adding *xunōi, toutesti tōi* at this point, giving the sense "'to follow what is public' (that is, common; for 'public' is 'common')." Clearly *xunos*, "public," was Heraclitus' word, one that for Sextus is archaic and needs explanation in terms of *koinos*, "common." But he may have *changed* Heraclitus' *xunos* to *koinos* in the quotation, and then be explaining this in the parenthetical phrase as an afterthought. Other scholars treat this entire sentence as a comment by Sextus, and only the next sentence as a quotation. But "he adds" certainly suggests that a quotation is about to begin.

[64] I.e., of the public reason.

Democritus (135–140) **(135)** This is what Heraclitus is like. But Democritus sometimes does away with the things that appear to the senses and says that none of these things appear truthfully, but only in the manner of opinion, while what is true in the things that there are is the fact that there are atoms and void. For he says "By convention sweet and by convention bitter, by convention hot, by convention cold, by convention color; in verity atoms and void." (I.e., perceptible things are thought – that is, held by opinion – to be, but it is not these things that truthfully are, but only atoms and void.) **(136)** And in *Strengthenings*, despite having promised to attribute strong trust to the senses, he is nonetheless found condemning them. For he says "In fact we understand nothing precise, but what changes according to the condition of the body and of the things that enter it and of the things that offer resistance to it." And again he says "It has been shown in many ways that in verity we do not understand what each thing is or is not like." **(137)** And in *On Ideas* he says "A human being must know by this rule that he is removed from verity"; and again: "This reasoning too shows that in verity we know nothing about anything, but opinion is for everyone a reshaping." And yet again: "However it will be clear that to know in verity what each thing is like is hopeless." In these places, then, he more or less removes all knowledge, even though it is only the senses that he singles out for attack.

(138) But in *Rules* he says that there are two forms of knowledge, one through the senses and the other through thought. Of these he calls the one through thought "legitimate," testifying to its reliability for the judgment of truth, while he names the one through the senses "bastard," not allowing it to be unerring in the discernment of what is true. **(139)** He says in so many words: "There are two forms of judgment, one legitimate, the other bastard. And all these are of the bastard kind: sight, hearing, smell, taste, touch. The other one is legitimate and separated from this." Then, ranking the legitimate kind before the bastard one, he goes on to say: "When the bastard one can no longer see any smaller or hear or smell or taste or perceive by touch, but < ... > more finely, < ... >."[65] So, according to this man, too, reason is the criterion, which he calls legitimate judgment.

---

[65] Clearly there are some words missing here. Presumably the sense was along the following lines: when the senses can proceed no further, but there is need for a means to judge more finely, then the "legitimate" kind of judgment (Sextus is surely correct that this is the intellect) must take over.

(140) But Diotimus said that according to him there are three criteria: for the apprehension of unclear things, apparent ones (for apparent things are a sight of things that are unclear, as Anaxagoras said, and Democritus praised him for this); for investigation, the conception ("for in every case, my boy, the only starting-point is knowing what the investigation is about";)[66] and for choice and avoidance, effects on us. For what we are at home with is to be chosen, and what we are alienated from is to be avoided.

The ancients' account concerning the criterion of truth, then, was something like this; (141) let us next deal with the schools after the physicists.

ii. Post-physicists (141–260)

Plato (141–144)   Well then, Plato in the *Timaeus*, having divided things into intelligible and perceptible, and said that intelligible things are comprehensible by reason, while perceptible things turn out to be opinable, clearly determined the criterion of the knowledge of objects to be reason, including with it the plain experience of sense-perception as well. (142) He says the following: "What is that which always is and has no coming into being, and what is that which is always coming into being and never is? The one is comprehensible by intelligence, with reason, the other by opinion, with sense-perception."[67] (143) And the Platonists say that the reason that is common to plain experience and the truth is called by him "comprehensive reason." For in judging the truth, reason has to start from plain experience, if indeed the judgment of true things comes about through plain things. But plain experience is not self-sufficient for knowledge of what is true. For it is not the case that if something appears in plain experience, this thing is also truly real. Rather, the thing that judges what merely appears and what, along with appearing, also truly exists – that is, reason – has to be present. (144) So both have to come together, plain experience in the role of a starting-line for reason in its judgment of the truth, and reason itself for a determination about plain experience. However, for applying itself to plain experience and determining what is true in it, reason again needs sense-perception to work with it. For it is by receiving the appearance through sense-perception that it creates

[66] A near-quotation from Plato, *Phaedrus* 237b7–c1.   [67] *Timaeus* 27d6–28a2 (virtually verbatim).

the understanding and the knowledge of what is true, so that it is comprehensive of both plain experience and the truth, which is equivalent to "apprehensive."[68]

Speusippus (145–146) **(145)** Plato's position was like this. But Speusippus (since some objects are perceptible, others intelligible) said that the criterion of intelligible things was knowledgeable reason, while that of perceptible things was knowledgeable sense-perception. And he supposed knowledgeable sense-perception to be the kind that has a share in truth by way of reason. **(146)** Compare the flute-player's or the harpist's fingers, which have a technical activity, yet not one that is perfected directly in the fingers themselves, but one that is completed by means of shared training in connection with reasoning. Or take the musician's sense, which has an activity capable of grasping what is in tune and what is out of tune, yet this does not develop on its own, but results from reasoning. In the same way knowledgeable sense-perception, too, naturally gets from reason a share in knowledgeable practice with a view to unerring discernment of the underlying things.

Xenocrates (147–149) **(147)** But Xenocrates says that there are three kinds of being: perceptible, intelligible, and composite and opinable. Of these, the perceptible one is that within the sky,[69] the intelligible one is that of everything outside the sky, and the opinable and composite one is that of the sky itself; for it is visible by sense-perception, but intelligible through astronomy. **(148)** Now, since these things hold in this way, he declared knowledge the criterion of the being that is outside the sky (that is, intelligible), sense-perception the criterion of the kind that is within the sky (that is, perceptible), and opinion the criterion of the mixed kind. And of these generally the criterion via knowledgeable reason is both firm and true, the one via sense-perception is true, but not *as* true as the one via knowledgeable reason, and the composite one is jointly both true and false; **(149)** for some opinion is true and some is false. Hence, too, the legendary three Fates: Atropos, the Fate of intelligible things (since she is immutable), Clotho, that of perceptible things, and Lachesis, that of opinable things.

---

[68] The notion of "apprehension" (*katalēpsis*), discussed below in the context of Stoic theory (227ff.; see also 150ff. on Arcesilaus and Carneades), becomes a major focus in the latter part of the book.
[69] I.e., the terrestrial region.

Arcesilaus (150–158) **(150)** Arcesilaus and his circle did not, as their main goal, define any criterion; those of them who are thought to have defined one delivered this by way of a hostile response against the Stoics.[70] **(151)** For the Stoics say that there are three interconnected things: knowledge, opinion, and the one positioned between these, apprehension. Of these knowledge is apprehension that is unshaken and firm and immutable by reason, opinion is weak and false assent, and apprehension is the one between these, namely assent to an apprehensive appearance. **(152)** And according to them, an apprehensive appearance is one that is true and such as could not be false. Of these, knowledge subsists only in the wise, opinion only in the inferior, and apprehension is common to both; and this is the criterion of truth. **(153)** This is what the Stoics say, and Arcesilaus rebutted them by showing that apprehension is no criterion between knowledge and opinion. For what they call apprehension, and assent to an apprehensive appearance, takes place either in a wise or an inferior person. But if it takes place in a wise person, it is knowledge, and if in an inferior person it is opinion, and beyond these nothing has been substituted other than a mere name. **(154)** And if apprehension is assent to an apprehensive appearance, it is unreal, first because assent takes place not toward appearance but toward speech (for assents are to propositions), and second because no true appearance is found to be such as could not be false, as is witnessed by many diverse cases. **(155)** But if there is no apprehensive appearance, apprehension will not take place either; for it was assent to an apprehensive appearance. But if there is no apprehension, everything will be inapprehensible. And if everything is inapprehensible it will follow even according to the Stoics that the wise person suspends judgment.

(156) Let us consider it like this: since everything is inapprehensible on account of the unreality of the Stoic criterion, if the wise person assents, the wise person will opine. For since nothing is apprehensible, if he assents to anything, he will assent to the inapprehensible, but assent to the inapprehensible is opinion. **(157)** So that if the wise person is among those who assent, the wise person will be among those who opine. But the wise person is *not* among those who opine (for according to them this goes with folly and is a cause of errors); therefore the wise person is not among those who assent. But if this is so, he will have to decline assent about

---

[70] For a rather different set of comments on Arcesilaus, compare *PH* 1.232–234.

everything. But declining assent is none other than suspending judgment; therefore the wise person will suspend judgment about everything.

(158) But since after this it was necessary also to investigate the conduct of life, which is not of a nature to be accounted for without a criterion, on which happiness too – that is, the end of life – depends for its trust, Arcesilaus says that, not[71] suspending judgment about everything, he will regulate his choices and avoidances and generally his actions by the reasonable, and by going forward in accordance with this criterion he will act rightly. For happiness comes about through insight, and insight lies in right actions, and the right action is that which, when done, has a reasonable justification. The person who pays attention to the reasonable will therefore act rightly and be happy.

Carneades (159–189)   (159) This is what Arcesilaus said. Carneades positioned himself on the criterion not only against the Stoics but also against everyone before him. In fact his first argument, which is directed against all of them together, is one according to which he establishes that nothing is without qualification a criterion of truth – not reason, not sense-perception, not appearance, not anything else that there is; for all of these as a group deceive us. (160) Second is the one according to which he shows that, even if there is this criterion,[72] it does not subsist apart from the effect on us from plain experience. For since an animal differs from inanimate things by its sensory ability, it is definitely through this that it will become capable of grasping both itself and external things. Now sense-perception that is unmoved, unaffected, and unchanged is not sense-perception at all, nor is it capable of grasping anything. (161) But when it is changed and somehow affected in accordance with the impact of plain things, then it does exhibit objects. Therefore the criterion is to be sought in the effect on the soul from plain experience. And this effect should turn out to be indicative of both itself and the apparent thing that produced it; and this effect is none other than the appearance. (162) Hence one should say that an appearance is a certain effect in the animal that is capable of displaying both itself and the other thing. For example, when we have looked at

---

[71] I retain the mss. *ou*. Mutschmann and many others alter to *ho*, giving the sense "The person who suspends judgment about everything will regulate his choices." But the mss. reading could very well represent a polemical aside on Sextus' part: Arcesilaus talks about regulating choices by the reasonable, and someone who does this does *not* in fact suspend judgment about everything.

[72] I retain the mss. *to* (and punctuate after *touto*, not before), instead of altering to *ti*.

something, says Antiochus,[73] our sense of sight is disposed in a certain way, and we do not have it in the same condition as we had before looking. And by way of this kind of alteration we grasp two things, one of them the alteration itself – that is, the appearance – and second the thing that brought about the alteration – that is, the thing seen. And similarly in the case of the other senses. (163) So, just as light shows both itself and everything in it, so too the appearance, being the originator of knowledge in the animal, ought (like light) both to reveal itself and to be indicative of the plain thing that brought it about. But since it does not always exhibit the truth, but often deceives and disagrees with the objects that sent it, like bad messengers, it necessarily follows that one cannot allow every appearance as a criterion of truth, but only, if at all, the true one. (164) Again, then, since there is no true one of such a kind as could not be false, but for every one that seems to be true an indistinguishable false one is found, the criterion will come to consist in an appearance that is common to both true and false. But the appearance that is common to these two is not apprehensive, and not being apprehensive, neither will it be a criterion. (165) And since there is no appearance capable of judging, neither could reason be a criterion; for this takes off from appearance. And this is likely enough; for the thing being judged first has to appear to it, and nothing can appear in the absence of non-rational sense-perception. Therefore neither non-rational sense-perception nor reason can be a criterion.

(166) These are the arguments for the unreality of the criterion that Carneades went through, deploying them against the other philosophers. But since he too requires some criterion for the conduct of life and for the achievement of happiness, he is in effect compelled for his own part to take a stand on this, helping himself to the persuasive appearance and the one that is persuasive as well as not turned away and gone over in detail. (167) It should be pointed out briefly what the difference between these is. The appearance, then, is an appearance of something – that is, of that *from* which it occurs and of that *in* which it occurs: that from which it occurs – namely, the externally existing sensed thing – and that in which it occurs – namely, a human being. (168) Being like this, it would have two states, one in relation to the thing that appears, the second in relation to the person having the appearance. As regards its state in relation to the

---

[73] This is an unexpected intrusion (cf. 201–202), since Antiochus has not previously been named in this context. But Sextus must be drawing directly or indirectly on Antiochus' account of these matters in his *Kanonika* (*On Rules*, cited in 201 – cf. also n. 13), which has not survived.

thing that appears, it is either true or false, true when it agrees with the thing that appears, false when it disagrees. (169) As regards its state in relation to the person having the appearance, one of them is apparently true and the other not apparently true. Of these, the apparently true one is called by the Academics "reflection" and "persuasiveness" and "persuasive appearance," while the not apparently true one is named "non-reflection" and "not persuasive" and "unpersuasive appearance"; for neither what immediately appears false, nor what is true but does not appear so, is of a nature to persuade us. (170) And of these appearances the one that is manifestly false and not apparently true is subject to objections and is not a criterion. [. . .]⁷⁴ (171) Of the apparently true kind, one is faint, as in the case of those who, because of the smallness of the thing being observed or because of the sizeable distance or even because of the weakness of their eyesight, grasp something in a mixed-up way and not distinctly. The other, in addition to appearing true, also has its appearance of being true to an extreme degree. (172) Of these, again, the faint and weak appearance could not be a criterion; for because of its not exhibiting clearly either itself or the thing that produced it, it is not of a nature to persuade us or to draw us to assent. (173) But the one that is apparently true and makes itself sufficiently apparent is the criterion of truth according to Carneades. And being the criterion, it has a sizeable breadth, and since it is extended, one has an appearance that is more persuasive and more striking in form than another.⁷⁵ (174) The persuasive, for the present purpose, is spoken of in three ways: in one way, applying to what both is true and is apparently true; in another way, to what is false but is apparently true; and in the third way, to what is <apparently> true, <which is> common to both.⁷⁶ Hence the criterion is the apparently true appearance, which the Academics call persuasive. (175) However, it sometimes happens actually to be false, so that it is necessary actually to use the appearance that is

---

⁷⁴ With Heintz and LS (69D), I delete the remainder of 170 as an ill-advised gloss. It contains the example of Orestes and Electra and closely resembles 249; the point clearly belongs in the Stoic context of the latter passage.

⁷⁵ This translates the manuscript text. But unless Sextus or his source is extremely confused, something must be wrong with this text; it makes no sense to speak of an appearance having an appearance. LS provide a lightly altered text, which they translate "and by admitting of degrees, it includes some impressions [i.e., appearances] which are more convincing and striking in their form than others." Heintz alters the text differently and a little more extensively; his text may be translated "and since it is extended, one specific appearance will be more persuasive and more striking than another."

⁷⁶ I follow LS's supplement *alēthes <phainomenon, hoper esti> koinon*, instead of deleting *alēthes*.

at times common to the true and the false. Yet one should not, because of the rare occurrence of this (I mean the one that merely imitates the truth), distrust the one that for the most part tells the truth. For both our judgments and our actions are, as a matter of fact, regulated by what applies for the most part.

The first and general criterion, then, according to Carneades, is like this. (176) But since an appearance is never monadic – rather, one hangs on another, like a chain – there will be added as a second criterion the appearance that is persuasive as well as not turned away.[77] For example, someone who catches an appearance of a human being necessarily also grasps an appearance of features that attach to him and of external features: (177) features that attach to him, such as color, size, shape, movement, talk, clothing, footwear, and external features, such as atmosphere, light, day, sky, earth, friends, and all the rest. Whenever none of these appearances distracts us by appearing false, but all of them in unison appear true, our trust is greater. (178) For we trust that this is Socrates from the fact that he has all his usual features too: color, size, shape, opinion, ragged cloak, and his being in a place where there is no one indistinguishable from him. (179) And just as some doctors detect the genuine fever patient not from one symptom, such as an excessive pulse or a severe high temperature, but from a cluster, such as a high temperature as well as pulse and soreness to the touch and flushing and thirst and similar things, so too the Academic makes his judgment as to the truth by a cluster of appearances, and given that none of the appearances in the cluster turns him away as being false,[78] he says that what strikes him is true. (180) And that the one that is not turned away is a cluster <. . .> of producing trust[79] is obvious

---

[77] I.e., as the sequel makes clear, not put into doubt by other conflicting appearances. But Sextus also makes clear that this label only applies to appearances that have in fact been subjected to a comparison with other relevant appearances; the coherence of multiple appearances is the point at issue.

[78] I.e., strikes him as false and so causes him not to trust it. Here it is the *person*, not the appearance itself, that is described as "turned away."

[79] I translate the words given in the manuscript, which are grammatically impossible as they stand; if we do not alter them, then something must have been lost between "cluster" and "of producing trust." Kayser's suggested alteration of *tou pistin empoiein* to *tōn pistin empoiousōn* would yield the sense "cluster of ones [i.e., appearances] producing trust." But this only reinforces another intractable problem that is in any case present, namely that "the one [i.e., the *appearance*] that is 'not turned away'" is being identified as a "cluster," i.e., a cluster *of appearances* (cf. n. 75). The text seems to be fundamentally garbled, and suggested reconstructions are bound to be speculative. Luckily, the overall train of thought is not obscured, since this clause is clearly supposed to be recapitulating the previous few sentences.

from Menelaus. For when he left on the ship the phantom Helen, which he brought from Troy under the impression that it *was* Helen, and set foot on the island of Pharos, he saw the true Helen. But while he caught a true appearance from her, nevertheless he did not trust such an appearance on account of its being turned away by another one, the one in virtue of which he knew he had left Helen on the ship. (181) So the appearance that is not turned away is like this; and it too seems to have breadth in view of the fact that one appearance is found to be not turned away to a greater degree than another.

Even more trustworthy than the appearance that is not turned away, and most perfect, is the one that produces judgment, which together with being not turned away is also gone over in detail. (182) What is the distinctive mark of this one should next be pointed out. In the case of the one that is not turned away, the requirement is simply that none of the appearances in the cluster should turn us away as being false, but that all of them should be true and apparently so and not unpersuasive. But in the case of the cluster associated with the one that is explored all round, we carefully scrutinize each of the appearances in the cluster – which is the kind of thing that happens in assemblies, too, when the people examine each of those who are in line to be office-holders or judges, to see if he is worthy of being entrusted with the office or the judgeship. (183) For example, at the place of judgment there are: the one judging, the thing being judged, and that through which the judgment occurs, distance and interval, place, time, manner, disposition, and activity. We distinguish precisely what each of these things is like: the one judging, whether its eyesight is not dulled (for if it is, it will be useless for judging); the thing being judged, whether it is not too small; that through which the judgment occurs, whether the atmosphere is not murky; the distance, whether it is not too great; the interval, whether it is not confused; the place, whether it is not immense; the time, whether it is not quick; the disposition, whether it is not observed to be crazy; the activity, whether it is not inadmissible.

(184) For all of these things one by one become the criterion: the persuasive appearance, and the one that is persuasive as well as not turned away, and besides these the one that is persuasive as well as not turned away and gone over in detail. For this reason, just as in ordinary life, when we are investigating a small matter we question one witness, when

it is a greater matter, several witnesses, and when it is an even more essential matter we examine each of the witnesses on the basis of the mutual agreement among the others, so, Carneades and his circle say, on random matters we use just the persuasive appearance as criterion, on more important matters we use the one that is not turned away, and on matters that contribute to happiness the one that is explored all round. (185) Besides, they say that just as they employ a different appearance in the case of different matters, so too they do not follow the same one in different situations. For they say that they attend to the persuasive one alone in cases where the situation does not give us an opportunity for exact consideration of the matter. (186) For example, someone is being pursued by enemies and, coming to a ditch, he catches an appearance as of his enemies lying in wait for him right there. Then being gripped by this appearance as persuasive, he turns away and flees the ditch, following the persuasiveness surrounding the appearance, before giving exact attention to whether there is in fact an ambush by his enemies at this place or not. (187) But they follow the one that is persuasive and explored all round in cases where time is available for employing one's judgment, on the matter that confronts one, with care and by going over it in detail. For example, someone observing a coil of rope in an unlit room immediately jumps over it, supposing it to be in fact a snake. But after this he turns round and examines what is true, and finding it motionless he already has in his thinking an inclination towards its *not* being a snake. (188) Still, figuring that snakes are sometimes motionless when they go stiff from winter cold, he pokes the coil with a stick, and then, after thus exploring from all angles the appearance that strikes him, he assents to its being false that the body made apparent to him is a snake. And again, as I said before, when we see something clearly we assent to the fact that this is true when we have previously found, by going over the matter in detail, that we have our senses in good order, that we are looking while awake and not in our sleep, and that there is a combination of clear atmosphere, moderate distance, and immobility of the thing striking us, (189) so that because of these things the appearance is trustworthy, since we have had sufficient time for going over in detail the things observed at its location. The same reasoning also applies to the one that is not turned away; for they accept it when there is nothing that has been capable of dragging it down, as was said earlier in the case of Menelaus.

Cyrenaics (190–200) (**190**) But now that the Academics' story has been given, from Plato onward, it is perhaps not beside the point also to review the Cyrenaics' position. For these men's school seems to have emerged from the discourse of Socrates, from which the Platonist tradition also emerged. (**191**) The Cyrenaics, then, say that effects on us[80] are the criteria, and that they alone are apprehended and turn out to be free from mistakes, but that of the things that have brought about the effects none is apprehensible or free of deceit. For, they say, that we are whitened and we are sweetened,[81] it is possible to say without deceit and truly and firmly and irrefutably; but that the thing productive of the effect is white or sweet, it is not possible to assert. (**192**) For it is probable that one is disposed whitely even by a thing that is not white and that one is sweetened even by a thing that is not sweet. For the person with vertigo or with jaundice is activated yellowly by everything, and the person with ophthalmia is reddened, and the person who presses on his eye is activated as if by two things, and the crazy person sees Thebes double and imagines the sun double,[82] (**193**) and in all these cases, that they are affected in this way (for example, they are yellowed or reddened or doubled) is true, but that the thing that activates them is yellow or reddish or double is thought to be false. And so, too, it very much stands to reason that we are not able to grasp anything more than the effects that belong to us.[83] Hence one must posit as apparent either effects on us or the things that are productive of the effects. (**194**) And if we say that effects on us are apparent, then it must be said that everything apparent is true and apprehensible; but if we declare as apparent the things that are productive of the effects, everything apparent is false and inapprehensible. For the effect that happens in us reveals to us nothing more than itself. Hence in fact (if we must tell the truth) only the effect is apparent to us; the external thing productive of the effect is perhaps a being, but it is not apparent to us.

(**195**) And in this way we are all unerring with respect to effects (the ones belonging to ourselves, anyway), but we all go wrong with respect to

---

[80] *Pathē*, often translated "feelings" or, in other contexts, "passions" or "emotions." But *pathos* is the noun cognate with *paschō*, "be affected," and may refer to anything that *happens to* one. To avoid begging the question on the nature of the entities under discussion, I translate *pathos* throughout as "effect" – sometimes adding "on us" to make clear that it is effects on human beings that are at issue.

[81] On this curious Cyrenaic terminology (see also 192, "disposed whitely," "activated yellowly," etc.), see V. Tsouna, *The Epistemology of the Cyrenaic School* (Cambridge University Press, 1998), esp. ch. 3. Such terminology is later employed on occasion by Sextus himself.

[82] A reference to Pentheus in Euripides' *Bacchae* (918–919).   [83] I.e., that occur in us.

the externally existing thing. And the former are apprehensible while the latter is inapprehensible, the soul being too weak to discern it as a result of the locations, the distances, the movements, the changes, and lots of other causes. Hence they say that there is not even a criterion common to humanity, but that common names are placed on objects.[84] (196) For everyone in common calls something white or sweet, but they do not *have* something white or sweet in common. For each person grasps the effect that is his own, but on the question whether this effect comes about in him and in his neighbor from a white thing, neither can he himself say, since he does not receive the effect on his neighbor, nor can his neighbor, since he does not receive the one that happens to the other person. (197) But since no common effect comes about in us, it is rash to say that what appears a certain way to me also appears that way to the next person. For perhaps I am put together in such a way as to be whitened by the thing that strikes me from outside, but the other person has his senses designed so as to be disposed differently. What is apparent to us, then, is absolutely not common.[85] (198) And that in fact we are not activated in the same way, given the different designs of our senses, is clear in the case of people with jaundice and people with ophthalmia and people in a natural condition. For just as the first group are affected yellowly, the second redly, and the third whitely from the same thing, so it is probable that even those in a natural condition are not activated in the same way from the same things, given the different design of their senses, but rather that the grey-eyed person is activated one way, the blue-eyed person another way, and the black-eyed person another way. So that we place common names on objects, but the effects that we get from them are our own.

(199) Similar, too, to what these men say about criteria seems to be what they say about ends. For effects on us extend also to ends. For of effects some are pleasant, some are painful, and some are in between. And the painful ones they say are bad, and their end is pain, while the pleasant ones are good, and their end (no mistake about it) is pleasure, and the things in between are neither good nor bad, and their end is the neither-good-nor-bad, which is an effect in between pleasure and pain. (200) Effects on us, then, are criteria and ends of everything that there is; and we live, they say, by following these and by paying attention to plain

---

[84] With Natorp I read *chrēmasin* for the mss. *krimasin*, instead of Mutschmann's *sugkrimasin*.
[85] I.e., common to more than one person.

experience and to satisfaction – plain experience as far as the other effects are concerned, but satisfaction as far as pleasure is concerned.

This is what the Cyrenaics' ideas are like. They go further than the Platonists in narrowing the criterion; for the latter made it a combination of plain experience and reason, while the former limit it only to plain experience – that is, effects on us.

Asclepiades (201–202) (**201**) Not far away from these people's opinion seem to be those who pronounce the criterion of truth to be the senses. For Antiochus of the Academy has made evident that there have been some who propose such a thing, writing the following (word for word) in the second book of his *On Rules*: "But someone else, second to none in medicine and involved also with philosophy, was persuaded that sense-perceptions in fact truly are apprehensions, and that we do not apprehend anything at all by reason." (**202**) For in these words Antiochus seems to be laying out the aforementioned position and to be hinting at Asclepiades the doctor, who does away with the leading part,[86] and who lived at the same time as himself. But we have gone through this person's line of thinking more intricately and separately in our *Medical Treatises*,[87] so that there is no need to repeat it.

Epicurus (203–216) (**203**) Epicurus says that there are two objects that are connected with one another – appearance and opinion – and that of these appearance, which he also calls plain experience, is in every case true. For just as the primary effects on us – that is, pleasure and pain – are produced from certain things liable to bring them about, and in accordance with the very things that are liable to bring them about (namely, pleasure from pleasant things and pain from painful things), and it is not possible for what is liable to bring about pleasure ever *not* to be pleasant, nor for what is liable to cause pain not to be painful, but it is necessary for what pleases, and what pains, to be in their underlying nature pleasant and painful respectively, so too in the case of appearances, which are effects that happen to us, the thing that is liable to bring each one about is in every way and entirely a thing that appears. And it is not possible for it, being a thing that appears, not to be in truth such as it appears <. . .> to be liable

---

[86] I.e., of the soul; cf. n. 22.   [87] This work has not survived.

to bring about an appearance.[88] **(204)** And one must reason similarly in the particular cases. For what is visible not only appears visible, but also is such as it appears; and what is audible not only appears audible, but also is in truth such, and similarly in the other cases. Therefore all appearances come to be true. And reasonably so. **(205)** For, the Epicureans say, if an appearance is said to be true whenever it comes about from a real thing and in accordance with just *that* real thing, and every appearance is produced from a real thing that appears and in accordance with the very thing that appears, necessarily every appearance is true.

(206) What fools some people is the difference in the appearances that seem to strike us from the same perceptible (e.g., visible) thing, in virtue of which the existing thing appears to be of varying color or varying shape or in some other way changed. For they supposed that, of the appearances that thus differ and compete, one of them must be true, while the other one of opposite origins turns out to be false. Which is silly, and typical of men who fail to see the nature of reality. **(207)** For (to give the argument in the case of visible things) it is not the whole solid body that is seen, but the color of the solid body. And of color, some is on the solid body itself, as in the case of things looked at close up or from a moderate distance, while some is outside the solid body, and exists in the neighboring locations, as in the case of things observed from a great distance. But this changes in the space in between, and takes on its own shape, and hence gives off an appearance of the same kind as it is itself in its true existence. **(208)** It is not the sound in the bronze instrument being struck that is heard, nor the sound in the mouth of the person yelling, but the one that strikes our sense; and no one says that the person who hears a faint sound from a distance hears it falsely given that on coming close he apprehends it as louder. Likewise, then, I would not say that one's eyesight tells a falsehood because from a great distance one sees the tower as small and round, but from close up as larger and square, but rather that it tells the truth. **(209)** Because when the perceptible thing appears to it small and of a such a shape, it is in fact small and of such a shape, since the edges of the images are broken off by their movement through the air; and when, by contrast, it appears large and of a different shape, it *is*, by contrast, equally large

---

[88] The text as it stands is not grammatically feasible. Suggested minor emendations do not seem to restore a feasible Greek sentence; either there is a more serious corruption or something is missing in the space indicated. If something is missing, the sense is probably "but it must be such as it appears, in order," or something of the kind (as suggested by Kochalsky).

and of a different shape. However, it is not any longer the *same* thing that has both sets of features. For this is left to distorted opinion to think – that the thing that appears when observed close up and the thing that appears when observed from far away were the same thing.

(210) The specific role of sense-perception is to apprehend only the thing that is present and affecting it (for example, color), not to judge that the existing thing here and the existing thing there are distinct. Hence for these reasons all appearances are true, but opinions are not all true but have a certain diversity. For of these some are true and others are false, seeing that they are judgments of ours applied to the appearances, and we judge in some cases correctly, and in other cases badly – either as a result of adding something and assigning it to the appearances or as a result of taking something away from them and, in general, falsifying the non-rational sense-perception. (211) Of opinions, then, according to Epicurus, some are true and some are false. The true ones are those that are testified in favor of, and not testified against, by plain experience, while false ones are those that are testified against and not testified in favor of by plain experience.

(212) "Testimony in favor" is an apprehension through plain experience of the fact that the thing on which the opinion is held is such as the opinion held it to be. For example, when Plato is approaching from a long way away, I conjecture and hold the opinion (given the distance) that it is Plato, but when he comes near there is additional testimony that it is Plato, now that the distance has been shortened, and there is testimony in favor of it through plain experience itself. (213) "Absence of testimony against" is consistency of the unclear thing on which the supposition or opinion was held with what appears. For example, when Epicurus says that there is void, which is unclear, he confirms this through a matter that is plain, namely motion. For if there is not void there should not be motion, since the moving body does not have a place into which it can progress, on account of everything being full and solid – (214) so that what appears does not testify against the unclear thing on which the opinion was held, since there *is* motion. "Testimony against," however, is something that conflicts with "absence of testimony against." For it is the exclusion,[89] by the supposed unclear thing, of what appears. For example, the Stoic says that there is not void, maintaining something unclear. But

---

[89] I retain the mss. *anaskeuē*, instead of altering to *sunanaskeuē*.

when that is what has been supposed about this,[90] the thing that appears (I mean motion) ought to be excluded along with it; for if there is not void, necessarily motion does not happen either, according to the method that we showed before. (**215**) "Absence of testimony in favor" is also opposed in the same way to "testimony in favor." For it is the impact through plain experience of the fact that the thing on which the opinion is held is not such as the opinion held it to be. For example, when someone is approaching from far away we conjecture (given the distance) that it is Plato, but when the distance has been shortened we get to know through plain experience that it is not Plato. And absence of testimony in favor is like this; for the thing that was opined was not testified for by what appeared. (**216**) Hence testimony in favor and absence of testimony against are the criterion of something's being true, while absence of testimony in favor and testimony against are the criterion of something's being false. But the grounding and foundation of all of them is plain experience.[91]

Peripatetics (216–226)   This is what the criterion is like according to Epicurus. But Aristotle and Theophrastus and in general the Peripatetics (**217**) also allow the criterion to be twofold (the nature of things being, at the highest level, twofold, since, as I said before, some things are perceptible, others intelligible): sense-perception for perceptible things, intelligence for intelligible things, (**218**) and common to both, as Theophrastus said, what is plain. First in order, then, is the non-rational and indemonstrable criterion, sense-perception, but first in power is intellect, even though it seems to come second in order as against sense-perception. (**219**) For the sense is activated as a result of perceptible things, but as a result of the activity (of the nature of plain experience) in the sense, there occurs an additional movement in the souls of those animals that are more powerful and better and capable of moving on their own. This is called by them both memory and appearance, memory of the effect in the sense, and appearance of the perceptible thing that brought about the effect on the sense. (**220**) For this reason they say that a movement of this kind is analogous to a footprint. And just as it (I mean the footprint) comes about both *by* something and *from* something – *by* something like the pressure

---

[90] I.e., about the void. By contrast, the "supposed unclear thing" two sentences back is the posited state of affairs, of which the *non-existence* of void, as posited by the Stoics, is then given as an example.

[91] For a discussion of difficulties in this passage, see LS vol. 1, commentary on sect. 18.

of the foot, but *from* something like Dion – so too the aforementioned movement of the soul comes about *by* something, namely the effect on the sense, but *from* something, namely the perceptible thing, to which it also retains a certain likeness. (**221**) And this movement, again, which is called both memory and appearance, has within itself, as another, third movement occurring in addition, that of rational appearance, which happens, finally, by way of our judgment and decision; and this movement is called both thought and intellect. For example, Dion strikes someone in the manner of plain experience, and the person is affected and altered in a certain way in his sense. By the effect on his sense there occurs a certain appearance in his soul, which we said before was memory and like a footprint; (**222**) and from this appearance an image is painted and fashioned (willingly on his part), namely the generic human being.

Well, a movement of the soul of this kind the Peripatetic philosophers name both thought and intellect (from different points of view) – thought in virtue of its potentiality, intellect in virtue of its actuality. (**223**) For when the soul has the potential to do this fashioning (that is, when it is of that nature), it is called thought, but when it is in fact actually doing it, it is named intellect.[92] However, from intellect and thinking arise conception and knowledge and skill. For thinking occurs sometimes about particular specific instances, at other times about both specific instances and genera; (**224**) but the gathering together of such images residing in the intellect, and the encapsulation of the particulars into the universal, is called conception. And lastly, in this gathering together and encapsulation knowledge and skill are constituted, knowledge being the one that has exactness and freedom from error, skill being the one that is not entirely like this. (**225**) And just as it is the nature of forms of knowledge and of skills to come into being later, so too is so-called opinion. For whenever the soul yields to the appearance that occurs in it from sense-perception, and is favorably disposed toward the thing that appeared and assents to it, this is referred to as opinion. (**226**) It appears, then, from what has been said, that the primary criteria of the knowledge of things are sense-perception and intellect, one having the status of a tool, the other that of a craftsman. For just as we cannot perform a test of heavy and light things without a pair of scales, nor grasp the difference between straight

---

[92] The words "thought" and "intellect" may seem ill suited to capture the potential/actual distinction. However, it is not clear that the Greek words *dianoia* and *nous* are inherently suited to this purpose either.

and crooked things without a ruler, so too intellect does not have a nature that allows it to scrutinize things without sense-perception.

Stoics (227–260) In summary, then, this is what the Peripatetics are like. (**227**) What is still left over is the Stoic opinion, so let us next speak about this. Well then, these men say that the apprehensive appearance is the criterion of truth. We will have knowledge of this after we have first learned what appearance is, according to them, and what are its specific differences. (**228**) Appearance, then, is, according to them, an imprinting in the soul. And right away they were at odds about this. For Cleanthes understood imprinting in terms of hollows and projections, like the imprinting that occurs in wax from signet rings, (**229**) while Chrysippus thought that sort of thing absurd. For first, he says, when thought is having appearances of something triangular and something square (both at once), the same body will need to have different shapes bordering it at the same time, and to become simultaneously both triangular and square, or even round, which is absurd. Then again, if many appearances subsist in us simultaneously, the configurations that the soul will have will also be very large in number, which is worse than the previous point. (**230**) So he himself suspected that "imprinting" was used by Zeno in place of "alteration," so that the statement is like this: "Appearance is an alteration of the soul" – since the same body's receiving a very large number of *alterations* at one and the same time,[93] when many appearances take shape in us together, is no longer absurd. (**231**) For just as air, when many people are speaking, receives an untold number of different impacts at once, and right away the alterations that it takes on are also many, so too the leading part, when it has a variety of appearances, will experience something analogous to this.

(**232**) But others say that not even the definition offered in accordance with his correction is correct. For if there is any appearance, it is an imprinting, i.e., an alteration of the soul; but if there is any imprinting in the soul, it is not invariably an appearance. For if a blow to the finger occurs, or a scratch to the hand happens, an imprinting, i.e., an alteration of the soul, is produced, but not also an appearance, since the latter result occurs not in any random part of the soul, but only in thought, i.e., the

---

[93] I follow Bekker's alteration of the mss. *hen kata* to *hena kai*, instead of deleting *kata ton auton chronon*.

leading part. (233) In confronting them, the Stoics say that along with "imprinting of the soul" is implied "in so far as it is in the soul," so that the full version is like this: "appearance is an imprinting in the soul in so far as it is in the soul." For just as "sun-eye"[94] is said to be a whiteness in the eye, and at the same time we imply that the whiteness is "in so far as it is in the eye" (that is, "in a certain part of the eye") – so that it is not the case that *all* human beings have "sun-eye" on the grounds that we all naturally have whiteness in the eye – so when we call appearance an imprinting in the soul, we also imply at the same time the fact that the imprinting occurs in a certain part of the soul, that is, the leading part, so that when expanded the definition becomes like this: "appearance is an alteration in the leading part." (234) Others, starting with the same resources, defended themselves more subtly. For they say that "soul" is spoken of in two ways, as what holds together the whole organism and as the leading part on its own. For when we say that the human being is composed of soul and body, or that death is the separation of soul from body, we are talking about the leading part by itself. (235) In the same way, when we say (in making a division) that of goods some are of the soul, some of the body, and some external, we are not referring to the whole soul but the leading part of it; for it is in this that the effects on us – that is, the goods – are produced. (236) Therefore when Zeno says that "appearance is an imprinting in the soul," again "soul" is to be understood not as the whole of it but as the part, so that what is said is of this sort: "appearance is an alteration in the leading part."

(237) But even if it is of this sort, some people say, it is again mistaken. For impulse and assent and apprehension are alterations of the leading part, but are different from appearance. For the latter is a certain way in which we are affected, or a condition, while the former are to a much greater extent activities of ours. The definition, then, is a bad one, since many different objects fit it. (238) And in the same way as the person who defines the human being and says that a human being is a rational animal has not marked out the conception of the human being in a sound way, given the fact that god too is a rational animal, so also the person who pronounced appearance to be an alteration of the leading part was in error; for it is no more an account of this than of any of the motions listed. (239) Since this objection, too, is of that kind, the Stoics again

---

94 *Ephēlotēs*, damage to the eye caused by the sun (*hēlios*).

have recourse to implications, saying that along with the definition one has to understand "by way of being affected." For as the person who says that sexual attraction is an attempt to form a relationship[95] implies at the same time "with young people in their prime," even if it does not express this in so many words (for no one is sexually attracted to old people or to people who are not at the peak of their prime), so, they say, when we speak of appearance as an alteration of the leading part, we imply at the same time the fact that the alteration occurs by way of being affected and not by way of activity. (240) But they do not seem even in this way to have escaped the charge. For when the leading part is nourished and grows, for God's sake, it is altered by way of being affected. But that kind of alteration in it, although it is by way of being affected, or a condition, is not appearance – unless they were in turn to say that appearance is a peculiar way of being affected, which is different from conditions of that kind, or they were to say this: (241) that since appearance comes about either from external things or from effects in us (and this is more properly called by them "empty attraction"), in the account of appearance there is absolutely implied at the same time the fact that the process of being affected occurs either by way of impact from outside or by way of effects in us – and in the case of alterations that take the form of growth or nourishment, this can no longer be understood as included.

Thus it is hard to give an account of appearance, as it figures in Stoicism. Now, among appearances there are many additional differences; (242) however, the ones about to be mentioned will be sufficient. Of appearances some are persuasive, some unpersuasive, some at the same time both persuasive and unpersuasive, and some neither persuasive nor unpersuasive. The persuasive ones, then, are those that produce a smooth movement in the soul – for example (right now) its being day, and my conversing, and everything that maintains a similar perspicuity. Unpersuasive ones are those that are not like this but that turn us away from assent, (243) such as "if it is day, the sun is not above the earth," "if it is dark, it is day." Persuasive and unpersuasive ones are those that, according to their state in relation to something, become sometimes of one kind and sometimes of the other kind, such as appearances of intractable arguments; neither

---

[95] For this Stoic definition see Stobaeus 2.91,15–16, translated on p. 218 of B. Inwood and L. Gerson, eds., *Hellenistic Philosophy: Introductory Readings* (Hackett Publishing, 1997); *erōs*, sexual attraction, is here listed as one of a great number of subspecies of passion (*pathos*) – all of which are in the Stoic view objectionable.

persuasive nor unpersuasive ones are, for example, those that are of such matters as "the number of stars is even," "the number of stars is odd." Of persuasive or unpersuasive[96] appearances some are true, (244) some false, some both true and false, and some neither true nor false. True ones are those of which it is possible to make a true predication: for example, "it is day" at present or "it is light"; false ones are those of which it is possible to make a false predication – for example, the oar under water being bent or the colonnade narrowing. True and false ones are like those from Electra that struck Orestes in his madness – (245) for in so far as it struck him as from some real thing it was true (for Electra was real), but in so far as it struck him as from a Fury it was false (for there was no Fury) – or again if someone while sleeping, when Dion is alive,[97] has in a dream a false and empty attraction as from him standing right there. (246) Neither true nor false are the generic ones. For of things whose specific instances are of this kind or that, the genera are neither of this kind nor of that. For example, some human beings are Greeks, others are barbarians, but the generic human being is neither Greek – since in that case all specific humans would be Greeks – nor barbarian, for the same reason.

(247) Of true appearances, some are apprehensive and some are not. Non-apprehensive ones are those that strike people when they are suffering an effect.[98] For millions of people when delirious or melancholic draw in an appearance that is true, yet not apprehensive, but occurring in this way externally and by chance; hence they often are not confident about it and do not assent to it. (248) An apprehensive one is the one that is from a real thing and is stamped and impressed in accordance with just *that* real thing, and is of such a kind as could not come about from a thing that was not real. For since they trust this appearance to be capable of perfectly grasping the underlying things, and to be skillfully stamped with all the peculiarities attaching to them, they say that it has each of these as an attribute.

(249) The first of these is its coming about from a real thing; for many appearances strike us from what is not real, as in the case of crazy people, and these would not be apprehensive. Second, its being from a real thing and in accordance with just *that* real thing; for again, some are from a real

---

96 I retain the mss. *ē apithanōn*, deleted by Mutschmann and most other editors.
97 With Heintz I delete *apo* before *Diōnos*.
98 Literally, "in a state of *pathos*," i.e. (as the sequel makes clear), in a diseased or otherwise abnormal condition.

thing, yet do not resemble just *that* real thing, as we showed a little earlier in the case of Orestes in his madness. For he drew in an appearance from a real thing, Electra, but not in accordance with just *that* real thing; for he supposed her to be one of the Furies, and so pushes her away as she approaches eager to take care of him, saying

Leave off! You are one of my Furies.[99]

And Heracles was activated from a real thing, Thebes, but not in accordance with just *that* real thing; for the apprehensive appearance also has to come about in accordance with just *that* real thing. (250) Not to mention its being stamped and impressed, so that all the peculiarities of the things that appear are skillfully stamped on. (251) For just as carvers tackle all the parts of the things they are completing, and in the same way as seals on signet rings always stamp all their markings exactly on the wax, so too those who get an apprehension of the underlying things ought to focus on all their peculiarities. (252) "Such as could not come about from a thing that was not real" they added because the Academics did not suppose, as the Stoics did, that it would be impossible for one that was in all respects indistinguishable to be found.[100] For the Stoics say that the person who has the apprehensive appearance skillfully gets in touch with the hidden difference in the objects, since this kind of appearance has a certain peculiarity, compared with other appearances, like what horned snakes have compared with other snakes. But the Academics say, on the contrary, that it would be possible for a falsehood that was indistinguishable from the apprehensive appearance to be found.

(253) Now, the older Stoics say that this apprehensive appearance is the criterion of truth. The later Stoics, on the other hand, added "if it has no obstacle." (254) For there are times when an apprehensive appearance does strike us, yet is not trusted because of the external circumstances. For example, when Heracles stood by Admetus, having brought Alcestis up from below the earth, Admetus did catch an apprehensive appearance from Alcestis, yet did not trust it. (255) And when Menelaus having come back from Troy saw the true Helen at Proteus' place (when he had left on the ship her phantom, over whom a ten-year war had been fought),

---

[99] Euripides, *Orestes* 264.

[100] I.e., that it would be impossible to find an appearance that was indistinguishable from one meeting the previous requirements, but false. Perhaps, as Heintz suggests, the word "false" has dropped out of the text.

he grasped an appearance that was from a real thing and in accordance with just *that* real thing, and stamped and impressed, but he did not have <trust>[101] in it. (256) So that the apprehensive appearance is the criterion *when it has no obstacle*; these ones were apprehensive, but had obstacles. For Admetus figured that Alcestis was dead and that a dead person does not rise up, but certain spirits do sometimes wander around. And Menelaus observed that he had left Helen under guard on the ship, and that it was not unlikely that the one found on Pharos was not Helen, but some phantom or spirit.

(257) Hence the apprehensive appearance becomes the criterion of truth not without qualification, but when it has no obstacle. For this one, they say, being plain and striking, all but grabs us by the hair, and draws us into assent, needing nothing else to strike us in this way or to suggest its difference from the others. (258) And this is why everyone, when eager to apprehend something with accuracy, seems spontaneously to go after an appearance of this kind – such as in the case of visible things, when the appearance he grasps of the underlying thing is weak. For he strains his sight and goes close up to the thing he is looking at, so as to be completely free of error; he rubs his eyes and in general does everything until he catches an appearance of the thing being judged that is clear and striking, as if considering that the trustworthiness of the apprehension lies in this. (259) And besides, it is impossible to say the opposite; and the person who is reluctant to maintain that appearance is the criterion, since he is affected in this way owing to the subsistence of another appearance, necessarily confirms the fact that appearance is the criterion, nature having given us the sensory capacity, and appearance, which comes about by means of it, as a sort of light for the recognition of the truth. (260) It is absurd, then, to reject so great a capacity and to deprive ourselves of the light (as it were). For in the same way as the person who admits colors and the differences among them, but does away with sight as unreal or untrustworthy, and who says that there are sounds, but maintains that hearing is not real, is totally absurd (for if the things through which we conceive colors and sounds are not there, we are not capable of experiencing colors and sounds), so too the person who accepts objects, but attacks sensory appearance, through which one grasps objects, is completely deranged and is putting himself on a par with inanimate things.

[101] With Kalbfleisch I read *eichē de autēi* <*pisti*>*n* for the mss. *eichē de autēn*.

3. *Counter-arguments against the criterion (261–445)*

(**261**) Well, the doctrine of the Stoics is like this. And since pretty much the entire disagreement about the criterion now lies in view, it would be a suitable moment to get our hands on the counter-argument and set sail against the criterion. As I said before, then, some allowed it to be located in reason, some in the non-rational senses, and some in both; and some have allowed the criterion "by which" (namely, the human being), some the one "through which" (namely, sense-perception and thought), and some the one in the manner of "impact" (namely, the appearance).[102] (**262**) We will try, then, as far as possible to make the impasses fit each one of the positions of this kind, so that we are not forced to repeat ourselves by attacking individually all the philosophers listed.

a. The criterion "by which" (the human being) (263–342)
i. *Problems in conceiving the human being (263–282)*

On the human being

(**263**) First in order, therefore, let us look at the criterion "by which" – that is, the human being. For I think that once this has been initially made intractable, there will be no further need to speak at greater length about the other criteria; for these are either parts of, or activities of, or effects on, a human being. If, then, this criterion is apprehensible, it ought, as a precondition, to be conceived, in so far as conception precedes every apprehension. But up to this point it has turned out, as we will establish, that the human being is inconceivable. (**264**) Therefore the human being is absolutely not capable of being apprehended; from which it follows that knowledge of the truth is undiscoverable, since the knower of it is inapprehensible. So, for example, of those who examined the conception, Socrates was in an impasse, remaining in a state of inquiry and saying that he did not know what he himself was or how he was related to the whole; "for I do not know," he says, "whether I am a human being or some other

---

[102] It is possible, as Heintz argued, that the second half of this sentence should be deleted as a gloss. In addition to some syntactical awkwardness, this part of the sentence fits very badly with the first half, which refers to a disagreement about what the criterion is; here, on the contrary, we are reminded of some alternative (but complementary) ways of conceiving of the criterion as such (cf. 35ff.). These latter alternatives are indeed appealed to in the discussion that follows (hence perhaps the gloss), but they seem wholly out of place here.

beast more convoluted than Typho."[103] (265) Democritus, the one who is likened to the voice of Zeus, and who said these things[104] about the whole, did try to lay out the conception, but came up with nothing more worthwhile than a commonplace assertion, saying "a human being is what we all know." (266) For, first of all, we all know a dog, too, but the dog is not a human being; and we all know a horse and a plant, but none of these things is a human being. Then again, he has taken for granted the thing being examined. For no one will lightly concede that what the human being is like is known, if indeed the Pythian[105] posed "know yourself" as the greatest object of search for humanity. And even if one were to concede it, one will not allow that *everyone* understands this, but only the most precise philosophers. (267) The Epicureans thought that the conception of the human being could be presented ostensively, saying "a human being is a shape like this, along with the possession of soul." But they did not realize that if the thing being shown is a human being, the thing not being shown is not a human being. And again, a showing of this kind is carried out either with a man or a woman, either with an old person or a young one, with someone snub-nosed or hook-nosed, straight-haired or curly-haired, and so on with other differences.[106] (268) And if it is carried out with a man, woman will not be a human being, while if with a woman, the male will be excluded, and if with a youth, other ages will be deprived of humanity.

(269) There were some philosophers who taught of the generic human being through a definition, thinking that from there the conception of particular human beings will come forth. Of these, some gave the following definition: "a human being is a rational mortal animal, capable of intelligence and knowledge." Now these people too have given us not the human being but the attributes of the human being. (270) But the attribute of something is different from the thing of which it is an attribute, since if it is not different, it would not be an attribute but the actual thing. Of course, some attributes are inseparable from the things of which they are attributes, like length, breadth, and depth for bodies (for without their

---

[103] Plato, *Phaedrus* 230a (not a verbatim quotation).
[104] It is not clear what the referent of "these things" is supposed to be. Democritus has already been mentioned; but this was much earlier (135–40) and the subject was epistemological, not cosmological. Perhaps this sentence has been lifted in isolation from a source in which the context was clear.
[105] I.e., Apollo, god of the oracle at Delphi, with which this saying was associated.
[106] I retain the mss. διαφορῶν, instead of altering to διαφόρων.

presence it is impossible to conceive a body). **(271)** On the other hand, some are separated from the thing of which they are attributes, and that thing remains when they are removed, like running, discussing, sleeping, or waking for the human being. For all of these are attributes of ours, but not all the time; for even when we are not running we remain the same, and when we are quiet, and the same applies in the other cases. So, given that there is a twofold distinction among attributes, we will not find either one of them to be the same as the underlying object, but always differing from it. **(272)** Therefore the people who say that the human being is a rational mortal animal, and so on, are foolish; for they have not defined the human being, but have enumerated his attributes. Of these "animal" is one of the attributes that belong to him all the time; for it is impossible to be a human being without being an animal. However, "mortal" is not even an attribute, but something that comes *after* the human being; for when we are human beings, we are alive and not dead. **(273)** "Reasoning and having knowledge," on the other hand, is an attribute, but not all the time. For even some non-reasoners are human beings (for example, those who are in the grip of "sweet sleep"),[107] and those who do not have knowledge have not been deprived of humanity[108] (for example, crazy people). When we were seeking one thing, then, they have presented another. **(274)** Besides, "animal" is not a human being, since then *every* animal will be a human being. And if "rational" stands for "reasoning," even the gods will, when reasoning, become human beings, and perhaps some other animals too. If, on the other hand, it stands for "uttering meaningful sounds," we will be saying that crows and parrots and the like are human beings,[109] which is absurd. **(275)** Again, if one were to say that "mortal" is a human being, it will follow that irrational animals are also humans (since they are mortal). And one needs also to think similarly about "reasoning and being capable of knowledge." For, first, such things also fall to gods; and second, if the human being is capable of these things, the human being is not these things, but the one capable of these things, whose nature they did not present.

(276) Some clever-seeming people of the dogmatic persuasion, though, meet this point by saying that while it is not the case that *each* of the things enumerated is a human being, all of them when collected together do make

[107] "Sweet sleep" (*hēdumos hupnos*) is a common Homeric phrase; from Sextus' perspective it is the language of archaic verse.
[108] I read the mss. text, instead of adding *hoi* before *ouk*.
[109] I do not accept the addition *kai* before *tous korakas*.

one – like what we observe in the case of parts and a whole. (277) For just as a hand, on its own, is not a human being, nor a head, nor a foot, nor any other such thing, but the composite of them is conceived as a whole, so too the human being is not merely an animal, nor rational on its own, nor mortal taken individually, but is the collection of all of them – that is, an animal *and* mortal *and* rational at the same time. (278) But a response to this,[110] too, is readily available. For first, if these things are not a human being when each one is taken on its own, how can they make a human being when collected together, without either exceeding what there is or falling short of what exists or going off course in some other way? In addition, they cannot even all coincide in the same place, so that the compound of them all can become a human being. (279) At any rate, "mortal" is not an attribute of ours when we are human beings, but is grasped by way of simultaneous recollection.[111] For on observing that Dion and Theon and Socrates, and in general particular people like us, have died, we reason that we too are mortal, even though dying is not yet present to us (after all, we are alive). (280) Again, "reasoning" is sometimes present to us, sometimes not; and, to repeat, "having knowledge" is not among the attributes belonging to the human being all the time, as we have already shown. It has to be said, then, that not even the combination of these things all together is a human being.

(281) Plato defines the human being worse than the others, saying "a human being is a wingless two-footed broad-nailed animal, capable of political knowledge."[112] Hence the things that ought to be said against him are indeed evident. For again, he has not explained the human being, but has enumerated his attributes and non-attributes. (282) For "wingless" is a non-attribute of his, whereas "animal" and "two-footed" and "broad-nailed" are attributes, and "capable of political knowledge" is sometimes an attribute and sometimes a non-attribute. So that when we were seeking to learn one thing, he presented another.

ii. Problems in apprehending the human being (283–313)
But let us just take the impossibility of readily conceiving the human being[113] to have been thus demonstrated. (283) The next thing to be said

[110] I do not accept the addition of *hē* before *pros touto*.
[111] Compare the notion of recollective signs, discussed in the next book; see esp. 2.151–152.
[112] This definition appears in the pseudo-Platonic *Definitions* (415a), which appears to derive from the Academy of Plato's successors.
[113] I do not accept the addition *heauton* after *anthrōpon*.

is that the apprehension of him is also something intractable, especially because in part this has already been inferred (for what is not conceived is not of a nature to be apprehended, either; but the human being *has* been shown to be inconceivable as far as the dogmatists' conceptions are concerned, and therefore inapprehensible as well). (**284**) However, it will be possible to construct a case of this kind in another way too.

By the whole of him (284–287)   If the human being is an apprehensible thing, either the whole of him wholly seeks and apprehends himself, or the whole of him is the object being sought and falling under the apprehension <. . .>,[114] just as if someone were to suppose sight was seeing itself. For either the whole of it will be seeing or seen, or it will be in part seeing itself and in part seen by itself. (**285**) But if the whole of the human being sought himself and was conceived along with this (along with the whole of him wholly conceiving himself), nothing will any longer be the object being apprehended, which is absurd. But if the whole of him were the object being sought and along with this (along with being sought) the whole of him were to be conceived, again nothing will be left over as the object seeking and going to produce the apprehension. (**286**) In addition, it is not possible to take turns, so that sometimes the whole of him is the object seeking, and sometimes the whole of him is the object being sought. For when the whole of him is seeking and along with this (along with the whole of him seeking) the whole of him is conceived, nothing will be left over that he will seek; and conversely, when the whole of him is wholly the thing being sought, there will not be the thing seeking.

(**287**) It remains, then, that it is not the whole of him that turns attention to himself, but that he produces the apprehension of himself by some part – which is also something intractable. For the human being is nothing over and above the body and the senses and thought. (**288**) Hence if he is going to apprehend himself with some part, he will either come to know his senses and his thought with his body, or on the contrary he will apprehend his body with his senses and his thought.

By the body (288–292)   Now, one cannot come to know one's senses and one's thought with one's body; for it is non-rational and dumb and not

---

[114] Scholars are agreed that there is a lacuna here; the context makes clear that a third alternative should be mentioned here, namely that of being partly the seeker/apprehender and partly the object sought/apprehended.

naturally suited to investigations of this kind. **(289)** Besides, if the body is capable of grasping the senses and thought, the thing that apprehends these[115] ought to be like these; that is, it should be in a similar condition and *become* both sense-perception and thought. For in grasping sight, in so far as it sees it will be sight, and in the course of apprehending taste tasting it will become taste, and similarly in the other cases. **(290)** For just as what grasps a hot thing as hot grasps it by being heated, and in being heated is right away hot, and as what produces knowledge of a cold thing as cold by being chilled is right away cold, so too, if the mass of flesh grasps the senses as senses, it senses, and in sensing it definitely becomes sense-perception, **(291)** and in this way the thing seeking will no longer exist, but it will be the thing being sought – along with the complete absurdity of the body's not differing from the senses and thought, when just about all those who have done philosophy dogmatically have introduced the distinction among these things. **(292)** The same argument also applies in the case of thought. For if the body grasps this as thought – that is, as intellectually active – the body will *be* thought, and in being thought it will not be the thing seeking but the thing being sought. Therefore the body is not capable of apprehending the human being.

By the senses (293–302) **(293)** Nor, again, are the senses. For they are merely affected and are imprinted in the manner of wax. They do not know a single additional thing, since if we attribute to them a seeking of anything, they will become no longer non-rational abilities, but rational ones, having the nature of seeking. But that is not how it is; for if being whitened and blackened and sweetened and made bitter and made fragrant – and generally, being affected – is peculiar to them, actively seeking will not belong to them. **(294)** Then again, how is it possible for the body to be apprehended through them, when they do not have the nature?[116] For example, sight is capable of grasping shape and size and color; but the body is neither shape nor size nor color, but if anything, the thing that these are attributes of. And for this reason sight cannot grasp the body, but only the attributes of the body, such as shape, size, and color. **(295)** Someone will say "Yes, but the product of their joint contributions is the body" – which is silly. For, first, we have shown that not even the combination of the

---

[115] I retain *to* before *tautas*, deleted by Mutschmann.
[116] I.e., presumably, the same kind of nature as what they are supposedly apprehending. But some words may well have dropped out of the text, as many scholars have supposed.

attributes of something all together *is* that of which they are attributes. (**296**) And then, even if this was so, it is again an impossibility for the body to be grasped by sight. For if the body is neither bare length, nor shape on its own, nor color taken separately, but the composite of these things, it will be necessary for sight, in grasping the body, to put these things together in itself one by one, and so to say that the collection of all of them together is body. (**297**) But putting something together with something, and grasping some size together with some shape, is the mark of a rational ability. But sight is *non*-rational; therefore it is not its job to apprehend the body. (**298**) Indeed, not only is it not naturally suited to conceive the combination as body, but it is also defective with regard to the apprehension of each of the latter's attributes. Length, for example: this is of a nature to be grasped by way of going over its parts,[117] where we begin at one and go through another and finish at another – which a non-rational nature is not capable of doing. (**299**) Or again, depth: for sight wanders over the very surface, and does not penetrate to depth. At any rate, it does not spot copper coins that are gilded over. And we mentioned, when we were doing away with the Cyrenaic position, that it was also unsuitable for knowledge of color.[118] (**300**) So, if sight is not even capable of grasping the attributes of the body, it is all the more incapable of observing the body itself. Yet this kind of thing is not the job of hearing or smell or taste or touch, either; for each of these knows only what is perceptible to itself, and that could not be the body. For hearing is capable of grasping only sound, but sound is not the body. And smell is the criterion only of what smells good or bad; but no one is so senseless as to admit the substance of our body in the category of things that smell good or bad. And (not to prolong the discussion) the same can be said about the other senses as well. So they do not grasp the body.

(**301**) Yet nor do they grasp themselves. For who has seen sight by sight? Or who has heard hearing by hearing? Who ever tasted taste by taste, or smelled smell by smell, or touched touch by touch? These things are inconceivable. Therefore it must be said that the senses are not even capable of grasping themselves – and thus not one another, either. For sight cannot see hearing in the process of hearing, and conversely hearing

---

[117] I retain the mss. *merōn*, instead of altering to *megethōn*.

[118] I.e., for knowledge of the actual colors of independently existing objects; see 190ff. (It is not really accurate of Sextus to claim that that passage was "doing away with" the Cyrenaic view; it was a simple exposition.)

is not of a nature to hear sight seeing, and the same mode of attack applies in the other cases, since if we say that hearing can be grasped as hearing (that is, as engaged in hearing) by sight, we will be conceding that sight is affected in the same way as hearing, so that it is no longer sight but hearing. (302) For how can it judge hearing in the process of hearing if it does not have a nature capable of hearing? And conversely, in order for hearing to grasp sight as engaged in seeing, it must itself, as a precondition, have become sight. But there is no extreme of absurdity that this seems to leave out. It has to be said, then, that the senses grasp neither the body nor themselves nor each other.

By thought (303–313)   (303) Yes, say the dogmatists, but thought comes to know the body and the senses and itself – which itself is also something intractable. For when they maintain that thought is capable of grasping both the whole body and the things within it, we will inquire whether it brings about apprehension by engaging with the whole body at once, or with its parts – and apprehends the whole by putting these together. (304) And they would not allow that it is the whole, as will be evident from what follows;[119] but if they were to say that it puts together the parts and thereby comes to know the whole, they will be pressured by an even greater impasse. For of the parts of the body some are non-rational, and the non-rational ones move us non-rationally. Therefore thought, by being non-rationally moved in relation to these, will become non-rational. But if it is non-rational it will not be thought; so that thought will not apprehend the body. (305) And in the same way, it cannot distinguish the senses either. For just as it cannot apprehend the body, given its participation in a rational capacity whereas the latter is non-rational, so again it will be unable to apprehend the senses, seeing that they are non-rational and for this reason move non-rationally the thing that apprehends them. Then again, in grasping the senses it will itself definitely be a sense. For in order to grasp the senses as senses (that is, in the process of sensing), it too will become similar in kind to them; in apprehending sight seeing it will, as a precondition, become sight, and in judging hearing engaged in hearing it will become none other than hearing. And the same argument applies in the case of smell and taste and touch. (306) But if the thought

---

[119] It is not clear what this is referring to. There is some talk of the whole in 310ff., but this is on a quite different topic.

that comes to know the senses is found to have made a transition into *their* nature, there will be nothing still existing that is the thing investigating the senses. For what we supposed was investigating has turned out to be identical with the things under investigation, and because of this is actually missing the thing that will do the apprehending.

(307) Yes, they say, but the same thing is thought and sense-perception, but not in the same respect; rather, in one respect it is thought while in another respect it is sense-perception. And in the way that the same drinking-cup is said to be both concave and convex, but not in the same respect – rather, in one respect it is concave (namely, the inside part) but in another respect convex (i.e., the outside) – and as the same road is conceived of as both uphill and downhill – uphill to the people going up it and downhill to the people going down – so the same capacity is in one respect intellect and in another respect sense-perception, and while being the same it is not barred from the apprehension of the senses that was mentioned before. (308) But they are completely silly, and are just vainly mouthing responses to the impasses that have been laid out. For we say that, even if these different capacities are agreed to exist in the same being, there still remains the impasse created by us a little earlier. (309) For I ask, how can this thing that is said to be in one respect intellect and in another respect sense-perception grasp that side of it that is sense-perception by that side of it that is intellect? For if it is rational and produces an apprehension of a non-rational thing, it will be moved non-rationally. But if it is moved non-rationally it will be non-rational, and if that is what it is like, it will not be an apprehender but a thing being apprehended – which is again absurd.

(310) By these means, then, let us consider it established that the human being cannot grasp either the senses through the body nor, conversely, the body through the senses, <. . .> neither themselves nor one another.[120] Next it has to be shown that thought is not even familiar with itself, as the dogmatic philosophers maintain. For if the intellect apprehends itself, either it will apprehend itself as a whole, or not as a whole, but by using some part of itself for this. (311) And it could not apprehend itself as a whole. For if it apprehends itself as a whole, it will as a whole be apprehension and apprehender; but if it is, as a whole, the apprehender,

---

[120] A few words, presumably giving further detail on what has just been shown, appear to have been lost; the text as it stands is clearly incomplete.

there will no longer be anything as the thing being apprehended. But it is the height of irrationality for there to be the apprehender, but for there not to be the thing that the apprehension is of. (312) Yet neither can the intellect use some part for this. For how does the part itself apprehend itself? If as a whole, there will be nothing as the thing being sought; but if by some part, how will *that* one come to know itself? And so *ad infinitum*. So that apprehension cannot get started, since either nothing is found in the first place to produce the apprehension, or there is nothing as the thing to be apprehended. (313) Then again, if the intellect apprehends itself, it will at the same time apprehend the place in which it is; for everything being apprehended is apprehended along with some place. But if the intellect also apprehends, along with itself, the place in which it is, this should not have been an object of disagreement among the philosophers, some saying that it is the head, others the chest, and in particular, some the brain, others the membrane around the brain, and some the heart, others the portal fissures of the liver or some such part of the body. But the dogmatic philosophers do disagree about this; therefore the intellect does not apprehend itself.

iii. Problems with the dogmatists' claim to be themselves the criterion (314–342)
(314) Well, let us take these to be the impasses facing the inquiry concerning the criterion, considered more generally as applying to every human being. But since the dogmatists egotistically refuse to allow other people the judgment of the truth, but say that they themselves are the only ones to have discovered this, all right: let us rest the argument on them, and teach that not even in this way is it possible for any criterion of truth to be found. (315) So, each of those who maintain that they have discovered what is true either just declares this by assertion or makes use of a demonstration. But he will not say it by assertion. For one of those who are in the opposite camp to himself will offer the assertion that maintains the opposite, and so his one will be no more trustworthy than theirs; for a bare assertion has equal force with a bare assertion. (316) But if it is with a demonstration that he declares himself the criterion, surely it will be a sound one. But in order for us to learn that the demonstration that he is using to declare himself the criterion is sound, we ought to have a criterion – and a previously agreed one at that. But we do *not* have an agreed upon criterion; that is what is under investigation. Therefore it is

not possible to find a criterion. (317) Again, since those who call themselves criteria of truth come from different schools, and *ipso facto* disagree with one another, we have to have available some criterion that we can use to judge the dispute, with the goal of assenting to some of them but not at all to others. (318) This criterion, then, is either in disagreement with all those who disagree, or in agreement with just one of them. But if it is in disagreement with all of them, it will itself become a party to the dispute; but if it is a party to this, it cannot be a criterion but is itself, too, in need of judgment, like the dispute as a whole. (For the same thing's simultaneously scrutinizing and being scrutinized is an impossibility.) (319) But if it does not disagree with all of them but agrees with one, <this one>, being derived from the dispute, has need of the one who is to scrutinize.[121] And for this reason the criterion that is in agreement with it, not being any different from it, will be in need of judgment, and being in need of judgment it will not be a criterion.

(320) But the most important thing of all is this. If we say that one of the dogmatists is judge of the truth, and that the truth belongs to him alone, we will say this focusing either on his age, or not on his age but on his hard work, or not on this, either, but on his cleverness and his thought, or not on his cleverness but on the testimony of the majority. But, as we will establish, it is not appropriate, in the search concerning the truth, to attend either to age or to love of hard work or to any other of the things mentioned; therefore it cannot be said that any of the philosophers is criterion of the truth. (321) One cannot attend to age, since most of the dogmatists were more or less the same age when they called themselves criteria of the truth. For all of them – like Plato, for example, and Democritus and Epicurus and Zeno – ascribed to themselves the discovery of the truth after they had reached old age. (322) Then again, it is not unlikely that, just as in the ordinary experience of life we observe that the young are often cleverer than the old, in the same way, too, in philosophy the young are more on the mark than the old. (323) For some people, Asclepiades the doctor among them, have said explicitly that the old are far behind the cleverness and mental agility found in the young. However, thanks to the false opinion

---

[121] Scholars are agreed in positing a lacuna in this sentence; the "it" in the next sentence seems to require the subject of the main verb in this sentence to be the "one" with which the alleged criterion agrees, not this criterion itself. I follow Kayser's suggestion *to hen touto*; Bekker suggests something more elaborate, but the effect is the same. But there may be more extensive corruption; there are other textual difficulties, and the entire section reads very awkwardly – as my translation does not attempt to conceal.

of the careless majority, things were assumed to be the other way round. The young were thought to fall behind in terms of cleverness on account of the great experience of the old, when in fact it is the other way round; for, as I said, people who have grown old *are* more experienced, but not cleverer than the young. So it cannot be said that any of the dogmatists is the criterion on account of age. (324) But not on account of love of hard work, either. For they are all equally hard-working, and there is no one who, having entered the competition for the truth and having said that he has found it, has taken it easy. But if all of them show evidence of equality in this respect, being inclined towards just one of them is an injustice.

(325) In the same way, no one could prefer one of them to another as far as cleverness is concerned. For, first, they are all clever; it is not that some are stupid and others not. In addition, the ones who are thought to be clever are often spokesmen not for the truth but for what is false. Among orators, at any rate, the ones who are outstanding at aiding the cause of what is false, and bringing it to equal credibility with what is true, we say are capable and smart, while the ones who are not like this, on the contrary, we say are slow and not clever. (326) So perhaps in philosophy, too, the most super-smart seekers of the truth are thought to be persuasive because of being naturally gifted, even if they speak on behalf of what is false, while those who are not naturally gifted are unpersuasive, even if they are on the side of what is true. Neither on account of age, then, nor on account of love of hard work, nor on account of cleverness is it appropriate to prefer any one to any other and say that this one has discovered what is true and that that one has by no means done so.

(327) The remaining option, therefore, is to pay attention to the majority of those who agree. For perhaps someone will say that the person in favor of whom the majority testifies with one voice is the best judge of the truth. But this is silly, and worse than the criteria that we attacked before. For (to leave the other points aside) in equal numbers to those who are in agreement about certain people are those who disagree with the same people – Epicureans against Aristotelians, for example, and Stoics against Epicureans, and similarly in the other cases. (328) If, then, the best person is the one who has seen what is true since all those who start from him[122] maintain the same thing, why are we to say that this one rather than that one is best, and is the criterion of truth? For example, if we say

---

[122] I.e., who adhere to his principles, belong to his school of thought.

it is Epicurus, because of there being a lot of people who are in agreement about him (that he found what is true), then why Epicurus rather than Aristotle – because there are no fewer fighting on *his* side?[123] (329) But regardless of that, again, just as in the affairs of everyday life it is not impossible that one clever person is better than many who are not clever, so too in philosophy it is not unlikely that one person is insightful and for this reason trustworthy, while many people are like geese and for this reason untrustworthy, even if they are in agreement in testifying in someone's favor. For the clever person is rare, while the careless person is common.

(330) Besides, even if we pay attention to the agreement and to the testimony of the majority, again we are led round to the opposite of the proposal; for necessarily there are more people who disagree about something than who agree about it. What I mean will become clearer when a suitable example has been put before us. (331) Let us make the supposition that, of the people who do philosophy according to each school, those who do philosophy according to the Stoic school are greater in number. And let us take it that these people are in agreement in saying that Zeno alone, and no one else, has discovered the truth. In that case the Epicureans will speak against them, the Peripatetics will say that they are lying, the Academics, too, will contradict them, and generally all those from the schools, (332) so that again, those who agree in preferring Zeno, compared with those who agree in saying that Zeno is *not* the criterion, are found to be fewer by far. And because of this very point: if we have to believe those who are in agreement in their declarations about someone because there are many of them, then no one should be said to have discovered the truth; for against everyone who is praised by some people there are many from the other schools who speak in opposition. (333) But here is the most essential point. Those who are in agreement about someone as having discovered the truth either have a differing condition in virtue of which they agree, or one that is not differing at all but one and the same. But they could not possibly have a differing condition, since that will undoubtedly require them to disagree. But if they have one condition, they come round to a position of equality with the person who declares the opposite. For just as that person has one condition in virtue of which he has objected to them, (334) so too they have a condition equal to that one, their numbers from now on being irrelevant as far as credibility is concerned. For

---

[123] With Heintz I delete *ē*, instead of *ouk*, in the mss. text *ē hoti ouk elassous.*

indeed, if our supposition was that there was *one* of them saying this, he would have had a force equal to all of them.

(335) But if the person who has discovered the truth in philosophy is said to have hit the mark on account of either age or love of hard work or cleverness or by having lots of people testifying for him, but we have established that he cannot be said, on account of any of these things, to be the criterion of truth, it appears that the criterion in philosophy is undiscovered.

(336) In addition, the person who says that he himself is the criterion of truth says what appears to himself, and nothing more. Therefore, since each of the other philosophers also says what appears to himself and is opposite to the point just put forward, it is clear that, such a person being equal to all of them, we will not be able to say definitely that any of them is the criterion. For if this person is trustworthy, because his being himself the criterion is apparent to him, the second one is trustworthy as well, since to him too it is apparent that he himself is the criterion, and so on with the third and the rest – from which it is concluded that no one is definitely the criterion of truth. (337) Besides this, someone says that he himself is the criterion either by assertion or using a criterion. But if by assertion, he will be checked by assertion, while if using a criterion he will be turned about. For this criterion is either in disagreement with him or in agreement. And if it is in disagreement with him, it will be untrustworthy, since it is in disagreement with the person who thinks he himself is the criterion. (338) But if it is in agreement, it will have need of someone judging. For just as this person who thinks he himself is the criterion was untrustworthy, so too the criterion that is in agreement with him, since it has in a certain way the same power as he does, will need some other criterion. And if this is so, we cannot say that each of the philosophers is the criterion; for everything that needs judgment is, taken by itself, untrustworthy. (339) Again, the person who says that he himself is the criterion maintains this either by assertion or by demonstration. And he cannot do so by assertion, for the reasons that I stated before. But if by demonstration, it must certainly be by a sound one; but that such a demonstration is sound is said either by assertion or by demonstration, and this goes on *ad infinitum*. Therefore for this reason too it has to be said that the criterion of the truth is undiscovered.

(340) The following question is also raised. Those who profess to judge what is true ought to have a criterion of what is true. This criterion, then,

either is not judged upon or has been judged upon. And if it is not judged upon, what is the source of its trustworthiness? For nothing that is disputed is trustworthy apart from a judgment. But if it has been judged upon, again the thing judging it either is not judged upon or has been judged upon. And if it is not judged upon, it is untrustworthy. But if it has been judged upon, again the thing judging upon it either has or has not been judged upon, and so on *ad infinitum*. (**341**) Again, the criterion, being a disputed thing, is in need of some demonstration. But since some demonstrations are true and others false, the demonstration that is employed toward the trustworthiness of the criterion also ought to be confirmed through some criterion, so that we fall into the reciprocal mode,[124] where the criterion is waiting for the trustworthiness supplied through the demonstration, but the demonstration is waiting for the confirmation derived from the criterion, (**342**) and neither of them can be made trustworthy by the other. And besides, the same thing becomes both trustworthy and untrustworthy. For the criterion is trustworthy because it judges the demonstration, and so is the demonstration, because it demonstrates the criterion. But the criterion is untrustworthy because it is demonstrated by the demonstration, and the demonstration because it is judged by the criterion.

b. The criterion "through which" (the senses or thought or both) (343–369)
(**343**) This, then, is the extent of the points by which the obscurity of the first criterion – that is, the "by which" – is put forward as an impasse in the skeptics' circles. The argument about the second one – I mean, the "through which" – is also easy to lay out. For if the human being discovers what is true, he finds this using either the senses alone or thought or the pair of them together, the senses and thought. But he cannot discover the truth using either the senses alone or thought by itself or both the senses and thought in combination, as we will establish; therefore the human being is not of a nature to discover what is true.

i. Problems with the senses as criterion (344–347)
(**344**) He cannot grasp what is true by the senses alone, as we showed before (and will now briefly explain). For they are by nature non-rational,

[124] The reciprocal mode (or the mode of circularity) is one of the Five Modes (or standardized ways of inducing suspension of judgment) of the later skeptics, summarized by Sextus at *PH* 1.164–177.

and not being able to do more than be imprinted by the things that appear, they are useless for the discovery of what is true. For the thing that is to grasp what is true in the underlying objects must not merely be activated whitely or sweetly, but must also be brought to an appearance of the corresponding state of affairs – "this is white" and "this is sweet." And likewise in the other cases. **(345)** But to fasten upon the corresponding state of affairs is no longer the job of sense-perception; for it is of a nature to grasp only color and flavor and sound – whereas "this is white" and "this is sweet," not being a color or a flavor, does not fall within the awareness of sense-perception. And in many cases the senses lie and disagree with one another, as we showed in going over the Ten Modes of Aenesidemus.[125] **(346)** But what is in disagreement and takes opposing sides is not a criterion, but is itself in need of something judging it. Thus the senses by themselves cannot judge what is true. And there has to be combination and memory for grasping of the underlying objects, such as a human being, a plant, and things like that. For the human being is a combination of color with size and shape and certain other peculiarities, **(347)** but sense-perception cannot combine anything in a memory-like way on account of the fact that the combination is neither a color nor a flavor nor a sound, which are the only things sense-perception is capable of grasping.

ii. Problems with thought as criterion (348–353)

(348) Not thought either, however. For if thought is familiar with what is true, it ought first to become familiar with itself. And just as the architect does not[126] judge the straight and the crooked apart from focusing on the design of his criteria (such as that of the ruler and the compass), so too thought, if it is capable of discerning what is true and what is false, must also have focused, as a precondition, on its own nature (such as[127] the being from which it is, the place in which it belongs, and all the other things). **(349)** But it *cannot* see such things at all, if in fact some say that it is nothing beyond the body in a certain state, like Dicaearchus,

---

[125] These are summarized at *PH* 1.35–163. Sextus there ascribes them to "the older skeptics" (36) rather than to Aenesidemus specifically. It is, however, very possible that Sextus is here referring back to an account of the Ten Modes in the lost general portion of the work (see the opening sentence of this book).

[126] With Heintz I read *ou chōris* for the mss. *kai chōris*.

[127] With Heintz I read *hoion*, instead of *di'hēn*, in place of the clearly corrupt mss. readings *dion* and *di'hon*.

while others have said that it is, but not that it is contained in the same place: some have said that it is outside the body, as did Aenesidemus in accordance with Heraclitus,[128] others that is in the whole body, like some people in accordance with Democritus, and others that it is in a part of the body – and their judgments are again highly divided. (350) And some say that it is different from the senses (like most people), whereas others say that it *is* the senses, i.e., peeping out from certain apertures (the sense-organs) – a position that was begun by Strato the physicist and Aenesidemus. Thought, therefore, is not the criterion. (351) And there are many bearers of thought,[129] and being many they are in disagreement, and being in disagreement they have need of that which judges upon them. This, then, is either thought again or something else over and above it. And it could not be thought; for being a part of the disagreement it will be in need of judgment and will no longer be a criterion. But if it is something else over and above it, it establishes the fact that thought is not the criterion. (352) It will also be possible now to use the reasonings spoken by these men;[130] for there is no need for us to say the same things again. In addition to these points, since according to most philosophers there is in us not only a thinking aspect, but along with this a sensing aspect as well, which lies in front of the thinking aspect, necessarily this thing that lies in front of it will not allow thought to grasp the external things. (353) For just as the body, which is situated between sight and what is seen, does not allow sight to grasp what is seen, so if sight, which is non-rational, lies between thought and the external thing seen, sight will not allow thought to grasp the external thing seen. And if hearing is between thought and the external thing heard, it will not permit thought to become familiar with the thing heard, and similarly in the case of the other senses. So thought, being shut off inside, and being kept in the dark by the senses, will not be capable of grasping any of the external things. Nor, therefore, can we say that this by itself is the criterion.

[128] Sextus several times suggests a philosophical association between Aenesidemus and Heraclitus; this is very surprising, since Aenesidemus is known as the originator of later Pyrrhonism. For a brief recent discussion of the issue see R. Bett, *Pyrrho, his Antecedents, and his Legacy* (Oxford University Press, 2000), ch. 4.5.

[129] Literally, "many thoughts (*dianoiai*)"; but the word "thought," as used to translate *dianoia*, refers to the thinking *capacity*, not to individual thoughts – hence "many thoughts" would be misleading.

[130] It is not clear what this refers to, and some scholars have suspected that the text is corrupt. But Sextus' own careless handling of his source material is another possibility.

iii. *Problems with the combination as criterion (354–363)*

(354) It remains, then, to say that it is both – that is, that thought grasps the external things using sense-perception as an assistant. But this is again impossible. For sense-perception does not supply the external things to thought, but announces the specific effect it undergoes. For example, touch, when warmed by fire, does not deliver the external, burning fire to thought, but the warmth from it – that is, the specific effect upon itself. **(355)** Yet not even this. For if intelligence is to grasp the effect upon sense-perception, it will *be* sense-perception. For what is capable of receiving a sight-like effect is moved in a sight-like way, but what is moved in a sight-like way is sight; and what is capable of receiving a hearing-like effect is moved in a hearing-like way, but what is moved in a hearing-like way is hearing; and similarly in the case of the other senses. **(356)** For this reason thought, too, if it picks up the effect upon each sense, is moved in a sensory way, and being moved in a sensory way it is sense-perception. But if it is sense-perception it is non-rational, and having become non-rational it will fall short of still being intelligence, and not being intelligence it will not, as intelligence, grasp the effect upon sense-perception. **(357)** And even if it does grasp the effect upon the senses, it will not know the external things. For the external things are not like the effects in us, and the appearance differs by a long way from the thing that appears – the appearance of fire, for example, from fire; for one burns, while the other is not capable of burning. In addition, even if we concede that the external things are like the effects in us, it is absolutely not the case that thought will apprehend the external things by grasping the effects in us. For what are like certain things are *other* than those things they are like. **(358)** For this reason, if thought comes to know the things that are like the external things, it does not come to know the external things, but the things that are like them. And in the same way as the person who does not know Socrates but is looking at the image of Socrates does not know whether Socrates is like the apparent image, so thought, in attending to the effects but not having viewed the external things, will know neither what kind of things these are, nor that they are like the effects. But if it does not know the apparent things,[131] nor will it understand the unclear

---

[131] I.e., presumably, including their relation to the things that caused them (as discussed in the previous sentence). The "apparent things" (*phainomena*) in this context must be the effects or

things that are deemed to be known by way of transition from these; so nor is it the criterion of the truth.

(359) But some of the dogmatists run on at the mouth, in the present case too, with the reply mentioned above, saying that these different parts of the soul – that is, the rational and the non-rational – are not separate, but just as honey is wholly and entirely both fluid and sweet at once, so too the soul wholly and entirely has the two powers coextensive with one another, of which one is rational and the other non-rational; (360) and that the rational one is moved by intelligible things, while the non-rational one is capable of grasping perceptible things. Hence, too, it is pointless to say that thought, or the soul in general, cannot grasp the other category among these different objects; for since the constitution that it has is diverse, it will right away be capable of grasping both of them. (361) But they are completely silly. For however much these powers seem to be combined in the same being and to be coextensive with one another and to permeate the whole soul, it is no less the case that they differ in kind from one another, and the former is one thing and the latter another. And it is possible to learn this from things that seem pretty clear; (362) for there are lots of things that are observed in connection with the same matter, but do not have the same nature. At least, weight and color both belong to the same body, but differ from one another; and again, shape and size are attributes of the same being, but the nature that they have is separate, size being conceived as one thing, shape as another. In this way, then, the rational power just mentioned, even if it occurs in a mixture with the non-rational power, will again differ from it. (363) Going along with this, additionally (for the reasons enumerated before), is the impossibility of one of them being moved in the same way as the other and being affected like it, since that will require both of them to become one – the rational one non-rational, if it is affected non-rationally, and the non-rational one rational, if it is moved rationally.

iv. Further problems with thought as criterion (364–368)
(364) But even if we suppose that thought peeps out through the sensory passages – as if through apertures, as it were – and gets in touch with

appearances; *phastaston*, "thing that appears," in 357 and elsewhere (e.g., 365), refers instead to the object causing the appearances. More commonly, *phainomena* also refers to objects (e.g., 404); but cf. 193–194 on the Cyrenaics, where both alternatives are considered.

the external objects independently of the senses that lie in front of it, the supposition will be found no less intractable even on these terms. For thought that grasps the underlying things in this way has to grasp the underlying things as plain. But nothing is plain, as we will establish; therefore it is not possible to grasp what is true in the underlying things. For a plain thing is deemed by the people on the other side to be what is grasped by means of itself and needs nothing else for assistance. (365) But nothing is of a nature to be grasped by means of itself; everything is grasped by means of an effect, which is other than what produces it, the thing that appears. For when honey has been brought to me and I have been sweetened, I guess that the externally existing honey is sweet, and when fire has been brought to me and I have been warmed, I take the condition in me as a sign that the externally existing fire is warm, and the same argument applies in the case of other perceptible things. (366) So, since what is grasped by means of another thing is agreed by everyone to be unclear, and all things are grasped by means of their effects on us (which are different from them), all external things are unclear and for this reason unknown to us. For to have knowledge of non-apparent things, something plain has to be present, and when this is not present, the apprehension of those things is gone as well. (367) Nor is it possible to say that, while they are unclear as far as this is concerned, they are apprehended by us in virtue of the fact that the use of their effects as a sign is firm. For if I am in a condition of sweetness after honey has been brought to my sense of taste, it is not definitely the case that the honey is sweet, nor, if I am in a condition of bitterness when wormwood has been brought, is it the case that the wormwood is bitter – as if, by necessity, the effects that occur in us ought also to be attributes of the causes that produce them.[132] (368) For just as the whip falling on flesh pains the flesh without also *being* pain, and as food or drink pleases the eater or drinker without being pleasure, so too fire can heat without necessarily also *being* hot, and honey can sweeten without also turning out to be sweet; and the same argument applies in the case of other perceptible things. But if, in order for us to know what is true, there has to be something plain, but

---

[132] "That occur" and "be attributes" render different forms of the same verb (*sumbainō*). In the first case the tense is present, denoting a process; in the second it is perfect, denoting a settled state. I have not found a way to reproduce this using the same English verb in both cases.

everything has been shown to be unclear, we must agree that what is true is not known.

v. A general problem stemming from disagreement (369)

(369) And how can it not be the case that the disagreement among the philosophers about the highest matters does away with the knowledge of the truth? For if some of the physicists, like Democritus, have done away with all apparent things, while others, like Epicurus and Protagoras, have posited all of them, and others, like the Stoics and Peripatetics, have done away with some and posited others, then whether one supposes thought or sense-perception or the pair of them together to be the criterion, it is altogether and absolutely necessary that either some apparent thing or some unclear thing be first employed for judgment among these people. But it is not possible for it to be an apparent thing; for if it comes from the material in dispute, it will be in dispute, and for this reason not a criterion. But if it is an unclear thing, matters are turned upside down, if what seems to be known is confirmed by means of what is not known – which is absurd.

c. The criterion "in virtue of which" (appearance) (370–439)

(370) But let us even concede the subsistence of the human being and of the senses and thought, for the purpose of the dogmatists' claim going forward. Still, in order for anything to be known through these, we have to agree on the third criterion – that is, appearance. For neither sense-perception nor the intellect can give its attention to things without being altered appearance-wise.[133] **(371)** But this criterion is also full of a great deal of impasse, as may be seen by those who have assembled the arguments in order right from the beginning. For since some of those who use appearance to rule on objects have settled on the apprehensive appearance, others on the persuasive one, we will take the kind common to both of them – that is, appearance itself – and do away with it. **(372)** For when this has been done away with, the different specific categories of appearances are done away with as well. And just as, if there is no animal, there is no human being either, so if there is no appearance, no apprehensive or persuasive appearance subsists either.

---

[133] I.e., altered by the impact of an appearance.

*i. Problems with the notion of appearance as an imprinting, understood
literally or metaphorically (372–387)*

For if appearance is an imprinting in the soul, either it is an imprinting
in the form of hollows and projections, as Cleanthes thinks, or it occurs
in the form of mere alteration, which was Chrysippus' opinion. (373)
And if it subsists in the form of hollows and projections, the absurdities
that Chrysippus speaks of will follow.[134] For if the soul, when affected
appearance-wise, is imprinted in the manner of wax, the last movement
will always obscure the previous appearance, just as the print of the second
seal is liable to wipe out the previous one. But if this is so, then memory,
which is a "storehouse of appearances," is done away with, and all skill is
done away with. For it is a "system and a collection of apprehensions,"
but it is not possible for many different appearances to subsist in the
leading part, since different prints in it are conceived at different times.
So imprinting, strictly conceived, is not an appearance. (374) Besides, if
"apparent things are a sight of things that are unclear,"[135] and we observe
bodies of apparent things that have much thicker parts than breath, but
are not capable of preserving any print on them whatever, it is reasonable
that breath[136] does not retain on itself one single print from an appearance
either. And in fact, water has thicker parts than breath; but when a finger
is pressed on it, it never turns out to be holding on to the print from the
pressure. (375) Why talk about water, though, when even the softest wax,
which is already solid by comparison, is imprinted by something with the
speed of thought, because of its wetness, but does not maintain the print?
If, then, the same body – which is firm by comparison with water – is
utterly incapable of holding on to any prints on it, it is surely obvious that
breath does not have a nature suitable for this either, having finer parts
and being fluid in comparison to such bodies.

(376) "Yes, but the appearance is not strictly an imprinting, but is
a mere alteration of thought." This in turn is worse than the previous
point. For one kind of alteration is in the form of an effect, the other
occurs as a change in the underlying thing. It occurs in the form of an
effect if, for example, a statue that is the same in terms of being and shape
is by turns heated at one time when the sun shines on it, and chilled at
another time when the dew of night falls. It occurs as a change in the

---

[134] Cf. 229–230.   [135] Cf. 140.
[136] The Stoics thought of the soul as breath (*pneuma*); see LS sect. 53.

underlying thing if, for example, this statue was melted and became a bronze sphere. (377) So, if appearance is an alteration of the soul, it is an alteration either simply in the form of an effect or in the form of a change in the underlying thing. And if it is in the form of an effect, then since corresponding to the different appearances the effect is different, the new effect changes the older one, and in this way there will not be a retention of any object in thought, which is absurd. But if it occurs as a change in the underlying thing, then at the same time as grasping an appearance of something, the soul, in being altered, will depart from being soul and will be destroyed, just as the statue that was melted into a sphere also departed at that point from being a statue. Therefore appearance is not an alteration of the soul, either – (378) in addition to the fact that they[137] are under pressure from the impasse about change. For if something changes and is altered, either what remains changes and is altered, or what does not remain. But neither what remains is altered and changes – for it remains in the state of being such as it was – nor what does not remain; for it has been destroyed and *has been* changed, but is not changing. For example, if white changes, either it changes while remaining white or while not remaining white. (379) But it does not change while remaining white; for it remains white, and in so far as it is white, it does not change. Nor does it change while not remaining white; for it has been destroyed and has been changed, but is not changing. Therefore white does not change. For this reason appearance too, if it is a certain change and alteration of the soul, is non-subsistent.

(380) But even if alteration is allowed, the subsistence of appearance will not also be conceded right away. For it was said to be an imprinting on the leading part; but it is not a matter of agreement whether there is this leading part, or in what place it is. Some people, like Asclepiades, say there is not any leading part at all, while some people think there is one, but do not agree about the place that contains it. For this reason, in so far as such disagreement is undecided, we have to remain in suspension of judgment, given that appearance's being an imprinting on the leading part is not accepted.

(381) But let us allow its being an imprinting on the leading part. But since such an imprinting is not reported to the leading part other than

---

[137] I.e., the proponents of the "alteration" view. The transition of thought in this part of the sentence is awkward and abrupt.

through sense-perception, such as sight, hearing, or some other such power, I ask whether the alteration that occurs in the leading part is of the same kind as the one that is in the sense, or different. And if it is the same, then since each of the senses is non-rational, the leading part too, in being altered, will be non-rational and no different from sense-perception. (382) But if it is different, it will not grasp the thing that appears in its underlying character, but the underlying object will be one thing, and the appearance that comes together in the leading part will be different – which is again absurd. So not even in *this* way can we say that appearance is an imprinting and alteration of the leading part.

(383) In addition to this, appearance is a product of the thing that appears, and the thing that appears is a cause of the appearance and is capable of imprinting on the sensory power, and the product is different from the cause that creates it. Hence, since the intellect fastens on the appearances, it will grasp the *products* of the things that appear, but not the *external* things that appear. (384) And if someone were to say that it fastens on the external things by means of the effects that happen in it, we will bring in the impasses mentioned above. For either the external things are the same as our appearances, or not the same, but similar.[138] <And they cannot be the same>; for how can the same thing be conceived as both a cause and its own product? (385) But if they are similar, then since what is similar to something is other than that to which it is similar, thought will know things that are similar to the things that appear but not the things that appear – along with the intractability of this as well: how will thought know that the things that appear are similar to the appearances? For it will come to know this very point either without appearance or with some appearance. And without appearance is impossible; for thought is not of a nature to grasp anything without having appearances. (386) But if it is with an appearance, then surely the appearance itself,[139] in order to know whether it is similar to the thing that appears, which creates it, ought to grasp itself and the underlying thing that appears. But, while the appearance will perhaps be able to grasp the underlying thing that appears (being from that thing), how will it grasp itself? In order for this

---

[138] I follow Kochalsky's deletion of *an eiē* in this sentence, coupled with his addition of the following sentence *kai ta auta men ouk an eiē.*

[139] With Heintz, I read *autē* instead of Mutschmann's *hautē,* and delete Mutschmann's *autē* after *ei.* (According to scholarship cited by Heintz, this has manuscript support and Mutschmann has misreported the manuscript readings.)

to occur, the same thing will have to become both appearance and thing that appears. (387) And since the thing that appears is one thing (for it is a cause), and the appearance is another thing (for it is a product), the same thing will be other than itself (both cause and product simultaneously) – each of which is absurd.

ii. Problems with supposing that all appearances are true/trustworthy or all false/untrustworthy (388–400)

(388) So, with these impasses created, let us move on: even given our agreement about there being appearance, of whatever kind the dogmatists want it to be, we can produce impasses in another way. If appearance is to be admitted as the criterion, either we must say that every appearance is true, as Protagoras said, or that every one is false, as Xeniades of Corinth said, or that some are true and some false, as the Stoics and Academics said, and also the Peripatetics. (389) But it cannot be said either that every one is true or that every one is false or that some are true and some false, as we will establish; therefore appearance cannot be said to be the criterion. One cannot say that every appearance is true because of the "turning about,"[140] as Democritus and Plato taught, speaking against Protagoras. (390) For if every appearance is true, then even *not* every appearance's being true, since it takes the form of an appearance, will be true, and thus every appearance's being true will become false. And even aside from such a turning about, saying that every appearance is true goes against what is apparent, and against plain experience, since a great many of them are false. (391) For we are not moved in the same way with regard to "it is day" (at present) and with regard to "it is night," or to Socrates living and being dead, nor do these things in any way deliver equally plain experience, but its now being day and Socrates' being dead seem to be trustworthy, whereas its being night and Socrates' being alive are not equally trustworthy but appear to be in the class of unreal things. (392) And the same argument applies to the following[141] as well as the conflict in certain things. For its being light obviously follows from its being day, and your moving follows from your walking, but its being night is clearly in conflict with its being day, and your *not* moving in conflict with your walking, and the assertion of the one is the negation of the other, and if something follows from

---

[140] Cf. n. 10.
[141] I.e., as the next few sentences make clear, to the fact that one thing follows from another.

something, then undoubtedly one thing also conflicts with another. But if there is something conflicting with something, then not every appearance is true; for what conflicts with something conflicts as true with false or as false with true. (393) And if it is an attribute of all appearances to be true, nothing is unclear to us. For if there is something true and something false, and it is unknown which of these is true and which false, then there arises what is unclear to us. And the person who says "The stars being odd or even in number is unclear to me" is in effect saying that he does not know which of the two is true and which false – the stars being even in number or odd. So that if everything is true and all appearances are true, nothing is unclear to us. But if nothing is unclear to us, everything is clear. And if everything is clear, there will be no such thing as investigating and being in an impasse about something. For a person investigates and is in an impasse about a matter that is unclear to him, not about what is apparent. But it is absurd to do away with investigation and impasse; therefore not every appearance is true, and not everything is true.

(394) Besides, if every appearance is true and everything is true, there is no truth-telling, or freedom from error, or teaching, or learning, or skill, or demonstration, or virtue, or any other such thing. Let us look at what I am saying. If every appearance is true, nothing is false. But if nothing is false, there will be no lying, nor being in error, nor being unskilled, nor being inferior; for each of these is related to what is false and receives its subsistence in the context of this. (395) But if no one is lying, no one will be telling the truth either, and if no one is in error, nor will anyone be free from error. In the same way, if no one is unskilled, the skilled person is done away with as well, and so is the wise person if there is no inferior person. For these things are conceived by way of comparison, and in the same way as there is no left if there is no right, and no up if there is no down, so, if there is not one of these opposing things, nor will the other subsist. Demonstration and the sign will also be gone. (396) For demonstration is of the fact of being true, but not false; but if *nothing* is false, there is no need of something to teach that it is not false. And the sign and the indication were declared to be capable of uncovering what is unclear; but if everything is true and plainly apparent by itself, we do not need something to disclose whether the thing that is not known is true or false.

(397) But why go on about these things, when neither animal nor universe in general will exist if it is agreed that all appearances are true?

For if everything is true, everything will become clear to us, and if this is so, everything's being *un*clear to us will also be sound and true – since it is one of "everything." But if everything's being unclear is true, we will not accept that either animal or plant or universe appears to us – which is absurd. (398) For all these reasons, then, it must be said that not all appearances are true and trustworthy – yet not that they are all false either, for analogous reasons; for their all being false is of equal force to their all being true. Because of this, in fact, it will be possible to apply just about all the points we mentioned before against this kind of position as well. (399) For if all appearances are false and nothing is true, "Nothing is true" is true. If nothing is true, therefore, there *is* a true thing. And so Xeniades, in saying that all appearances are false and that nothing at all in the things that are is true, has been brought round to the opposite of his thesis. For generally it is impossible, in calling any particular thing false, not to determine something as true as well. For example, when we say that P is false, we are affirming that the falsehood of P is itself so, and we are positing "P is false," so that in effect we are declaring something like "P's being false is true." At the same time as calling something false, then, we are necessarily determining that there is a true. (400) In the same way it is possible also to teach here that the differences among appearances are more or less plain, in virtue of which some induce our assent, while others repel it, and neither do they all in common induce it, nor do they all collectively repel it – since, no doubt, if there was no difference, but they were all equally untrustworthy or trustworthy, there could never be either skill or lack of skill, no praise, no criticism, no deceit. For skill and approbation and immunity to deceit are conceived in terms of true appearances, deceit and criticism in terms of false ones. So we cannot say either that all appearances are true and trustworthy or that they are all false and untrustworthy.

iii. Problems with supposing that some appearances are trustworthy and others not (401–438)
(401) It is left, then, to maintain that some are trustworthy and others untrustworthy, as the Stoics and the Academics said, the Stoics accepting apprehensive appearances and the Academics those that seem to be persuasive. But once we have carefully looked into it, this itself also seems to us more like wishful thinking than the truth.

The apprehensive appearance (402–435) (**402**) For an apprehensive appearance (to start with this) is the one that is from a real thing and is stamped and impressed in accordance with just *that* real thing, and is of such a kind as could not come about from a thing that was not real. Carneades says that he will allow the Stoics the rest of this, but that "of such a kind as could not come about from a thing that was not real" is impermissible. For appearances come about from unreal things as well as from real ones. (**403**) And an indication of their indistinguishability is their being found equally plain and striking, while an indication of their being equally striking and plain is the fact that the corresponding actions are connected with them. For just as in waking life the thirsty person who is taking in drink is pleased, and the person who is fleeing a wild animal or some other horror shouts and yells, so too in dreams people who are thirsty and think they are drinking from a spring have relief, (**404**) and likewise people facing horrors have fear:

> Achilles leapt up amazed,
> Clapped his hands, and spoke a sorrowful word.[142]

And just as, in a healthy condition, we trust and assent to very clearly apparent things – for example, we relate to Dion as Dion and Theon as Theon – so too in madness some people are affected in a similar way. (**405**) At any rate Hercules in madness, after grasping an appearance from his own children as if they were Eurystheus', put the corresponding action together with this appearance. The corresponding action was doing away with his enemy's children – which he did. So if certain appearances are apprehensive in so far as they lead us on to assent and to putting the corresponding action together with them, then since there have also appeared false ones of this kind, it has to be said that non-apprehensive appearances are indistinguishable from apprehensive ones. (**406**) And in the same way as the hero grasped an appearance from the bow and arrows, so too he grasped an appearance from his own children – that they were Eurystheus' children. For one and the same appearance preexisted, and for a person in the same state.[143] But the one from the bow and arrows was true, whereas

---

[142] After dreaming of Patroclus (*Iliad* 23.101–2).

[143] Clearly something is wrong with this sentence; either the text is corrupt or Sextus is being very careless. The surrounding context clearly speaks of a comparison between *two* appearances; and what can it mean to speak of an appearance "preexisting"? To restore clarity to the train of thought, it is best simply to ignore this sentence.

the one from the children was false. **(407)** Since they both moved him equally, then, it must be agreed that the one was indistinguishable from the other. And if the one from the bow and arrows is called apprehensive, because the corresponding action was connected with it (when he used the bow and arrows as bow and arrows), we should also say that the one from the children does not differ from this, in so far as the corresponding action was connected with it as well – that is, the need to do away with his enemy's children.

(408) So then, this indistinguishability between apprehensive and non-apprehensive appearances, in terms of the property of being plain and intense, is established. But the Academics show equally well their indistinguishability in terms of stamp and print. They bring the Stoics up against things that are apparent. **(409)** For in the case of things that are alike in shape, but that differ in terms of what is underlying, it is impossible to distinguish the apprehensive appearance from the false and non-apprehensive one. For example, if there are two eggs exactly alike, and I give them to the Stoic one after the other, will the wise person, after fastening upon them, have the capacity to say infallibly whether the egg he is being shown is a single one, or the one and then the other?[144] **(410)** The same argument also applies in the case of twins. For the superior person will grasp a false appearance, even though he has the appearance as from a real thing and stamped and impressed in accordance with just *that* real thing, if he gets an appearance from Castor as if from Polydeuces. From here, too, came the "veiled" argument.[145] When a snake has poked its head out, if we want to give our attention to the underlying object, we will fall into a great deal of impasse, and will not be able to say whether it is the same snake that poked its head out before or another one, since many snakes are coiled up in the same hole. **(411)** The apprehensive appearance,

---

[144] I.e., whether he is being shown the same egg or a different egg each time. With LS (partially following Heintz), I transpose *ei* from before *epibalōn* to before *enallax*. But there may be more extensive corruption; the Greek does not submit to any acceptable translation without considerable strain.

[145] Chrysippus wrote a book on this topic; Diogenes Laertius 7.198. Diogenes also lists this argument alongside the sorites argument (cf. n.146) and several others (7.82), but the portion of the text in which he explained it has been lost. However, Lucian (*Auction of Lives* 22) gives a vignette of Chrysippus employing it. The argument, as Sextus' example suggests, seems to center around problems with identifying objects in situations of incomplete information; the point of the title is brought out by the question "If you see someone who is veiled, do you know that person or not?"

then, does not have any peculiarity by which it differs from false and non-apprehensive appearances.

In addition, if anything else is apprehensive of anything, sight is. But not even this is apprehensive of anything, as we will establish; therefore there is nothing that is apprehensive of anything. (412) For sight is thought to grasp colors and sizes and shapes and motions; but it does not grasp any of these things, as will be apparent right away when we start with colors. If sight apprehends any color, then – say the Academics – it will also apprehend that of a human being. But it does not apprehend this; therefore it does not apprehend any other color, either. (413) And that it does not apprehend it is clear. For it changes according to seasons, activities, natures, ages, conditions, diseases, health, sleep, waking, so that we know that it varies in this way, yet we are ignorant of what it truthfully is. And in this way, if this color is not apprehensible, nor will any other one become known. (414) Again, we will find the same kind of impasse in the case of shape. For the same one strikes us as both smooth and rough, as in the case of pictures, both round and square, as in the case of towers, both straight and bent, as in the case of the oar out of and in the water, and, in the case of motion, both moving and still, as in the case of people sitting on a ship or standing on the shore.

(415) Besides, if the non-apprehensive appearance is attached to the apprehensive appearance, the apprehensive appearance cannot be the criterion of truth. For just as what is attached to crooked cannot be the criterion of straight, so if the apprehensive appearance is attached to false and non-apprehensive appearances, it cannot be the criterion. But the apprehensive appearance *is* attached to non-apprehensive and false things, as we will establish; therefore the apprehensive appearance is not the criterion of true and false. (416) For in the case of the "heap" problem,[146] since the last apprehensive appearance lies next to the first non-apprehensive one, and is just about impossible to distinguish from it, Chrysippus says that, in the case of appearances where the difference between them is so small, the wise person will hold fast and keep quiet, whereas in cases where a greater difference strikes him, he will assent to one of them as true. (417) So if we establish that there are many false and non-apprehensive things

---

[146] Also known (in philosophical English) by the original Greek word *sorités*; the classic form of the problem is expressed by the question "How many grains make a heap?"

lying next to the apprehensive appearance, it is clear that we will be in a position of having proved the necessity of not assenting to the apprehensive appearance, so that we do not, by agreeing to it, also fall into assenting to the false and non-apprehensive ones because they are in the same neighborhood – however much difference in the appearances may seem to strike us.

(418) This statement will be clear with an example. Suppose there is an apprehensive appearance, "fifty is few," which appears to be separated by a long way from this other one: "ten thousand is few." Well then, since the non-apprehensive "ten thousand is few" is very far away from the apprehensive "fifty is few," the superior person will not suspend judgment when this great difference strikes him, but will assent to the apprehensive appearance, "fifty is few," and will not assent to the non-apprehensive one, "ten thousand is few." (419) But if the wise person does not assent to "ten thousand is few," in so far as it is separated by a long way from "fifty is few," it is surely clear that he will assent to "fifty-one is few." For there is nothing in between this one and "fifty is few." But since "fifty is few" is the apprehensive appearance in the last position, "fifty-one is few" is the first non-apprehensive one. Therefore the superior person will assent to the non-apprehensive appearance "fifty-one is few." And if he assents to this one, which has no difference from "fifty is few," he will also assent to the non-apprehensive "ten thousand is few." (420) For *every* non-apprehensive appearance is equal to a non-apprehensive appearance. So, since the non-apprehensive "ten thousand is few" is equal to "fifty-one is few", and it was in no way different or separated from "fifty is few," the apprehensive appearance "fifty is few" will become equal to the non-apprehensive appearance "ten thousand is few." (421) And in this way the apprehensive appearance makes its exit along with the false and non-apprehensive appearance, because of their indistinguishability.

Nor is it possible to say that not every non-apprehensive appearance is equal to *every* non-apprehensive appearance, but that one of them is more non-apprehensive and another less, (422) since, first of all, the Stoics will then be fighting with themselves and with the nature of things. For just as a human being, in so far as he is a human being, does not differ from a human being, nor does a stone differ from a stone, so a non-apprehensive appearance, as being non-apprehensive, does not differ from a non-apprehensive appearance, nor does a false one, as being false, differ from a false one. It was starting from here that Zeno taught that faults are equal. (423) Then again, let it be the case that one is more apprehensive and another less. How can this help them? For it will follow that the wise person does not assent to the more non-apprehensive one, but does assent to the less non-apprehensive, which is absurd. For according to them the wise person has an unerring criterion, and is deified in every respect because of not having opinions – that is, assenting to a falsehood, in which lie the peak of unhappiness and the downfall of the inferior.

(424) Now, in order for a sensory appearance to occur, such as a visual one, five things must come together, according to them: the sense-organ, the thing sensed, the place, the manner,[147] and thought, since if a single one of these is missing while the others are present – for example, if thought is in an unnatural state – the apprehension, they say, will not be preserved. Hence some people have said that even the apprehensive appearance is not a criterion in general, but when it has no obstacle of <this> kind.[148] (425) But this is something impossible. For given the differences in the places and given the external circumstances and given a multitude of other factors, objects do not appear to us as the same or in the same way (as we argued above) – so that while we can say that it appears to this sense and in this circumstance, we are not in a position to authenticate whether it is in truth such as it appears, or whether it *is* one way but appears another, and for this reason there is *no* appearance without an obstacle.

(426) And how can they avoid falling into the reciprocal mode? For when we are investigating what the apprehensive appearance is, they define it by saying "the one that is from a real thing and is stamped and impressed in accordance with just *that* real thing, and is of such a kind as could not come about from a thing that was not real." Then again, since everything that is taught by means of a definition is taught from things that are known, when we go on to ask what "the real thing" is, they turn around and say "a real thing is what activates an apprehensive

---

[147] I follow the mss. reading *pōs*, rather than Heintz's conjecture *phōs*, adopted by Mutschmann (about which Heintz had second thoughts – *Studien zu Sextus Empiricus* [Max Niemeyer Verlag, 1932], 147).

[148] I follow LS's reading *kata <touton> ton tropon*. For explanation of the "no obstacle" point, cf. 253ff.

appearance." So that in order to learn of the apprehensive appearance, we need to have previously grasped the real thing, yet to achieve this, we need to proceed to the apprehensive appearance. And in this way neither one becomes clear, since it is waiting for assurance from the other. (427) And just as, since some things that appear both appear and are real, whereas others appear but are *not* also real, we need some criterion that will establish which are the ones that appear and are at the same time real, and which are the ones that appear and are not real, in the same way, since some appearances are apprehensive and some are not, we need a criterion that will sort out which are of this kind and which are non-apprehensive and false. (428) Now, this criterion will be an appearance that is either apprehensive or not apprehensive. And if it is not apprehensive, it will follow that a non-apprehensive appearance is, purely and simply, the criterion of everything; its job is the examining even of the apprehensive one, which they will not want. But if it is apprehensive, first of all that is silly (for we were seeking to judge when this very appearance is apprehensive), (429) and second, if for distinguishing apprehensive and non-apprehensive appearances we take as a criterion the apprehensive appearance, the fact that the one judging them is in fact an apprehensive appearance will also need to be scrutinized – by means of an apprehensive appearance – and then that one by means of another, and so on *ad infinitum*.

(430) But perhaps someone will say that the apprehensive appearance is the criterion both of the thing that appears (that it does truly exist) and of itself (that it is apprehensive). But this is no different from saying, conversely, that the thing that appears is a test both of itself and of the appearance. For just as, when apparent things are in disagreement, one seeks the means by which we are to judge what is real and what is not real, so too, when appearances are not in harmony with one another, we inquire into the means by which we are to judge the apprehensive one and the one that is not of that kind. (431) For this reason, since these matters are similar, if the appearance, despite not being in harmony, can be the criterion of itself, the thing that appears will also be trustworthy by itself, however much it is in disagreement – which is absurd. (432) Or if this does need something to judge it, in so far as it is in disagreement, then the appearance too will need something to scrutinize it and establish whether it is in fact apprehensive.

Besides, if every supposition of the inferior person is ignorance, according to them, and only the wise person tells the truth and has firm knowledge of what is true, it follows that, since so far the wise person is undiscovered, what is true is necessarily undiscovered as well. And for this reason everything also turns out to be inapprehensible, since we are all inferior, and so do not have a firm apprehension of the things that there are. **(433)** And since this is the case, the things said by the Stoics against the skeptics are available to be said, in turn, by the skeptics against them. For since among the inferior, according to them, are numbered Zeno and Cleanthes and Chrysippus and the rest of their school, and every inferior person is gripped by ignorance, then undoubtedly Zeno was ignorant as to whether he was contained in the universe or whether he himself contained the universe, and whether he was a man or a woman, and Cleanthes did not know whether he was a human being or some beast more crafty than Typhon.[149] **(434)** Again, Chrysippus either knew this doctrine, which is a Stoic one (I mean, "The inferior person is ignorant of everything"), or he did not even know *this*. And if he knew it, then it is false that the inferior person is ignorant of everything; for Chrysippus, being an inferior person, knew this very thing – the inferior person's being ignorant of everything. But if he did not even know this very fact, that he is ignorant of everything, how does he lay down doctrines about lots of things, positing that there is one world-order, and that this is administered by providence, and that being is entirely changeable, and a great many other things? **(435)** And it is possible, if it is to anyone's liking, for the cross-questioner to bring forward the other impasses, as they have the habit of doing against the skeptics.[150] However, since the character of the attack has been shown, it is not necessary to go on at length.

The persuasive appearance (435–438)   Against the people who accept persuasive appearances the argument is brief. For it is one of these two: these criteria are supposed by them to be useful either for the conduct of life or for the discovery of the truth in the things that there are. **(436)** And if they say the first, they will be absurd; for none of these appearances

---

[149] Cf. 264 on Socrates.

[150] Mutschmann (following Kochalsky) prints a lacuna in this sentence, and this may well be correct; even after their change of the mss. *autois* to *autoi*, the Greek as it stands is very awkward. However, the general sense is clear enough.

can contribute by itself to the conduct of life, but each one also needs the observation in light of which this one is, for this reason, persuasive, and another one, for this reason, gone over in detail and not turned away.[151] (437) But if it is for the discovery of what is true, they will fall down. For the persuasive appearance alone is not the criterion of what is true either. In order for what is true to be discovered, the appearance needs <to be>[152] gone over in detail, on account of the fact that in going over each of the things observed in its neighborhood, we are definitely led to a suspicion that one of the things that ought to be examined in this neighborhood may have been left aside – because, if a "turning away" happens in our thought, the knowledge of the truth is destroyed. (438) And on the whole, it looks as if they are overcome by their own refutations. For just as, in casting aspersions on the apprehensive appearance, they said that this is not the criterion of truth, because other indistinguishable but false ones lie next to it, so it is not unlikely that in our careful consideration of the persuasive appearance, certain other false things also lie next to the objects that have been gone over in detail – so that, for example, we *seem* to have a sound soul and body, but do not, or the thing that appears *seems* to be viewed from a suitable distance, but that is not how it is.

iv. Conclusion to 3c, and to 3 in general (439)

(439) But let us get to the main point: if it is not the case either that all appearances are trustworthy, or that they are all untrustworthy, or that some are trustworthy and some untrustworthy, then appearance cannot be the criterion of the truth. From which it follows that nothing is the criterion, given that neither the "by which," nor the "through which," nor the "in virtue of which"[153] is firm in its knowledge.

---

[151] For explanation of these notions see 176–189.
[152] At least a verb is missing from the text; all editors have supplied *einai*, "to be." But many have suspected a more extensive lacuna; a translation of Mutschmann's suggestion (not actually incorporated into his text) would be "needs <to be> gone over in detail, <and for the one that is gone over in detail to be 'not turned away'>". This entire sentence, in fact, is a mess. There are several other textual difficulties; I follow Mutschmann's text, but the language and thought are strained on any reading.
[153] This is the only place in the book in which the third way of conceiving the criterion is explicitly referred to by this term (though cf. 37 for its use in this context); elsewhere, instead of a phrase parallel with the labels for the other two, Sextus resorts to a more cumbersome paraphrase – cf. 35–37, 261, 370. By contrast, the parallel passage at *PH* 2.14–79 consistently refers to it in this way.

d. Final reply to dogmatist counter-attack (440–445)

(440) But the dogmatists typically reply by asking how on earth the *skeptic* declares that nothing is a criterion. For he says this either without a criterion or with a criterion. And if it is without a criterion, he will become untrustworthy; but if it is with a criterion, he will be turned about, and in saying that nothing is a criterion he will agree to employ a criterion for the purpose of showing this. (441) And again, when we raise the question "If there is a criterion, either it has been judged or it is unjudged," and we reach one of two conclusions – either infinite regress or that something is said, absurdly, to be its own criterion – they lead the counter-attack by saying that it is *not* absurd to admit something as its own criterion. (442) For the straight is capable of testing both itself and other things, and the pair of scales is capable of measuring both the equality of other things and its own equality, and light appears capable of uncovering not only other things but itself too – which means that the criterion *can* be a criterion both of other things and of itself.

(443) But against this it must be said, first, that the skeptic's procedure is to refrain from making the case for things that are trusted, but, in their case, to be content with the common preconception as a sufficient basis – but to make the case for the things that seem *not* to be trustworthy, and to bring each of them into equal strength with the trust surrounding the things deemed worthy of acceptance. In the present case too, then, we are not abolishing the criterion when we avail ourselves of the arguments against it, but we want to show that there being a criterion is not entirely reliable, since equal resources are mustered for the opposite case. (444) Then again, even if we do seem to join in doing away with the criterion, we can use the currently available appearance for this purpose – but not as a criterion. In putting forward, by way of this, the persuasive arguments that strike us in favor of there being no criterion, we do put them forward, but we do not do this with assent, given the fact that the opposing arguments are also equally persuasive. (445) "But for God's sake, something can be its *own* criterion, as happens with the ruler and the scales." But this is juvenile. For with each of these there is a criterion over and above it, such as sense-perception and intellect – which is why we even get into constructing them. But they do not want there to be any criterion over and above the one that has now come under examination. Therefore when it says something about itself, and does

not have anything that gives additional testimony of its truthfulness, it is untrustworthy.

C. Transition to Book 2 (446)

(446) That is enough on the criterion. And since this treatise is of sufficient length, we will make a new beginning, and try to create impasses separately about the true itself.

Book 2

A. The true (1–140)

(1) In the treatise that we have now finished, we have gone over the impasses that are usually recounted by the skeptics with a view to doing away with the criterion of truth. Having also given the account that they trace from the original physicists up to more recent figures, we promised, on top of all this, to speak separately about the true itself. Hence, in fulfilling that promise now, let us first look into whether there is anything true.

Whether there is anything true

(2) It is apparent to everyone right away that, if there is no obvious criterion, the true is also necessarily made unclear at the same time. But still, it will be possible for good measure to explain that even if we say nothing directly against the criterion, the disagreement about the true itself is sufficient to bring us into suspension of judgment. (3) And in the same way as, if there is nothing straight or crooked in the nature of things, neither is there a standard capable of testing them; and if there is no heavy or light body, the setting up of scales is also done away with; so if there is nothing true, the criterion of truth is also gone. And that there is nothing true or false – if we go by the dogmatists' words – we can learn once we have laid out the disagreement on this subject that has developed among them.

1. Disagreements about the true (4–13)

a. About what kinds of things are true (4–10)
(4) Of those who have inquired into the true, some say that there is nothing true, others that there *is* something true. And of those who say that

there is, some say that only intelligible things are true, some that only perceptible things are true, and some that both perceptible and intelligible things are true. (5) Xeniades of Corinth, as we pointed out earlier,[1] says that nothing is true, and perhaps also Monimus the Cynic when he says that "everything is vanity" – which is thinking of things that are not, as if they are. (6) Plato and Democritus supposed that only intelligible things are true, Democritus because nothing perceptible exists by nature (the atoms that comprise everything having a nature bereft of every perceptible quality), (7) but Plato because perceptible things are always becoming, but never are, since being flows like a river, so that it does not remain the same for two of the smallest instants, nor (as Asclepiades also said) does it permit demonstrative reference twice, because of the speed of the flux. (8) Aenesidemus[2] and Epicurus, on the other hand, both resorted to perceptible things, but disagreed on specifics. For Aenesidemus says that there is a difference among apparent things, and says that some of these appear in common to everyone, while others appear privately to someone, and that the ones that appear in common to everyone are true, while the ones not like this are false. Hence "true" [*alēthes*] is named after what *does not escape* [*mē lēthon*] common judgment. (9) But Epicurus spoke of all perceptible things as true and as beings. For there is no difference between saying that something is true and saying that it is real; hence, too, in delineating the true and the false he says "That which holds in the way in which it is said to hold is true," and he says "That which does not hold in the way in which it is said to hold is false." He adds that sense-perception, being capable of grasping the things that impinge on it, and neither taking away nor adding nor changing anything (since it is non-rational), continually tells the truth and grasps the thing that is, in the way in which that very thing is in its nature. And though all perceptible things are true, opinable things differ, and some of them are true and others false, as we showed earlier.[3] (10) But the Stoics say that both some perceptible things and some intelligible things are true – the perceptible ones not straightforwardly, though, but by way of reference to the intelligible things related to them. For, according to them, what is real and

---

[1] Cf. 1.53–54.
[2] I delete the words *kai Hērakleiton*, "and Heraclitus," altered by Mutschmann and others to *kath'Hērakleiton*, "in accordance with Heraclitus"; either way, they are out of place in this passage. On "Aenesidemus 'in accordance with Heraclitus'," see 1.349.
[3] 1.203–216.

contradicts something is true, and what is not real and contradicts something is false; and this, being an incorporeal proposition, is an intelligible thing.

b. About the locus of the true (11–13)

(11) So the first disagreement about the true was something like this. But there was another disagreement among them; some placed the true and false in the region of the thing signified, others in that of utterance, others in that of the motion of thought. And the Stoics stood for the first opinion, saying that three things were connected with one another, the thing signified and the signifier and the object. (12) Of these the signifier is the utterance (for example, the utterance "Dion"); the thing signified is the actual state of affairs revealed by it, and which we apprehend as it subsists in our thought, and which foreigners do not understand even though they hear the utterance; and the object is the externally existing thing (for example, Dion himself). And of these, two are bodies, namely the utterance and the object, while one is incorporeal, namely the state of affairs signified and sayable, which is true or false. This is not the case universally, but some sayables are deficient and some self-sufficient.[4] And belonging to the self-sufficient kind is the so-called proposition, which they delineate by saying "a proposition is what is true or false." (13) But Epicurus and Strato the physicist accept only two of these, the signifier and the object; so they appear to hold the second position and to locate the true and false in the utterance. The last opinion (I mean, the one that places the true in the movement of thought), seems to be a scholarly fiction.[5]

2. *Difficulties about the true (14–140)*

(14) Now that an account of this topic, covering the main points, has been given, let us move on to the particular impasses,[6] some of which will be aimed more generally against all the positions that have been laid out, and others more specifically against each one.

---

[4] On "sayables" (*lekta*) see 70ff. and LS sect. 33.
[5] The significance of this is not quite clear. It does not apparently mean that no one held the view in question; cf. 11, 137.
[6] Somewhat confusingly, this term is later used (55) to introduce the second sub-category of difficulties mentioned here – the ones said to be aimed "more specifically."

a. General difficulties (15–54)

i. *Difficulties in establishing something as true either by assertion or by demonstration (15–16)*

(**15**) And let us speak about the general ones first. The person who says that there is something true, then, either just declares that there is something true or demonstrates it. And if he merely declares it, he will hear the opposite of his mere assertion, namely that *nothing* is true. But if he demonstrates that there is something true, he demonstrates this either with a true demonstration or with one that is not true. But he would not say that it is with one that is not true; for something of that kind is untrustworthy. But if with a true one, by what means does it come about that what demonstrates that there is something true is true? If by means of itself, there will also be the possibility of saying, by means of itself, that it is *not* true; (**16**) but if from a demonstration, it will be asked in turn how *this* is true, and so *ad infinitum*. Since, then, in order for us to learn something true it is necessary first to grasp an infinity, but it is impossible to grasp an infinity, it is impossible to know securely that there is anything true.

ii. *Difficulties in supposing that what is true is apparent, or unclear, or each in a certain respect (17–31)*

(**17**) Then again, if there is anything true, it is either apparent, or unclear, or in a certain respect apparent and in a certain respect unclear. But it is neither apparent, as we will establish, nor unclear, as we will show, nor in a certain respect apparent and in a certain respect unclear, as we will explain; therefore it is not the case that there is anything true. (**18**) For if it is apparent, either everything apparent is true or something apparent[7] is true. But it is not the case that everything apparent is true (for example, what strikes us in sleep or in madness is not true); in that case, since apparent things involve a lot of conflict, one would have to agree that conflicting things are both real and are equally true – which is absurd. Not everything apparent, then, is true. (**19**) But if one apparent thing is true and another one false, we ought to have a criterion for distinguishing which apparent thing is true and which one false. This criterion, then, is either apparent to everyone or unclear. And if it is apparent, then since not

---

[7] I.e., *just* something apparent (as opposed to everything); this language recurs several times in the following sections.

every apparent thing is true, it too, being an apparent thing, will have to be scrutinized by another apparent thing, and that one by a different one, and so *ad infinitum*. (**20**) But if it is unclear, then not only apparent things will be true, but unclear things as well. For if we grasp the unclear thing that is employed to give trust to the apparent thing, something unclear has to be true; for what is true is not judged by what is false. (**21**) But if something unclear is true, what is apparent is not the only thing that is true, which was the original hypothesis. Then again, by what means does it come about that this unclear thing, too, is true? If by means of itself, then *all* unclear matters will also be true by means of themselves. But if on the grounds of being demonstrated, it will certainly be demonstrated true either by an unclear thing or by an apparent thing. And if by an unclear thing, that one will again need to be judged by something else, and the third one by a fourth, and so *ad infinitum*. (**22**) But if by an apparent thing, we will fall into[8] the reciprocal mode, guaranteeing the apparent thing by the unclear one, and conversely confirming the unclear thing by the apparent one. (**23**) But if neither everything apparent is true nor something apparent, *nothing* apparent is true.

Yet it is not unclear either. (**24**) For again, if what is true is unclear, either everything unclear is true or not everything. But neither is everything unclear true nor something unclear, as we will establish; therefore what is true is not unclear either. For if everything unclear is true, then first, the dogmatists should not have taken opposing positions – some saying, for example, that there is one element, others two, and some a definite number, others an infinite number – nor should they have shown up each others' opinions as false. (**25**) And if everything unclear is true, conflicting things will be true – for example, the stars being even and being odd in number; for they are equally unclear, and everything unclear is[9] true. But conflicting things *cannot* be true; therefore not everything unclear is true. (**26**) Nor, however, are some unclear things true. For this unclear thing's being true, and that one's being false, is asserted either all by itself and without a criterion, or with a criterion. And if it is asserted without hesitation, we will have nothing to say to the person who declares the opposite to be true. (**27**) But if with a criterion, this criterion is definitely either apparent or unclear. And if it is apparent, the original hypothesis

---

[8] Following Heintz, I read *empesoumetha* for the mss. *ekpesoumetha* ("we will be wrecked on"); cf. 1.341 for this usage.

[9] With Bekker, I read *estin* for the mss. *estai*.

(that only the unclear is true) will be false. **(28)** Then again, by what means does it come about that that by which we judge the apparent thing is true? If by means of itself, then the assertion (made by means of itself) that it is *not* true will also be trustworthy. If by an apparent thing, that apparent thing will also be grasped by another apparent thing, and so *ad infinitum*. **(29)** And if by an unclear thing, the reciprocal mode will arise: we will be able neither to hold the apparent thing trustworthy without the unclear thing nor to hold the unclear thing firm apart from the apparent thing. Nor, then, can the unclear be true.

(30) It remains to say, therefore, that what is in a certain respect true and in a certain respect unclear is true; <. . .>.[10] For if we suppose that this apparent thing is true in so far as it is apparent, then we suppose it true either in so far as everything apparent is true, or not everything. And if the unclear thing is assumed to be true in so far as it is unclear, then it is assumed true either in so far as everything unclear is true, or not everything. And from this point on, we will pile on the same impasses.[11] **(31)** Hence if neither what is apparent is true, nor what is unclear, nor what is in a certain respect apparent and in a certain respect unclear, and there is nothing else besides these, necessarily nothing is true.

iii. Difficulties stemming from the status of the highest genus (32–36)

(32) Some people also raise the impasse stemming from what is most generic: what is.[12] For this is a genus higher than all of them, while it is itself subordinate to no other. Now, this is either true, or false, or true and false both at once, or neither true nor false. **(33)** And if it is true, all things will become true, in so far as they are specific instances of it. And just as, given that the genus of human beings is human being, the specific ones are also human beings, and given that the genus is rational, all the particular ones are rational, and given that it is mortal, they similarly are mortal, so, if the genus of everything is true, it is necessary that all beings are also true.

---

[10] A phrase such as "which is also absurd" seems to have dropped out of the text at this point.

[11] I.e., the ones raised in the previous two paragraphs.

[12] The Stoics are elsewhere recorded as proposing not "what is" (*to on*) as the highest genus, but "the something" (*to ti*), with "what is" subordinate to it; see LS sect. 27. (The parallel passage of *PH* [2.86–87] does talk of this standard Stoic view.) For this reason some have suspected the text at this point; but "all beings" at the end of 33 suggests that "what is" is what Sextus actually wrote. However, he does not say here that he is reporting a Stoic view; and in any case Diogenes Laertius (7.61) says that Stoics did consider "what is" as the highest genus, so there was apparently some confusion on the point.

(34) But if all beings are true, nothing will be false, and if there is no false, neither will there be anything true, as we mentioned earlier in showing that each of these is conceived in terms of a comparison with the other one.[13] Besides, if everything is true we will be positing conflicting truths; but that is absurd. Therefore the most generic is not true. (35) Yet nor is it false, because of similar impasses. For if it is false, everything that partakes of it will also be false. But *everything*, both bodies and incorporeal things, partakes of it; so everything will become false. And analogous impasses will follow from everything's being false. (36) It is left, then, to say that it is true and false both at once, or neither true nor false. But that is worse than what has been indicated above, because it follows from this that all the particulars are true and false both at once, or neither true nor false – which is absurd. So there is not anything true.

*iv. Difficulties in supposing that what is true is either absolute
or relative (37–39)*

(37) Then again, what is true is either among the things that are in virtue of a difference and by nature, or among the things that are in relation to something.[14] But it is neither of these, as we will establish; therefore it is not true.[15] Now, what is true is not in virtue of a difference and by nature, in so far as what exists in virtue of a difference and by nature affects things that are in a similar state in the same way. For example, the hot is not hot for one person and cold for another, but is hot for everyone who is in the same state. (38) However, what is true does not affect everyone similarly, but the same thing seems to be true considered in relation to this person, and false considered in relation to another person. Therefore what is true is not among the things that are in virtue of a difference and by nature. But if it is among the things in relation to something, then since the things in relation to something are only conceived and are not also real, then what is true, too, will certainly be only conceived, and will not be real. (39) Besides, if what is true is among the things in relation to something, the same thing will be true and false both at once. For just as the same thing is both right and left (right in relation to this thing, left in relation to that one), and the same thing is both up and down (up considered in relation to what lies under it, and down considered in relation to what lies above

---

[13] Cf. 1.394–400.   [14] For further explanation of these terms see 161ff.
[15] I retain the mss. reading *estin alēthes*, altered by Bekker and Mutschmann to *esti t'alēthes*.

it), so we will call the same thing true and false both at once. And if this is so, it will be no more true than false – and surely not true.

v. Difficulties is supposing that what is true is either perceptible
or intelligible or both (40–50)

(40) Aenesidemus in effect puts forward similar impasses on the topic. If there is anything true, either it is perceptible, or it is intelligible, or it is perceptible *and* it is intelligible. But neither is it perceptible nor is it intelligible, nor the combination of both, as will be established; therefore it is not the case that there is anything true. (41) That it is not perceptible we will reason as follows. Of perceptible things some are genera and some are specific instances; and genera are the common features that extend among the particulars – as human being is what runs through particular human beings, and horse through particular horses – while specific instances are the particular individual characteristics – for example, of Dion, Theon, and the rest. (42) Now, if what is true is perceptible, it too will surely be a perceptible thing that is common to multiple things or that has the status of an individual characteristic. But neither is it common nor does it have the status of an individual characteristic; therefore what is true is not perceptible. (43) Moreover, in the same way as what is visible is grasped by sight, and what is audible is known by hearing, and what is smellable by smell, so too what is perceptible is known by sense-perception in general. But what is true is not known by sense-perception in general; for sense-perception is non-rational, and what is true is not known non-rationally. Therefore what is true is not perceptible.

(44) Yet it is not intelligible either, since in that case none of the perceptible things will be true – which is again absurd. For either it will be intelligible to everyone in common or to some people specifically. But what is true cannot be intelligible either to everyone in common or to some people specifically. (45) For its being understood by everyone in common is impossible, and its being understood by a person or some people specifically is untrustworthy and disputable. Therefore what is true is not intelligible. But nor is it perceptible and intelligible both at once. For either everything perceptible and everything intelligible is true or something perceptible and something intelligible. (46) But saying that everything perceptible and everything intelligible is true is not feasible. For perceptibles conflict with perceptibles and intelligibles with intelligibles and, by a further permutation, perceptibles with intelligibles; and if

everything is true, the same thing will have to be and not be, and be both true and false. But to maintain that something perceptible and something intelligible is true is again something intractable; for this is what is being investigated. (47) And besides, it is consistent to say either that all perceptible things are true or that all of them are false; for they are equally perceptible – it is not that one is more so and another less so – and again intelligible things are equally intelligible, not one more so and another less so. But perceptible things are not all said to be true, nor all false; therefore it is not the case that there is anything true.[16]

(48) "Yes, but the truth is grasped not in so far as it appears, but in virtue of another cause." Well, what is this cause? Let the dogmatists put it forward publicly, so that it can either draw us to assent or turn us away to avoidance. (49) Then again, how do they grasp this very cause? As apparent to them or as not apparent? If as apparent, then they are lying when they say that the truth is not real in so far as it appears; but if as not apparent, how have they grasped what is not apparent to them? All by itself or through something else? (50) All by itself is impossible; for nothing that is not apparent is graspable all by itself. But if it is through something else, that thing again is either apparent or not apparent; and since the investigation goes on in this way *ad infinitum*, what is true becomes undiscoverable.

vi. *Difficulties in supposing that the persuasive is true (51–54)*

(51) What then? Is what persuades us, the persuasive, to be called true – whatever kind of being it has, whether perceptible or intelligible or the combination, perceptible and intelligible both at once? (52) But this too is intractable. For if the persuasive is true, then since the same thing does not persuade everyone, nor the same people all the time, we will be conceding that the same thing is both real and not real, and that the same thing is simultaneously true and false. In so far as it persuades some people, it will be true and real, but in so far as it does not persuade other people, false and unreal. But it is impossible for the same thing both to be and not to be, or to be both true and false; (53) therefore the persuasive is not true either. Unless we are to say that what persuades many people is true; after all, honey, which persuades many healthy people that it is sweet, but does not

---

[16] The arguments in this paragraph are unusually crabbed and unconvincing. Textual problems may be part of the difficulty (here I do not depart from Mutschmann's text at any point), but can hardly be the whole story.

persuade the one person who has jaundice, we truly call sweet. But this is silly. For when we are inquiring about truth, we should not look to the number of people who agree but to their conditions. The sick person is in one condition, and all the healthy people are in one state. **(54)** This condition, then, is no more to be relied on than that one, since if it is supposed, conversely, that many people are embittered by the honey (people in a fever, for example), and that the one person who is healthy is sweetened,[17] it will certainly follow that we call the honey bitter – which is absurd. So, just as we here put aside the evidence based on the numbers, and nonetheless say that honey is sweet, so too when many people are sweetened, and one person is embittered, let us leave off calling honey sweet because of the number of people thus affected, and examine what is true in another way.

b. Particular difficulties (55–140)
i. Not everything is false (55)
(55) The general impasses about what is true are somewhat of this sort. Following them, let us go on to the particular ones. Now, we showed earlier[18] that the people who say that everything is false are turned about. For if everything is false, "everything is false" will be also false, since it belongs to "everything." And if "everything is false" is false, its opposite, "not everything is false," will be true. Therefore if everything is false, not everything is false.

ii. Difficulties for truth created by Democritus' and Plato's rejection of the senses (56–62)
(56) And Democritus and Plato, in rejecting the senses and doing away with perceptible things and following only intelligible things, make matters confused, and shake not only the truth of the things that there are, but even the conception of them. For every concept comes into being from sense-perception or not without sense-perception, and either from experience or not without experience. **(57)** Hence we will find that not even the so-called false appearances – for example, those in sleep or those in madness – are distinct from the things known to us through sense-perception by way of experience. Indeed, the person who in madness imagines Furies,

> Bloody-looking, dragon-shaped girls,[19]

---

[17] For the terms "embittered" and "sweetened," compare 1.190ff. on the Cyrenaic position.
[18] 1.398–399 (though the reasoning is not exactly the same as in this passage).
[19] Euripides, *Orestes* 256.

conceives a shape put together out of the things that have appeared to him. In the same way, the person who dreams in his sleep of a winged human does not have this dream without having seen something winged and a human being. (58) And generally it is impossible to find anything to do with conception that one does not have for oneself as something known by way of experience. For this will be grasped either in virtue of similarity to the things that have appeared in experience, or in virtue of augmentation or diminution or combination. (59) In virtue of similarity, as when we conceive Socrates, who has not been seen, from the image of Socrates that has been observed; in virtue of augmentation, when proceeding from the common human being we conceive a kind of being who is not like

> A bread-eating man, but a wooded peak
> Of the high mountains;[20]

(60) in virtue of diminution when, on the contrary, we reduce the size of the common human being and grasp a concept of a pygmy; and in virtue of combination, when from a human being and a horse we conceive the Hippocentaur, which we have never encountered. Experience through sense-perception, then, has to precede every conception, and for this reason if perceptible things are done away with, every concept is necessarily done away with as well. (61) And the person who says that all apparent things are false and that only intelligible things are real "in verity"[21] (that is, in truth) will say this either relying on mere assertion or with a demonstration. But if he is speaking by assertion he will be held back by assertion, while if he tries to employ a demonstration he will be turned about. (62) For he will teach that "in verity" there are only intelligible things either by something apparent or by something unclear. But he will not teach this by something apparent – for it is not real – nor by something unclear – for the unclear ought to be made trustworthy beforehand by something apparent. Therefore the position of Democritus and Plato is not sound.

---

[20] *Odyssey* 9.191–2.
[21] Cf. 1.135–137 on Democritus. The word *eteēi*, "in verity," frequently used there in the quotations from Democritus, is archaic and not part of Sextus' normal usage; Sextus clearly intends it here as a quotation.

*iii. Difficulties in establishing what is true in Epicureanism
and Stoicism (63–68)*

(63) Epicurus said that everything perceptible is true, and that every appearance is from a real thing, and is of the same kind as what activates the sensation, and that those who say that some appearances are true and others false are in error through not being able to separate opinion from plain experience. In the case of Orestes, anyway, when he thought he was looking at the Furies, the sensation that was activated by images was true (for the images did exist), but the intellect in thinking that they were solid Furies had a false opinion. (64) And besides, he says, the people just mentioned, who introduce a difference in the appearances, do not have the ability to confirm that some of them are true and others false. For they will not teach any such thing by something apparent – for apparent things are under investigation – nor by something unclear – for what is unclear ought to be demonstrated through something apparent. (65) Of course, in saying such things Epicurus has unintentionally fallen into[22] a similar impasse. For if he agrees that some appearances come from solid bodies and others from an image, and concedes that plain experience is one thing but opinion another, then, I ask, how does he distinguish the appearances that strike us from a solid body and those from an image? Not by plain experience – for that is under investigation – nor by opinion – for opinion ought to be confirmed through plain experience. (66) It is especially absurd that he tries to demonstrate things that are less under investigation by means of things that are more under investigation. For while we are inquiring about the reliability of apparent things, he introduces this monstrous and mythical opinion about images.

(67) Nor does the Stoics' account go smoothly. For they want there to be a difference among both perceptible and intelligible things, in virtue of which some are true and others false, but they do not have the ability to draw such a conclusion. For they have agreed that some appearances are empty, such as the ones that struck Orestes from the Furies, and that others are fraudulent – the ones that are from existing things, but not in accordance with just *those* existing things, like the ones that happened to Heracles in his madness; they were from his own children, but were as if from those of Eurystheus. For it came from the children, who did exist,

---

[22] With Heintz I read *empeptōken* for the mss. *ekpeptōken*; cf. 22 above.

but not in accordance with just *those* existing things; for he did not see the children as his own, but says

> There, one of Eurystheus' youngsters dies;
> He has fallen to me, paying for his father's enmity.[23]

(68) And since this is so, appearances become indistinguishable, and the Stoics are not able to say which are in truth apprehensive and come from existing things and in accordance with just *those* existing things, and which are not like this, as we showed earlier at greater length.[24]

iv. Difficulties in supposing that the locus of the true is the sayable (69–129)
(69) The argument about this position is similar to the argument we would introduce about the remaining position,[25] according to which some suppose that what is true and what is false belong in the thing signified – that is, in the incorporeal sayable – others that they belong in the utterance, and others in the movement of thought. (70) For example (to begin with the first one), the Stoics maintained that the true and the false belong in common in the sayable. They say that a sayable is what subsists in virtue of a rational appearance, and that a rational appearance is one by way of which it is possible to present what appeared to reason. And they call some sayables deficient and others self-sufficient. Let us leave aside the deficient ones for now, but of the self-sufficient ones they say that there are numerous types.

Distinctions among sayables (71–74) (71) They call some "imperatives," which we speak in giving orders, such as

> Come here, dear girl;[26]

and others "assertives," which we speak in making assertions, such as "Dion is going for a walk"; and questions, which we speak in asking about

---

[23] Euripides, *Hercules* 982–983.   [24] Cf. 1.402ff.

[25] This transition is very awkward, since what is being introduced is not a single position but a set of mutually exclusive positions (that will, in fact, occupy the remainder of the discussion of the true); cf. 11ff. In addition, it is far from clear in what respect the discussion to follow is "similar" to what has preceded it. Heintz proposed to alter *staseōs*, "position," to *diastaseōs*, "disagreement." But this introduces difficulties of its own, and I incline rather to regard this as a clumsy piece of editing by Sextus or his source.

[26] *Iliad* 3.130.

things, such as "Where does Dion live?"; **(72)** to some they also give the name "cursings", which we speak when we make curses –

> May their brains pour out on the ground, just like this wine;[27]

and "prayings," which we speak when we pray, as in

> Father Zeus, ruler on Ida, noblest and greatest,
> Let Ajax gain victory and the glory that he prays for.[28]

(73) And they also refer to some of the self-sufficient ones as propositions; when we speak these we either tell the truth or lie. Some are also more than propositions. For example, one of this kind –

> The herdsman is like Priam's sons –

is a proposition; for in saying it we either tell the truth or lie. But one like this –

> How like Priam's sons the herdsman is – [29]

is something more than a proposition and not a proposition. **(74)** However (since there is quite enough difference among sayables), in order for something to be true or false, they say, it first of all has to be a sayable, then also self-sufficient, and not just of any kind quite generally but a proposition. For it is only in speaking *this* one, as I said before, that we tell the truth or lie.

Difficulties in establishing that there are sayables (75–78) **(75)** And so, say the skeptics, by what means are they able to establish that there is any incorporeal sayable, which is separate both from the signifying utterance, such as "Dion," and from the object – for example, Dion himself? For either the Stoics will say all by itself that this is real, or they will confirm its reality through a demonstration. **(76)** And if they were to say all by itself that this incorporeal sayable is real, it will also be open to us to say, all by itself, that there is[30] no such thing. For just as they are trustworthy without

---

[27] *Iliad* 3.300. [28] *Iliad* 7.202–203.

[29] This line of tragic verse (in the original the second version is identical with the first except for an additional word) is of unknown origin.

[30] The strict Stoic view actually denied that there *are* (*einai*) sayables; instead, they only "subsist" (*huphistanai*) – cf. 70, and see LS sect. 27. As for whether sayables could be said to "be real" (*huparchein*), the evidence is more ambiguous; for discussion see A. A. Long, "Language and Thought in Stoicism," in A. A. Long, ed., *Problems in Stoicism* (Athlone Press, 1971), esp. 84–94.

a demonstration, so too the bringers of impasse[31] will be trustworthy when they put forward the opposite in a bare statement; or, if they are not trusted, the Stoics will also be equally untrustworthy. **(77)** But if they confirm such a thing through a demonstration, a worse impasse will follow for them. For demonstration is speech, and speech consists of sayables. It is by sayables, then, that the Stoics will be establishing that there is some sayable, which is inconsistent, since the person who does not allow that there is any sayable will not allow that there are many sayables. **(78)** And since it is a matter of investigation whether there are the sayables in the demonstration, if they immediately grasp the fact that there are these, the bringers of impasse will also immediately grasp the fact that there are not; the same trust or distrust applies in both cases. But if they grasp it from a demonstration, they will run on *ad infinitum*. For they will find a demonstration demanded of the sayables that are contained in the second demonstration, and of the ones in the third when they provide a third, and of the ones in the fourth when they provide a fourth, so that their demonstration of there being a sayable cannot get started.

Or that there are propositions (79–84) **(79)** One can say lots of other things on this topic; but it will be more suitable for us to go through them in the section on demonstration.[32] For now, though, this should be said – that they want the self-sufficient proposition to be composite. For example, "it is day" is put together out of "day" and "[it] is."[33] But nothing incorporeal can be either put together or divided; for these things are peculiar to bodies. Therefore nothing is a self-sufficient object or proposition.[34] **(80)** And every sayable has to be *said* (this is how it came by this name). But no sayable is said, as the bringers of impasse establish; so there is no sayable. And it follows from this that there is no proposition either, true or false. For saying is, as the Stoics themselves claim, bringing forth the utterance that is capable of signifying the conceived object – for example, this line:

Sing, goddess, of the fury of Achilles son of Peleus.[35]

---

[31] I.e., the skeptics themselves; see *PH* 1.7 for this term in a list of labels applied to skepticism.

[32] 299–481.

[33] In Greek the sample sentence contains just two words; there is no separate word corresponding to "it."

[34] Some have deleted the words "object or" (*pragma oude*), and this may be right; it is hard to understand their point.

[35] The opening line of the *Iliad*.

(81) But there is no way to bring forth the utterance that is capable of sig-nifying *this*, given the fact that a thing whose parts are not simultaneously real is not itself real, and the parts of this object are not simultaneously real, so that it is not real either. That its parts are not simultaneously real is shown immediately. For when we bring forth the first half-line, there is not yet the second one, and when we bring forth the second one, there is no longer the first one, so that we do not bring forth the whole line. (82) Yet the same applies even to the first half-line. For again, when we are saying the first part of the half-line, we are not yet bringing forth the second part of it, and when we are bringing forth the second, we are no longer saying the first, so that the half-line is not real either. And if we look into it, nor is even a single word, like "fury"; for when we say the syllable "fu," we are not yet bringing forth the "ry," and when we are bringing forth the "ry," we are no longer bringing forth the "fu." (83) If, then, it is impossible for anything to be real whose parts are not simulta-neously real, and it has been shown that even in the case of a single word the parts are not simultaneously real, it must be said that no word is real. And for this reason, nor is a proposition, which they say is composite – like "Socrates is," for example. For when "Socrates" is being said, there is not yet the "is," and when the "is" is being said, there is no longer the "Socrates." Therefore the proposition as a whole is never real – only parts of the whole; but the parts of this are not propositions. Therefore there is no proposition. (84) Indeed, why are we going over the whole proposition "Socrates is," when even the case-form "Socrates,"[36] taken on its own, itself cannot be conceived as belonging to reality for the same reason (I mean, the fact that its component parts are not simultaneously real)?

Or that there are true or false propositions (85–86)   (85) But even if it is allowed that there is some proposition, the skeptics will not agree <that there is any proposition>[37] that is true and any that is false, because this is not easy for the targets of their argument to explain. For they say that a true proposition is what is real and contradicts something, while a false one is what is not real and contradicts something. And when they are asked "What is the real?" they say "What activates an

---

[36] That is, the word "Socrates" in the nominative case (as opposed to its other possible inflections).
[37] Following Kochalsky's supplement *to axiōma einai ti*.

apprehensive appearance"; (86) and then, when they are questioned about the apprehensive appearance, they resort again to what is real, which is equally unknown, saying "An apprehensive appearance is one that is from a real thing and in accordance with just *that* real thing." But this amounts to teaching the unknown through an unknown, and to falling into the reciprocal mode. For in order for us to learn of what is real, they refer us to the apprehensive appearance, saying that a real thing is what activates an apprehensive appearance. But in order for us to gain knowledge of the apprehensive appearance, they refer us back to what is real. So, not knowing either the latter or the former, nor will we understand the true and false proposition that is taught from them.[38]

Difficulties concerning the relation between true and false in Stoicism (87–90) (87) And even if one passes up this impasse, another one beyond it will emerge for those who accept the Stoic technicalities. If we want to learn what a human being is, we ought first to know what "animal" and "rational" and "mortal" are (for the concept of the human being is constituted from these). Or, if we decide to find out what a dog is, we will again need first to have apprehended "animal" and "capable of barking" (for the dog is conceived from these). (88) So, in the same way, if true is, according to the Stoics, what is real and contradicts something, and false is what is not real and contradicts something, then for the conceiving of these things we ought necessarily to know what "that which contradicts" is. But the Stoics are absolutely unable to establish "that which contradicts" for us; therefore what is true and false will not be known either. (89) For they say "Things that contradict are those of which one goes beyond the other by a negative" – for example, "It is day"/"It is not day." For the proposition "It is not day" goes beyond the proposition "It is day" by the negative "not," and for this reason it is in contradiction with that one. But if "that which contradicts" is this, things like this will be in contradiction: "It is day and it is light" and "It is day and it is not light." For the proposition "It is day and it is not light" goes beyond the proposition "It is day and it is light" by a negative. But these things are *not* in contradiction, according to them; therefore things in contradiction are not those of which one goes beyond the other

[38] Cf. 1.426.

by a negative.[39] **(90)** Yes, they say, but they are in contradiction if we add this – that the negative is placed at the *front* of one of them;[40] for then it governs the whole proposition, while in the case of "It is day and it is not light," since it is a part of the whole, it does not govern to the extent of making the whole negative. Well then, we will say, there should have been an addition to the conception of things that are in contradiction: that they are in contradiction not merely when one goes beyond the other by a negative, but when the negative is placed at the front of the proposition.

Platonic difficulties concerning the negative (91–92) **(91)** Someone else will also employ Plato's argument, which he uses in *On the Soul*,[41] and will teach that it is not possible for the proposition, by participation in the negative, to be more than what does not have the negative. For just as nothing becomes cold by participation in hot, so nothing becomes large by participation in small (it becomes small); and just as something becomes large by participation in the larger, so too something becomes small by participation in the small. Hence, too, nine does not become larger in virtue of the addition of the unit. For one is less than nine; **(92)** by gaining this in addition, then, nine will not become more than nine, but rather less. Since, then, the negative "not" is something smaller than the proposition, it will not make the proposition larger, given that just as something becomes larger by participation in some largeness, so too it is made smaller by participation in something smaller.

Distinctions among types of propositions (93–98) In this way, then, Plato's argument will be borrowed by some for this topic. **(93)** But as for ourselves, let us add to the preceding points and say the following: if what is true is a proposition, it is definitely either a simple proposition or a non-simple one or one that is both simple and non-simple. For almost the first and most crucial difference among propositions that the dialecticians[42] bring forward is the one in terms of which some of them

---

[39] Following Von Arnim and LS, I adopt the supplement *hōn* (instead of Mutschmann's *tōi*), and alter the mss. *pleonazein* to *pleonazei*.

[40] The canonical placing of the negation in Stoic logic was at the beginning of the sentence; see sect. 2 of S. Bobzien, "Logic," in B. Inwood, ed., *The Cambridge Companion to the Stoics* (Cambridge University Press, 2003). (This word order is quite acceptable in Greek, whereas "Not it is day" is not feasible English.)

[41] I.e., the *Phaedo*; see 100c–103d.

[42] Some have seen this term, here and over the next several pages (as well as in a few other authors), as the name of a specific school, centered around Philo and Diodorus (cf. 112–118). The fullest

are simple and some non-simple. And the simple ones are those that are constituted neither from a single proposition taken twice, nor from different propositions by means of one or more conjunctions – such as "It is day," "It is night," "Socrates is having a discussion," and everything of a similar form. (94) For just as we call the warp[43] simple, although it is constituted from threads, since it is not woven out of warps (which are like it in kind), so propositions are called simple, since they are constituted not from propositions but from certain other things. For example, "It is day" is simple in so far as it consists neither of the same proposition taken twice nor of different ones, but is a combination of certain other things, namely "day" and "[it] is."[44] Furthermore, there is no conjunction in it either. (95) Non-simple propositions are those that are, for example, double – those that are constituted from a proposition taken twice or from different propositions by means of a conjunction or conjunctions – such as "If it is day, it is day," "If it is day, it is light," "If it is night, it is dark," "It is day *and* it is light," "Either it is day or it is night."

(96) Of the simple ones some are definite, some indefinite, and some intermediate. Definite ones are those that are expressed in terms of a demonstrative reference, such as "This person is walking," "This person is sitting" (for I am "demonstrating" some particular human being). (97) Indefinite ones, according to them, are those in which some indefinite term governs, such as "someone is sitting." And intermediate ones are those that are of this sort: "A human being is sitting" or "Socrates is walking." "Someone is walking" is indefinite, since it has not marked off any of the particular people walking; for it can be uttered in the case of each of them. But "This person is walking" is definite, since it has marked off the person being demonstrated. "Socrates is sitting" is intermediate, since it is neither indefinite (for it has marked off the specific case) nor definite (for it is not expressed with a demonstrative reference), but seems to be intermediate between the two of them, the indefinite and the definite. (98) And they say that the indefinite – "Someone is walking" or "Someone is sitting" – becomes true, when the definite – "This person

---

treatment is T. Ebert, *Dialektiker und frühe Stoiker bei Sextus Empiricus* (Vandenhoeck & Ruprecht, 1991). But the matter is controversial – for some doubts, see Jonathan Barnes, "A Big, Big D?" *Classical Review* 43 (1993), 304–306 – and "dialecticians" may simply be equivalent to "logicians," with no particular group intended by the term itself.

[43] I.e., the lengthwise threads in a loom.   [44] Cf. n. 33.

is sitting" or "This person is walking" – is found to be true. For if no particular person is sitting, the indefinite "Someone is sitting" cannot be true.

Difficulties surrounding simple propositions (99–107) **(99)** These are the kinds of things (to cover just the main points) that the dialecticians say on the subject of simple propositions. But the bringers of impasse ask first whether the definite can be true. For if this is done away with, neither can the indefinite be true, and if the indefinite is also done away with, the one that is intermediate between these will not subsist either. But these are, as it were, the elements of simple propositions; therefore if they are rejected, simple propositions will be gone as well, and it will not be possible to say that the true belongs in simple propositions. **(100)** Now, they say that this definite proposition – "This person is sitting" or "This person is walking" – is true whenever the predicate, such as "sitting" or "walking," is an attribute of the thing that falls under the demonstrative reference. But when some particular human being is demonstrated in the saying of "This person is walking," it is either (say) Socrates who falls under the demonstrative reference or some part of Socrates. But it is neither Socrates who falls under the demonstrative reference nor some part of Socrates, as we will establish; therefore the definite proposition cannot be true. **(101)** Socrates does not fall under the demonstrative reference, in so far as, while he is constituted of soul and body, the whole does not fall under the demonstrative reference whether the soul is demonstrated or the body.[45] Yet a part of Socrates does not fall under the demonstrative reference either. For if they say that the predicate ("walking" or "sitting") is an attribute of the thing that falls under the demonstrative reference, but the predicate (such as "walking" or "sitting") is *never* an attribute of the part being demonstrated (which is very small), then, necessarily, neither will the part be a thing that falls under the demonstrative reference. **(102)** But if it is neither this nor Socrates, and there is nothing besides these, the definite proposition, expressed in terms of a demonstrative reference, is gone, along with the fact that it virtually becomes indefinite itself. For if the part of Socrates being demonstrated admits of being this one, but

---

[45] The text at the end of this sentence (after "while he is constituted of soul and body") is corrupt. I translate Mutschmann's conjecture *eith'hē psuchē deiknutai eite to sōma, ouchi kai to holon hupo tēn deixin piptei*. But this does not yield a remotely plausible argument, nor does any other conjecture based on the words in the mss. Perhaps there is a larger portion of text missing.

admits of being *not* this one but another one, the whole necessarily becomes indefinite. If there is not the definite proposition, then, nor will there be the indefinite one. And for this reason neither will the intermediate one subsist.

(103) In addition to this, when they say that the proposition "It is day" is true in the present, while "It is night" is false, and "It is not day" is false, while "It is not night" is true, one will be curious as to how a negative which is one and the same, in coming together with true things makes them false, and in coming together with false things makes them true. For this is like Silenus in the riddle of Aesop: when he saw the same person in the winter season blowing with his mouth both so that his hands would not be cold and so that he would not be burnt, said that he could not stand to live with a beast of such a kind as to have complete opposites coming out of it. (104) In this way the same negative[46] making real things unreal and unreal things real also partakes of a magical nature. For either they want it to be real, or not to be real, or to be neither real nor not real, or to be real and not real at the same time. And if it is real, how, in coming together with a real thing, does it make the whole unreal and not, rather, real? For a real thing added to a real thing secures its reality even more. (105) But if is unreal, then when it comes together with what is not real, for what reason does it make it real and not, rather, unreal? For an unreal thing added to an unreal thing produces not reality but unreality. Or how, being unreal, does it change the real into unreality, but does not make it in one respect real and in another respect unreal? For just as white and black, when put together, do not make black or white, but something that is in one respect white and in another respect black, so too an unreal thing coming together with a real thing will make the whole in one respect real and in another respect unreal. (106) Besides, what makes something unreal *does* something, and what does is and is real.[47] Therefore the negative, if it is not real, will also not make anything unreal. It remains, then, to say that it is neither real nor not real. But if it is like that, then again, how, if it is neither real nor not real, does it create unreality on coming together with what is real, and reality when coming together with what is not real? (107) For just as what is neither hot nor cold, on coming together with what is hot, cannot make it cold, nor on coming together with what is cold make

---

[46] Following Heintz's alteration of the mss. *autē hē apophasis* to *hē autē apophasis*.

[47] Mutschmann posits a lacuna at this point. This is unnecessary; the argument as it stands is readily intelligible.

it hot, so it is unreasonable that what is neither real nor not real should create unreality on coming together with what is real, or reality when coming together with what is unreal. And it will be possible to create the same impasses even if they say that the negative is in a certain respect real and in a certain respect unreal.

Descriptions of and difficulties surrounding non-simple propositions (108–129) (**108**) Now that we have a feel (up to a point) for the dialecticians' laying down of the law with respect to simple propositions, let us move on to that of the non-simple ones.[48] Now, non-simple propositions are the ones mentioned above, which are constituted from a differentiated proposition[49] or from different propositions and in which a conjunction or conjunctions prevail. (**109**) Out of these let us take for the present the so-called conditional.[50] This, then, is constituted from a differentiated proposition or from different propositions by means of the conjunction "if [*ei*]" or "if indeed [*eiper*]." For instance, from a differentiated proposition and the conjunction "if," a proposition like this is constituted: "If it is day, it is day"; (**110**) and from different propositions and the conjunction "if indeed," we get one of this character: "If indeed it is day, it is light." Of the propositions in the conditional, the one in the position after the conjunction "if" or "if indeed" is called both "leader" and "first," and the other one "finisher" and "second," even if the whole conditional is expressed the other way round, like this: "It is light, if indeed it is day." For in this case, too, "It is light" is called "finisher" although it was expressed first, and "It is day" is called "leader" although it is spoken second, because of being in the position after the conjunction "if indeed." (**111**) In concise terms, then, the composition of the conditional is like this, and a proposition of this kind seems to promise that the second one

---

[48] I retain the mss. reading *epi tēn tōn ouch'haplōn*; Mutschmann alters to *tēn epi . . .*

[49] With Mutschmann I retain the mss. *diaphoroumenou*, on which the manuscripts agree here and twice in 109; cf. 281, 294, 466. Elsewhere the Stoics are reported as calling this type of proposition "duplicated," *diphoroumenou* (see *SVF* vol. 2, texts 261, 263), which clearly makes much more sense (and cf. "taken twice" in 95 above); but Mutschmann suspects that the mistake is Sextus' own (see his app. crit.), and this may well be right. The topic also comes up at *PH* 2.112; again the verb is "differentiated," but in this case the single letter (alpha) that distinguishes the two Greek verbs is erased in one manuscript.

[50] Literally, "connected (proposition)." But as the sequel makes clear (cf. Diogenes Laertius 7.71), this refers to what we call conditionals; Sextus' sarcastic "so-called" is perhaps meant to suggest that the term is not entirely lucid (since other kinds of propositions besides conditionals might be called "connected").

within it follows from the first one within it, and that if the leader is so, the finisher will be so. Hence, if such a promise is kept, and the finisher follows from the leader, the conditional becomes true; but if it is not kept, it is false. (112) And so, starting from this, let us look at whether any conditional can be found that is true and that keeps the promise just mentioned.

All the dialecticians in common say that a conditional is sound when its finisher follows from its leader. But on the question of when it follows, and how, they disagree with one another and lay out competing criteria of following. (113) Philo, for example, said that the conditional is true when it does not begin with a true proposition and finish with a false one, so that a conditional, according to him, is true in three ways and false in one way. For when it begins with a true one and finishes with a true one, it is true, as in "If it is day, it is light." And when it begins with a false one and finishes with a false one, it is again true – for example, "If the earth flies, the earth has wings." (114) In the same way, too, the conditional that begins with a false one and finishes with a true one is true, such as "If the earth flies, the earth is." But it is false only when it begins with a true one and finishes with a false one, as does "If it is day, it is night." For when it is day, "It is day" is true, while "It is night," which was the finisher, is false. (115) Diodorus, on the other hand, says that a conditional is true which neither was nor is *able to* begin with a true one and finish with a false one – which conflicts with Philo's position. For a conditional such as "If it is day, I am having a discussion," when it is day at present, and I am having a discussion, is true according to Philo, since it begins with the true "It is day" and finishes with the true "I am having a discussion," but false according to Diodorus. For it *is able* to begin with the true "It is day" and finish with the false "I am having a discussion" (when I have become quiet), and it *was* able to begin with a true one and finish with the false "I am having a discussion." (116) For before I began having a discussion, it began with the true "It is day" and finished with the false "I am having a discussion." Again, one of this character – "If it is night, I am having a discussion" – when it is day and I am silent, is in the same way true according to Philo (for it begins with a false one and finishes with a false one), but false according to Diodorus. For it it is *able* to begin with a true one and finish with a false one, when night has come, and when, further, I am not having a discussion but am quiet. (117) But in addition, "If it is night, it is day," when it is day, is true according to Philo for this reason:

that it begins with the false "It is night" and finishes with the true "It is day"; whereas according to Diodorus it is false for this reason: that it is *able*, when night takes over, to begin with the true "It is night" and finish with the false "It is day."

(118) Since there is this kind of opposition, then – to speak by way of example – among the criteria for the conditional proposition, it may be that the distinguishing of the sound conditional is intractable. In order for us to learn this, the dispute among the dialecticians about its soundness needs first of all to be decided on. And to the extent that that is not decided on, it[51] too is bound to remain in suspension of judgment. (119) And this makes sense. For either we will pay attention to all the dialecticians' criteria or to one of them. But it is not possible to pay attention to all of them. For they conflict, as I have shown in the case of the two spoken of before, and things that are in conflict cannot be equally trustworthy. But if we pay attention to one of them, we will pay attention to it either all by itself and without judgment, or with reasoning that shows that this kind of criterion is sound. (120) And if we assent to some criterion without judgment and all by itself, why will we assent to this one rather than that one? And this amounts to assenting to none of them, because of the conflict. But if it is with reasoning that shows that the criterion of the conditional accepted by us is sound, this reasoning either is inconclusive and non-terminating or conclusive and terminating.[52] (121) But if it is inconclusive and non-terminating, it is untrustworthy and bad for preferring some criterion of the conditional. But if it is conclusive, it is surely conclusive for this reason, that the consequence follows from the premises, so that it is itself certified through a certain following. (122) But the following that was sought from the beginning in the case of the conditional should have been certified by reasoning. This, therefore, amounts to falling into the reciprocal mode. For in order for us to learn about the conditional, which needs to be certified as a result of its following, we have to resort to some reasoning, and in order for this reasoning to be sound, its following, from which it is judged that it is sound, has to have been previously confirmed. (123) If, then – at least on the basis of this kind of impasse – we do not

---

[51] I.e., the sound conditional (the gender of the Greek pronoun makes this clear).

[52] "Conclusive" (*sunaktikos*) and "terminating" (*perainōn*) appear to be equivalent terms, as are their opposites. "Terminating" and "non-terminating" recur at 428ff., but nowhere else in the book; and the passage parallel to 428ff. in *PH* (2.146ff.) uses "conclusive and inconclusive" throughout.

have the sound conditional, nor will we have conclusive reasoning. But if we do not have this, nor will we have demonstration; for demonstration *is* conclusive reasoning. But if demonstration is not real, dogmatic philosophy is done away with.

(124) From these one can make a transition to conjunctions and to disjunctions, and in general to the remaining forms of non-simple propositions. For the conjunction should be constituted either from simple or from non-simple or from mixed ones, but all of these are put into impasse when the simple ones have been put into a prior impasse. (125) And indeed, when they say that a conjunction that has all its components true is sound, such as "It is day and it is light," and that one that has a single false proposition in it is false, they are again laying down the law for themselves. For if a proposition that is a composite out of all true ones is true, it would be consistent that one that is a composite of all false ones should right away be false, and that one that consists of false and true ones simultaneously should be no more true than false. (126) For if it is possible for them to lay down the law on whatever they want and to arrange matters for themselves as they choose, then it must be allowed that the conjunction that has a single component false is called by them false – but it will also be possible for others to make opposing arrangements, and to say that the conjunction made out of a majority of true components but one false one is true. (127) But if one should pay attention to the nature of things, it is presumably consistent to say that the conjunction that has something false in it and something true is no more true than false. For just as what is a mixture of white and black is no more white than black (for the white was white and the black was black), so what is solely true turns out to be true, what is solely false is false, and what is a composite of both should be called no more true than false. (128) But, they say, just as in life we do not say that the piece of clothing that is sound in most parts, but torn in a small part, is sound (on the basis of its sound parts, which is most of them), but torn (on the basis of its small torn part), so too the conjunction, even if it has only one false component and a majority of true ones, will as a whole be called false on the basis of that one. (129) For in life we have to allow people to use words loosely; after all, they are not seeking what is true in reference to nature, but what is true in reference to opinion. I mean, we talk of digging a well and of weaving a cloak and of building a house – which

is not legitimate. For if there is a well, it is not being dug but has been dug, and if there is a cloak, it is not being woven but has been woven. So that in life and in common usage loose talk has its place; but when we are investigating things in reference to their nature, then we need to maintain precision.

v. Difficulties in supposing that the locus of the true
is the utterance (130–136)
(**130**) From these points it has been sufficiently shown that the argument[53] is intractable, and creates a lot of trouble, for those who let the true and false reside in some incorporeal sayable. That it is also not readily manageable for those who place them in the utterance is easy to discover. (**131**) For every utterance, if it is, is either coming into being or in silence. But it is not the case either that one that is coming into being is (given the fact that it does not subsist) or that one that is in silence is (given that it is not yet coming into being); therefore it is not the case that there is utterance. The one that is coming into being is not, as is shown from similar cases. For a house that is coming into being is not a house, and the same applies to a ship, or anything else of this kind – and so to utterance as well. And that the one that is in silence does not subsist either is a matter of agreement. If, then, utterance is either coming into being or in silence, but it is not the case, at either of these times, that it is, there cannot be utterance.

(**132**) Besides, if the true is in utterance, it is either in the shortest utterance or in a long one. But it is not in the shortest one; for the shortest thing is partless, but the true is not partless. Nor is it in a long one; for that is non-subsistent given the fact that, when the first part of it is being expressed, the second part is not yet, and when the second part is being expressed, the first part is no longer. Therefore the true is not in utterance. (**133**) In addition, if it is in utterance, it is either in one that signifies or in one that does not signify. But it could not be in one that does not signify anything, like "blah-blah" and "gobbledegook"; for how is it possible to apprehend as true an object that does not signify? (**134**) It remains to say, therefore, that it is in one that signifies. Which is again impossible;

---

[53] I take "the argument" here to refer to the course of the discussion in general, rather than to some particular argument; two distinct groups are mentioned, and it is the same "argument" that is said to create trouble for both of them.

for no utterance is capable of signifying *as utterance*, since in that case all the Greeks and foreigners who apprehended an utterance must also have apprehended what is signified by it. So that as far as this point is concerned, too, the true is not to be placed in utterance. (135) And some utterances are simple, others composite – simple ones such as "Dion," composite ones like "Dion is walking." If, then, the true is in utterance, it is either in simple or in composite utterance. But it is not in simple and non-composite utterance; for what is true has to be a proposition, and no proposition is non-composite. (136) But it could not be in composite utterance given the fact that no composite speech, such as "Dion is," subsists. For when we are saying "Dion," we are not yet saying "is," and when we are expressing the latter we are no longer saying the former. So that the true is not in utterance either.

vi. *Difficulties in supposing that the locus of the true is the movement of thought (137–139)*

(137) Nor, however, is it in the movement of thought, as some have suspected. For if what is true is in the movement of thought, none of the external things will be true; for the movement of thought is in us and not external. But it is absurd to say that none of the external things is true; therefore it is also absurd to allow what is true to be in the movement of thought.

(138) And since the movements of thought are private to each person, nothing will be true in common. But if nothing is true in common, everything will be indistinct and in disagreement. For what this person has that is true (that is, the movement of his thought) another person does not have, and conversely, what that person has, this person has not apprehended.[54] But it is absurd to say that there is nothing agreed upon as true; (139) therefore it is also absurd and not sound to maintain that what is true exists in the movement of thought. And it follows that those who allow what is true to be in the movement of thought accept that *all* of them are true – the movement of Epicurus' thought, for example, and that of Zeno and of Democritus and of all the others; for all of them have the attribute of being movements of thought. But it is impossible for all of them to be true, just as it is impossible for all of them to be false. Therefore the movement of thought is not true either.

---

[54] I translate the mss. *ou kateilēphen*; Bekker, followed by Mutschmann, alters to *ouk eilēphen*.

3. Transition to B and C (140)

(**140**) Well then, having created so many impasses about the criterion and about what is true, let us inquire after this into the approaches that are constructed, using the criterion, for the apprehension of what is true but does not impinge on us all by itself – that is, sign and demonstration. And taking them in order let us speak first of sign; for it is by participating in this that demonstration becomes capable of uncovering the conclusion.

B. The sign (141–299)

1. Introductory remarks (141–144)

Whether there is any sign

(**141**) Since there is, at the highest level, a dual distinction among things, in terms of which some things are clear, others unclear (clear things being the ones that impinge on the senses and thought all by themselves, and unclear things being those that are not grasped by themselves), our discussion of the criterion, directed toward the impasse over plain things, proceeded according to a sound method (**142**) (for if the criterion is shown to be infirm, it also becomes impossible to state confidently about apparent things that they are in their nature such as they appear). Now, since the side of the distinction involving unclear things is still left, we think it is fine to use a concise approach for the rejection of this as well, one that does away with both sign and demonstration. For when these in turn are done away with, the apprehension of what is true by means of them also becomes infirm. But perhaps it is appropriate, before dealing with the particulars, to go over some brief points about the nature of the sign.

(**143**) "Sign," then, is said in two ways, general and specific. In general it is what seems to reveal something; thus, we regularly call a sign what produces a renewal[55] of the object that was observed together with it. Specifically, it is what is indicative of an object that is unclear, which

---

[55] I.e., a reminder; cf. 152–153 for this terminology of "renewing". The idea seems to be that one's *memory* of previous associations between objects of types A and B is "renewed" or reactivated, as a result of which one's *current* observation of an object of type A leads to an expectation of an object of type B.

is the kind that it is our task at present to examine. (**144**) But if one is paying attention to its nature distinctly, one must again first grasp, as we said above, that clear objects are those that come to our knowledge by themselves – such as, at present, its being day and my having a discussion – while unclear ones are those that are not like this.

2. *Matters of taxonomy and methodology (145–161)*

a. Distinctions among ways of being unclear (145–150)

How many different kinds of unclear things there are

(**145**) Some unclear things are unclear pure and simple, others are unclear by nature, and some are unclear for the moment. Of these, the ones called "unclear for the moment" are those that, while having a plain nature, are at times unclear to us because of certain external circumstances, as the city of Athens is to us now; for it is by nature plain and clear, but is unclear because of the distance in between. (**146**) Unclear by nature are those that are hidden away for all time and cannot fall within our plain experience, such as intelligible[56] pores and the unlimited void that is deemed by certain physicists to be outside the cosmos. (**147**) And the ones said to be unclear pure and simple are those that are of a nature never to fall within human apprehension, such as whether there is an even or an odd number of stars and that there is such-and-such number of grains of sand in Libya. (**148**) Since, then, there are four different kinds of object – first that of plain things, second that of things unclear pure and simple, third that of things unclear by nature, and fourth that of things unclear for the moment – we do not say that every kind needs a sign, but that some of them do. (**149**) For of course neither the things that are unclear pure and simple allow of any sign, nor do the plain things – the plain things because they strike us by themselves and do not need anything else for their disclosure, and the things that are unclear pure and simple because they escape all apprehension quite generally and do not allow of apprehension through a sign. (**150**) But those that are unclear by nature and those that are unclear for the moment do have need of the observation that comes from a sign – the ones that are unclear for the moment because in certain circumstances they are removed from our plain experience, and

---

[56] I.e., not perceptible (accessible *only* to the intellect).

the ones that are unclear by nature because they are non-apparent all the
time.

b. Distinction between indicative and recollective sign, and declaration
that the skeptic's critique is limited to the indicative sign (151–158)
(**151**) So, since there are two different kinds of objects that need a sign,
the sign, too, proves to be of two kinds. One kind is the recollective, which
appears useful especially in the case of things that are unclear for the
moment; the other kind is the indicative, which, it is maintained, deserves
to be employed in the case of things that are unclear by nature. (**152**) Now,
the recollective sign, when it has been observed through plain experience
together with the thing signified, leads us, immediately it impinges on
us when the other thing is unclear, to a recollection of the thing that has
been observed together with it but is not now striking us plainly, as in the
case of smoke and fire. For having often observed these things connected
with one another, immediately we see one of them (that is, the smoke)
we renew the rest (that is, the unseen fire). (**153**) The same account also
applies in the case of the scar that comes after a wound and the trauma to
the heart that precedes death. For on seeing the scar we renew the wound
that preceded it, and on looking at the trauma to the heart we predict
that death is to come. The peculiar character of the recollective sign is
like this; (**154**) but the indicative sign differs from this. For it does *not*
admit of being observed together with the thing signified (for the object
that is unclear by nature is from the beginning not within our awareness,
and for this reason cannot be observed together with any of the apparent
things), but it is said to signify that of which it is indicative simply by
means of its own nature and constitution, all but giving voice. (**155**) For
example, the soul is one of the objects that is unclear by nature. For it is
not of a nature ever to fall within our plain experience. And being of this
kind, it is revealed indicatively by means of the motions of the body; for
we reason that a certain power, clothed by the body, endows it with such
motions.

(**156**) Well then, while there are two signs – the one that is recollective
and is thought to be useful mainly in the case of things that are unclear for
the moment, and the indicative, which is adopted in the case of things that
are unclear by nature – we intend to conduct the entire investigation and
create all the impasse not about the recollective sign (for this is generally
trusted by everyone in ordinary life to be useful), but about the indicative

sign. For this has been invented by the dogmatic philosophers and rationalist doctors,[57] as being able to provide them the most necessary service.
(157) Hence we are not in conflict with the common preconceptions of
humanity, nor are we throwing life into confusion, saying that nothing is
a sign, as some people falsely accuse us of doing. For if we were doing
away with every sign, perhaps we would be in conflict with life and with
all humanity. But in fact we ourselves judge this way, assuming fire from
smoke, a previous wound from a scar, death from previous trauma to the
heart, and oil from a previous headband.[58] (158) Since, then, we do in fact
posit the recollective sign, which is used in ordinary life, but do away with
the one falsely believed in by the dogmatists, in addition to our not being
in conflict with ordinary life we actually even speak on its side, seeing that
we are refuting – by means of signs through an inquiry into nature! – the
dogmatists who have risen up against the common preconception and say
that they know things that are unclear by nature.

c. Reminder as to the skeptical procedure (159–161)
(159) Enough has been said, then – to give the main points – about the
sign that falls under our investigation. But we need at present to bear in
mind the skeptical procedure. This is to lay out the arguments against the
reality of the sign not with confidence or assent (for doing that would be
equivalent to maintaining, like the dogmatists, that there is a sign), but so
as to bring the investigation into equal strength,[59] and to show that it is just
as believable that there is no sign as that there is one, and conversely that
the reality of a sign is just as unbelievable as the unreality of any sign. For
in that way equilibrium and suspension of judgment is produced in our
thinking. (160) And of course, for this reason even the person who seems
to be contradicting us, when we say that nothing is an indicative sign, is a
help, and this very person anticipates us in constructing the position that
ought to be constructed skeptically. For if the arguments compiled against

---

[57] On the major approaches to medicine in later antiquity see Galen, *On the Sects for Beginners*,
translated in Galen, *Three Treatises on the Nature of Science* tr. R. Walzer and M. Frede (Hackett
Publishing, 1985). "Rationalist" does not name a single school (hence the term is neither capitalized
nor cited in the Index of Names). Rather, it covers anyone who believes, as against the Empiricists,
that theorizing about the underlying workings of the body is possible and useful (cf. 327); thus
Galen freely alternates between the terms "rationalist" and "dogmatist".

[58] Both worn by athletes.

[59] On the important skeptical concept of "equal strength" (*isostheneia*) see especially *PH* 1.8ff. In
the present work cf. 298, 363, 1.443.

the sign by the bringers of impasse are extremely powerful and virtually impossible to oppose, while those of the dogmatists postulating its reality do not fall short of these, we should immediately suspend judgment about its reality and not adhere unfairly to either side. (**161**) However, now that the skeptical procedure has been presented, let us move next to setting out the topic that lies before us.

3. *Difficulties concerning the sign (161–299)*

a. Identification of the sign's relative status, and difficulties surrounding this (161–175)

Of the things that there are, say the skeptics, some are in virtue of a difference, while others are in a certain state in relation to something. In virtue of a difference are any that are conceived in virtue of their own subsistence and absolutely, such as white, black, sweet, bitter, and everything like these; for we focus on them alone and individually, and without conceiving anything else as well. (**162**) In relation to something are those things that are conceived in virtue of their state in relation to another thing and are no longer grasped absolutely – that is, on their own – such as whiter and blacker and sweeter and bitterer and everything that is of the same kind. For what is whiter or blacker is not conceived in virtue of its own individuality, in the same way as what is white or black or bitter. Rather, in order to conceive this, we need to focus at the same time on the thing than which it is whiter or than which it is blacker. And the same account applies in the case of the sweeter and the bitterer.

(**163**) Since, then, there are two different kinds of objects, one that of the things in virtue of a difference, the second that of the things in a certain state in relation to something, the indicative sign too is necessarily among either the things in virtue of a difference or the things in relation to something; for there is no third kind between these two. But it could not be among the things in virtue of a difference, as is agreed right away even by those of the other opinion. It will, then, be among the things in relation to something. (**164**) For just as the thing signified, being conceived in virtue of its state in relation to the sign, is among the things in relation to something, <. . .>;[60] for it is a sign *of something*, namely the thing

---

[60] Here some words have dropped out; the sense must be "so too the sign is among the things in relation to something."

signified. At any rate, if (let us suppose) we do away with one of them, the remaining one will also be done away with at the same time, which is the kind of thing also apparent in the case of the right and the left. For if there is no right, neither will there be a left, on account of the fact that each of these is a thing in relation to something, and if there is no left, the conception of right is also canceled along with it. (165) Well now, things in relation to something are apprehended together with one another. For it is not possible, as I said, to recognize something whiter without the thing than which it is whiter being encountered along with it, nor something blacker without the thing than which it is blacker being conceived along with it. So, since the sign is among the things in relation to something, as we explained, together with the sign there is apprehended the thing of which it is a sign. But what is apprehended together with it is not a sign of it. For the supposition that it is possible for what is apprehended together with something to be a sign of that thing is completely unhinged. For if both are grasped on a single occasion, neither is this one capable of uncovering that one, nor is that one capable of revealing this one, but each one, since it strikes us by itself, lacks this kind of power.

(166) Again, one might put together an argument of this kind. If the sign is apprehensible, it is apprehended either before the thing signified or together with it or after it. But it is not apprehended before it or together with it or after it, as we will establish; therefore the sign is not apprehensible. (167) Now, to say that the sign is apprehended after the thing signified is right away plainly absurd. For how can the sign still be capable of uncovering, when the thing it is capable of uncovering, the thing signified, is apprehended before it? Besides, if they say this, the dogmatists will be accepting something that conflicts with the dogma they usually propound. For they say that the thing signified is unclear and not apprehended by itself. But if it is *after* the apprehension of this that the sign is apprehended, this thing, which has been discovered *before* the presence of what reveals it, will not be unclear. So that the sign is not apprehended after the thing signified. (168) Yet nor is it apprehended together with it, for the reason mentioned a little earlier. For things that are apprehended together with one another do not need to be revealed by one another, but strike us by themselves, at the same time, and for this reason neither could the sign be said to be a sign, nor could the thing signified be said any more to be signified. (169) It remains to say, then, that the sign is apprehended before the thing signified. But this again spirals

into the same refutations. For the dogmatists ought first to show that the sign is not among the things in relation to something, or that things in relation to something are not apprehended together with one another, and *then* extract from us the possibility of the sign being apprehended before the thing signified. (170) But the starting-points are unchanged: it is not possible to testify in favor of the sign's being apprehended beforehand, since it is from the class of things in relation to something and ought to be apprehended together with the thing of which it is the sign. But if, in order for the sign to be apprehended, it has to be apprehended either before the things signified or together with it or after it, and it has been shown that none of these is possible, it has to be said that the sign is inapprehensible.

(171) Some people also call the dogmatists into question by means of another argument with the same force, which goes like this. If there is any sign that is indicative of something, either it is an apparent sign of an apparent thing, or a non-apparent sign of a non-apparent thing, or an apparent sign of a non-apparent thing, or a non-apparent sign of an apparent thing. But it is neither an apparent sign of an apparent thing, nor a non-apparent sign of a non-apparent thing, nor an apparent sign of a non-apparent thing, or the reverse; therefore there is no sign. (172) Such is the argument, and its layout is clear. And it will become even clearer when we have indicated the opposition that the dogmatists bring to bear on it. For they say that they only go along with two of these combinations, and that they disagree with us about the remaining two. (173) For they say that while it is true that the apparent is a sign of the apparent and that the apparent is a sign of the non-apparent, it is false that the non-apparent is capable of showing the apparent or that the non-apparent is capable of showing the non-apparent. For example, an apparent thing as the sign of an apparent thing is the shadow as the sign of the body; for, being a sign, it is itself an apparent thing, and the body, being a thing signified, is also plain. And an apparent thing is capable of showing a non-apparent thing – for instance, blushing is capable of showing shame; for it is plain and discovered by itself, whereas shame is hidden. (174) But the people who say this are completely silly. For if it is agreed that the sign is in relation to something and that things in relation to something are necessarily apprehended together with one another, it is not possible that, of the things that are equally encountered together with one another, one is the sign and the other the thing signified. Rather, because of the plain

simultaneous encountering of them both, it is absolutely in every way impossible that either one of them can be either a sign or a thing signified, one of them having nothing to uncover, the other not needing anything to uncover it. (175) And the same things should be said about the remaining combination – the one where they maintain that the apparent is a sign of the non-apparent. For if this is so, the sign has to be apprehended before the thing signified and the thing signified apprehended after the sign, which is impossible because of their being from the class of things in relation to something and needing to be apprehended together with one another.

b. Difficulties stemming from disagreements about whether the sign is perceptible or intelligible (176–182)
(176) Now, of the objects that are apprehended by a human being, some seem to be apprehended through sense-perception and others through thought: through sense-perception, such as white, black, sweet, or bitter; through thought, such as fine, shameful, lawful, unlawful, pious, or impious. The sign too, then, if it is apprehensible, is among either perceptible or intelligible objects, so that if it is not from one of these two classes, it will not be real at all to begin with. (177) And this, of course, is an indication of its not being graspable – I mean the fact that up to now its nature is torn apart, some people supposing that it is perceptible, some intelligible. Epicurus and the leaders of his school said that the sign was perceptible, the Stoics that it was intelligible. And this disagreement remains undecided virtually for all time, and since it remains undecided, there is every necessity for the sign to be kept in suspension of judgment, since it has to be either perceptible or intelligible. (178) And the strangest thing of all is that it fails in its promise, seeing that it promises to be capable of uncovering something else, but it is itself now found, conversely, to need something else that will uncover it. For if everything that is a matter of disagreement is unclear, and the unclear is graspable by means of a sign, undoubtedly the sign too, being a matter of disagreement, will need some sign for its manifestation (since it is unclear).

(179) Nor yet can they say that it is possible to establish and make trustworthy the object of disagreement itself by a demonstration. For, first, when they have demonstrated it, let them *then* take it as trustworthy; but in so far as it is a mere promise on their part and not a demonstration, the matter of suspension of judgment stands. (180) Then again, demonstration

is a thing that is in dispute, and since it is a matter of disagreement it itself has need of something to render it trustworthy; but to want to show what is under investigation by means of what is under investigation is completely absurd. Besides, speaking generically, demonstration *is* a sign; for it is capable of revealing the conclusion. (**181**) In order for the sign to be confirmed, then, demonstration has to be trustworthy, but in order for demonstration to become trustworthy, the sign has to be confirmed first, so that each of them is waiting for the trust given to it by the other one, and so is just as untrustworthy as the other. (**182**) In addition to this, what is used in the role of demonstration for the confirmation of the sign is either perceptible or intelligible. And if it is perceptible, again the question that was there from the beginning remains, given that perceptible things are in general a matter of disagreement. But if it is intelligible, it is equally untrustworthy – for it cannot be grasped apart from perceptible things.

c. Difficulties in supposing that the sign is perceptible (183–243)
i. Difficulties stemming from disagreements about the nature of perceptibles (183–187)
(**183**) However, let it be agreed and granted, as an added bonus, that the sign is either perceptible or intelligible. Even so, it is impossible for its subsistence to be trustworthy. We should speak about each one in turn, starting with its being perceptible. In order for this to be accepted, then, the reality of perceptible things must be previously agreed to and accepted by all the physicists, so that the inquiry into the sign can go forward from this accepted point. (**184**) But it is not agreed to, but

As long as water flows and tall trees flourish[61]

the physicists will never stop fighting about it, since Democritus says that no perceptible thing exists, but our apprehensions of them are empty effects on our senses, and nothing sweet is really in external things, or bitter or hot or cold or white or black, or any other of the things that appear to everyone; for these are names for effects on us. (**185**) But Epicurus said that all perceptible things exist such as they appear and strike us in sense-perception, since sense-perception never lies (but we are of the *opinion* that it lies). The Stoics and Peripatetics take a middle road, and say that

---

[61] From an epigram on Midas (see Plato, *Phaedrus* 264C–D); Sextus also uses this line at *PH* 2.37 and *M* 1.28.

some perceptible things exist as true, while others are not real – sense-perception lies about them. (186) But now the main point: if we want the sign to be perceptible, first of all the subsistence of perceptible things has to be agreed and firmly established, so that the sign too may be granted to be solidly apprehensible. Otherwise, if it turns out that *that* has been a matter of dispute for all time, we have to agree that the sign too is involved in the same discord. (187) For just as the color white cannot be securely apprehended if the subsistence of perceptible things is not agreed to, in view of the fact that it is itself among perceptible things, so neither will the sign, if it is in the class of perceptible things, be said to be solid while the battle about perceptible things goes on. But let us say there is agreement about perceptible things and that there is no dispute at all about them. I ask, how can the people with the other opinion teach us that the sign is in fact perceptible? For every perceptible thing is of a nature to impinge on everyone in the same condition, and to be grasped equally. The color white, for example, is not apprehended in one way by Greeks and in another way by foreigners, or differently by craftsmen and by ordinary people, but in the same way by everyone who has unimpaired senses.

ii. Difficulties surrounding the fact that signs do not affect everyone equally (188–191)

(188) Again, bitter and sweet do not taste one way to this person and another way to that person; they taste similar to everyone who is similarly disposed. But the sign, as sign, does *not* seem to affect all who are similarly disposed in the same way, but for some people it is not a sign of anything at all, even though it strikes them plainly, while for others it is a sign – not, however, of the same thing, but of a different thing. For in medicine (for example) the same apparent things are signs of one thing to this person (say, Erasistratus), or another thing to that person (such as Herophilus), and of another thing to that person (say, Asclepiades). It should not be said, then, that the sign is perceptible; for if what is perceptible affects everyone similarly, but the sign does not affect everyone similarly, the sign cannot be perceptible. (189) Again, if the sign is perceptible, then just as fire, which is perceptible, burns everyone who can be burnt, and snow, which is perceptible, chills everyone who can be chilled, so too the sign, if it is among perceptible things, ought to lead everyone to the same signified thing. But it does *not* lead them to the same

signified thing; therefore it is not perceptible. (**190**) In addition to this, if the sign is perceptible, unclear things are either apprehensible by us or inapprehensible. If, then, they are inapprehensible by us, the sign is gone. For given that there are two kinds of objects, plain ones and unclear ones, if neither what is plain has a sign because of being discovered by itself, nor do unclear things because of being inapprehensible, there is no sign. (**191**) But if they are apprehensible, then again, since the sign is perceptible and what is perceptible affects everyone equally, unclear things ought to be apprehensible by everyone. But some people, such as the Empiricist doctors and the skeptical philosophers, say that they are not apprehended, while others say that they are apprehended, but not in the same way. Therefore the sign is not perceptible.

iii. Dogmatic counter-arguments and responses to them (192–202)
(**192**) Yes, they say, but just as fire, which is a perceptible thing, displays different powers depending on differences in the underlying matter, and when it is next to wax melts it, when next to clay hardens it, and when next to wood burns it – in the same way it is likely that the sign, too, since it is perceptible, is capable of revealing different objects depending on differences in the people apprehending it. (**193**) And it is not surprising that this is also observed to happen in the case of recollective signs. For the lifting of a torch signifies the approach of enemies to some people, but shows the arrival of friends to others, and the sound of a bell is to some people a sign of the selling of prepared food, to others of the need to sprinkle the roads.[62] The indicative sign too, then, since it has a perceptible nature, will be capable of revealing a variety of things. (**194**) But here too, one might expect those who use the inference from fire to show that what happens to occur in the case of fire occurs in the case of the sign. For it is accepted that fire has the powers mentioned before, and there is no one who differs about the fact that wax is melted by it, clay is hardened, and wood is burned. (**195**) But if we accept that the equivalent occurs in the case of the indicative sign, we will put ourselves into a position of extreme absurdity, saying that each of the things indicated by it is real, so that, for example, excess and acridness in the humors and physical constitution are causes of a disease. (**196**) Which is absurd; for it is not

---

[62] Apparently for the purpose of settling the dust. See Suetonius, *Caligula* 43 (although Suetonius implies that this was a grossly extravagant activity performed on a single occasion).

possible for causes that are so conflicting and destructive of one another to be real simultaneously. So, let the dogmatic philosophers either agree to this, even though it is impossible, or that the sign, which is perceptible, is indicative of nothing considered in itself, (**197**) but that we, who are in different conditions, are not affected in the same way by it. But they could not stand to agree to this – quite apart from the fact that these powers of fire are not agreed upon but are a matter of impasse. (**198**) For if fire had a nature such as to burn, it ought to burn everything, and not burn some things but others not at all; and if it had a nature such as to melt, it ought to dissolve everything, as opposed to some things but not others. (**199**) But in fact, it seems to do these things not as a result of its own nature, but as a result of the forms of matter that are exposed to it.[63] For example, it burns wood not because it is itself such as to burn, but because wood is in a suitable condition for burning when it gets the help of fire; and it melts wax not because it has a melting power, but because wax possesses a tendency to melt when it gets the help of fire.

We will teach about this more precisely when we inquire into the reality of such things.[64] (**200**) For now, against those who make an inference from the recollective sign and bring in the torch and also the sound of the bell, we should say that it is not surprising if signs of this kind are capable of showing multiple things. For they are determined, as they say, by the people who lay down the conventions, and it is up to us whether we want them to reveal one thing or to be capable of showing multiple things. (**201**) But the indicative sign is thought to be by its nature suggestive of the thing signified, and so necessarily has to be indicative of one object, and this must undoubtedly be of a single form – since if it is common to many things, it will not be a sign. For it is impossible for one thing to be firmly grasped by means of something when there are many things being shown by it. For example, becoming poor after being wealthy is equally a result of squandering one's resources, getting into trouble at sea, and giving to friends; but if it is equally a result of many things, it can no longer be revelatory of any one of them in particular. For if of this one, *why* of this one rather than of that one; and if of that one, why of that one rather than of this one? (**202**) Yet nor can it be revelatory of all of them; for they cannot all be real at once. Therefore the indicative sign differs from the

---

[63] I delete *tōn kaiomenōn*, present in all mss.; I suspect this is a gloss. (Bekker, followed by Mutschmann, substitutes *tōn hupokeimenōn*, but this is very awkward.)
[64] See *M* 9.237ff.

recollective sign, and one cannot infer from the latter to the former, in so far as one of them has to be revelatory of one thing alone, while the other can be capable of displaying many things and of signifying as *we* decide.

iv. Three further miscellaneous difficulties (203–207)

(203) Besides, every perceptible thing, considered as a perceptible thing, is unteachable. For one is not taught to see the color white, and one does not learn to taste sweet, or to grasp hot, or anything else of this kind; rather, knowledge of all these things comes to us from nature and without being taught. But the sign, considered as a sign, is taught, they say, with a lot of effort – like the one in navigation which is indicative of winds and storms or fine weather. (204) The same applies to the ones used by the people who busy themselves with the heavens, such as Aratus and Alexander the Aetolian, and likewise with those used by the Empiricist doctors, such as flushing and bulging of the vessels and thirst and other things, which the person who has not been taught does not grasp as signs. (205) Therefore the sign is not perceptible; for if what is perceptible is unteachable, but the sign, considered as a sign, is teachable, the sign cannot be perceptible. (206) And what is perceptible, in so far as it is perceptible, is conceived in virtue of a difference[65] – such as white, black, sweet, bitter, and everything of that kind. But the sign, in so far as it is sign, is one of the things in relation to something; for it is considered in terms of its state in relation to the thing signified. The sign, therefore, is not among perceptible things. (207) What is more, every perceptible thing, as the name makes clear, is grasped by sense-perception; but the sign, considered as a sign, is not grasped by sense-perception but by thought. At any rate, we say that a sign is true or false, but the true and false are not perceptible; for each of them is a proposition, and the proposition does not belong to perceptible but to intelligible things. It has to be said, therefore, that the sign is not among perceptible things.

v. Difficulties in supposing that like indicates like or unlike indicates unlike (208–214)

(208) The issue can be attacked in this way, too: if the indicative sign is perceptible, the perceptible ought, as a precondition, to be indicative of something – which is not so. For if the perceptible indicates something,

---

[65] Cf. 161–162.

either what is like in kind will be indicative of what is like in kind, or what is unlike in kind of what is unlike in kind. But neither is the like in kind indicative of the like in kind, nor is the unlike in kind of the unlike in kind; therefore the perceptible is not indicative of anything. (209) For example, let us suppose that we have never encountered the color white, nor the color black, and we see white for the first time. From our apprehension of this we would not have the power to apprehend the color black. (210) For while it is perhaps possible to have a conception of the fact that black is another color, and not like white, to produce an apprehension of the color black from the presence of white is impossible. And the same argument applies in the case of sound, and generally in the case of the other perceptible things. A perceptible thing that is like in kind, then, cannot be indicative of what is like in kind – that is, the visible of the visible or the audible of the audible or the tastable of the tastable. (211) Yet neither can the unlike in kind be indicative of the unlike in kind, such as the visible of the audible or the audible of the tastable or smellable. For if one smells something fragrant, one does not proceed to an apprehension of the color white, nor, if one apprehends a sound, is one's sense of taste sweetened.

(212) In fact, it is superfluous to ask whether the like in kind can be a sign of the like in kind and the unlike in kind of the unlike in kind, when anyone with any intelligence would give up on something more immediate than this – I mean, the fact that the perceptible cannot even be indicative of itself. (213) For, as we have shown many times, of those who have inquired into the perceptible, some say that it is not grasped by sense-perception as it is by nature; for it is neither white nor black, neither hot, nor cold, nor sweet, nor bitter, nor does it have any other such quality, but it seems to exist as such when our sense experiences empty effects and tells lies. But some have thought that some perceptible things do truly exist and others not at all; and others have testified in favor of the equal reality of all of them. (214) So, since there is so much undecided disagreement[66] about the subsistence of perceptible things, how is it possible to say that the perceptible is capable of displaying itself, when it is not yet known which of the positions that are in such discord is the true one? But this point, anyway, has to prevail – that if neither the perceptible thing that is

[66] Following Heintz, I alter *staseōs* to *diastaseōs*.

like in kind is indicative of the perceptible thing that is like in kind, nor is the unlike in kind indicative of the unlike in kind, nor is it itself indicative of itself, it is impossible, therefore, to say that the sign is perceptible.

vi. Aenesidemus' argument against signs being apparent things (215–238)
Initial statement and explanation (215–216)   **(215)** Aenesidemus, in the fourth book of his *Pyrrhonist Discourses*, puts forward an argument to the same purpose and with virtually the same force, as follows: if apparent things appear alike to all who are similarly disposed, and signs are apparent things, signs appear alike to all who are similarly disposed. But signs do *not* appear alike to all who are similarly disposed; yet apparent things do appear alike to all who are similarly disposed; therefore signs are not apparent things. **(216)** Now, Aenesidemus seems to be calling perceptible things "apparent things," and he is putting forward an argument in which a second indemonstrable overlaps with a third – its pattern is like this: "If the first and the second, then the third; not the third, but the first; therefore not the second."[67]

Initial validation of premises as true and conclusion as following from them (217–222)   **(217)** That it is in fact this way we will show a little later;[68] for now we will demonstrate more simply that its premises are sound and that the consequence follows from them. To begin with, then, the conditional is true; for the finisher[69] follows from the conjunction – that is, from "apparent things appear alike to all who are similarly disposed, and signs are apparent things" there follows the fact that signs appear alike to all who are similarly disposed. **(218)** For if everyone who has unimpaired eyes apprehends the color white similarly, not differently, and if everyone who has a sense of taste in a natural state apprehends the sweet sweetly, then necessarily everyone who is in a similar condition ought to apprehend the sign in a similar way as well, if it belongs among perceptible things like the white and sweet. **(219)** So that the conditional is sound. And the second premise – "signs do not appear alike to all who are similarly disposed" – is also true. In the case of people with a fever, at any rate, flushing and prominence of the vessels and wet skin and higher temperature and racing

---

[67] For the classification of arguments presupposed here, cf. 223–227.
[68] 234ff.   [69] I.e., the consequent of the conditional; cf. 110.

pulses and the remaining signs do not strike those who are similarly disposed (in terms of their senses and the rest of their constitution) as signs of the same thing, nor do they appear alike to everyone, (**220**) but to Herophilus (for example) they appear straightforwardly as signs of good blood, to Erasistratus as signs of a transfer from the veins to the arteries, and to Asclepiades as signs of intelligible[70] bodies obstructing intelligible pores. The second premise, then, is also sound. (**221**) But so is the third, too – that apparent things appear alike to all who are similarly disposed. For the color white, for instance, does not strike the person with jaundice, and the person who has bloodshot eyes, and the person whose disposition is in line with nature, in the same way (for they are differently disposed, and for this reason it appears yellow to one, reddish to the next, and white to the next). But to people in the same condition – that is, healthy people – it only appears white. (**222**) The premises, then, are true, and from them will be drawn the consequence "Therefore the sign is not an apparent thing."

Taxonomy of indemonstrable arguments and identification of Aenesidemus' argument within this taxonomy (222–238) So, now that we have gone over it, the argument has right away been shown to be true; (**223**) that it is indemonstrable and deductive will become clear when we have analyzed it. For, to go back a little, arguments are spoken of as "indemonstrable" in two ways, covering both arguments that have not been demonstrated and those that have no need of demonstration (given that in their case it is immediately clear that they reach a conclusion).[71] And we have often mentioned[72] that the arguments laid out by Chrysippus at the beginning of his first *Introduction to Deductions* qualify for this label in the second sense. (**224**) Now, taking this as accepted, one must realize that the first indemonstrable argument is the one made out of a conditional and its leader,[73] having as its conclusion the finisher in that conditional. That

---

[70] Cf. n. 56.

[71] In the first of these usages (not the important one here) "undemonstrated" might be a better translation for the Greek *anapodeiktos*; many Greek adjectives ending in – *tos* are ambiguous between English words ending "-able" and ending "-ed."

[72] Possibly a reference to lost works, or perhaps a result of Sextus' incomplete adaptation of his source. *PH* 2.156 provides a loose parallel, but says nothing about Chrysippus or about two senses of "indemonstrable."

[73] I.e., the antecedent of the conditional; cf. 110.

is, when an argument has two premises, of which one is a conditional and the other is the leader in the conditional, and has as consequence the finisher in the same conditional, then an argument of this kind is called a first indemonstrable – for example: "If it is day, it is light; but it *is* day; therefore it is light." For this has a conditional as one of its premises ("If it is day, it is light"), the leader in the conditional as the other premise ("But it *is* day"), and, third, "Therefore it is light" as the consequence, which is the finisher of the conditional.

(225) The second indemonstrable is the one made out of a conditional and the contradictory of the finisher in that conditional, having as its conclusion the contradictory of the leader. That is, when an argument, again consisting of two premises, of which one is a conditional and the other is the contradictory of the finisher in the conditional, has as its consequence the contradictory of the leader, then an argument of this kind is a second indemonstrable – such as "If it is day, it is light; but it is *not* light; therefore it is not day." For "If it is day, it is light" (which is one premise of the argument) is a conditional, and "But it is *not* light" (which is the other premise of the argument) is the contradictory of the finisher in the conditional; and the consequence, "Therefore it is not day," is the contradictory of the leader.

(226) The third indemonstrable argument is the one made out of a negative conjunction and one of the items in the conjunction, having as its conclusion the contradictory of the remaining item in the conjunction – such as "It is not both day and night; it is day; therefore it is not night." For "It is not both day and night" is the negation of the conjunction "It is both day and night," "It is day" is one of the items in the conjunction, and "Therefore it is not night" is the contradictory of the remaining item in the conjunction.

(227) Well then, this is what the arguments are like; and the modes and, as it were, patterns in which they are put forward are as follows: for the first indemonstrable "If the first, the second; but the first; therefore the second"; for the second one "If the first, the second; but not the second; therefore not the first"; for the third one "Not both the first and the second; but the first; therefore not the second."

(228) One also has to realize that some indemonstrables are simple, others non-simple. Simple ones are those that make immediately clear that they reach a conclusion – that is, that the consequence is drawn from

their premises. The ones just laid out are like this; for, in the case of the first, if we allow that "If it is day, it is light" is true – I mean, that its being light follows from its being day – and we suppose that the first part, its being day, which is the leader in the conditional, is true, its also being light, which was the conclusion of the argument, will necessarily follow. (**229**) Non-simple ones are those that are connected together out of simple ones, and need to be analyzed into the latter in order for us to recognize that they too reach a conclusion. And of these non-simple ones some consist of parts that are like in kind, others of parts that are unlike in kind. Examples of the former would be those connected together out of two first indemonstrables or two seconds, (**230**) and of the latter those consisting of a first <. . .>,[74] or a second and a third, and in general ones like these. For example, an argument such as this consists of parts that are like in kind: "<If it is day, then> if it is day, it is light; but it *is* day; therefore it is light." For it is connected together out of two first indemonstrables, as we will know after analyzing it. (**231**) For one should realize that there is a dialectical rule handed down for the analysis of deductions, as follows: "When we have the premises that are capable of reaching a certain conclusion, we in effect have that conclusion in them, even if it is not stated explicitly." (**232**) Since, then, we have two premises, the conditional "If it is day, <then if it is day, it is light>," which begins with the simple proposition "It is day" and finishes with the non-simple conditional "If it is day, it is light," and also its leader "It is day," from these we will conclude, by the first indemonstrable, the finisher of the first conditional, namely "Therefore if it is day, it is light." (**233**) In effect, then, we have this being concluded in the argument, but it is left out in terms of the explicit wording; and if we line <it>[75] up with the minor premise of the argument as laid out – "It is day" – we will have "It is light" concluded by the first indemonstrable – which was the consequence of the argument as laid out. So that there are two first indemonstrables, one like this: "<If it is day, then> if it is day, it is light; <but it *is* day; therefore if it is day, it is light>," and the other like this: "If it is day, it is light; but it *is* day; therefore it is light."[76]

---

[74] Presumably the words "and a second" or "and a third" have been lost.

[75] Following Kochalsky, I add *ho* before *taxantes*; this is the simplest way of correcting the syntax. I also insert a stop after *kata de tēn ekphoran paraleleimenon*, which clearly belongs with what precedes rather than with what follows.

[76] The text from 230–233 is severely defective; the copyists clearly had no idea what Sextus was talking about. Mutschmann despairs of restoring the correct text. But in fact there is no serious

(234) Such is the character, then, of the arguments that are connected together out of parts that are like in kind. There remain the ones made out of parts that are unlike in kind, such as the one that Aenesidemus put forward about the sign, which goes like this: if apparent things appear alike to all who are similarly disposed, and signs are apparent things, signs appear alike to all who are similarly disposed. But signs do *not* appear alike to all who are similarly disposed; yet apparent things do appear alike to all who are similarly disposed; therefore signs are not apparent things. (235) For an argument like this consists of a second and a third indemonstrable, as we can learn from its analysis, which will become even clearer after we have made our explanation at the level of its mode, which is like this: "If the first and the second, the third; not the third, but the first; therefore not the second." (236) For since we have a conditional in which a conjunction of the first and second leads, and the third finishes, and we have the contradictory of the finisher, "Not the third," we will reach as a conclusion the contradictory of the leader, "Therefore not the first and the second," by the second indemonstrable. Now, this itself is in effect present in the argument, since we have the premises that are capable of concluding to it, but it is missing in terms of explicit statement. And when we have lined this up with the remaining premise – the first – we will have the conclusion "Therefore not the second," reached by the third indemonstrable. So that there are two indemonstrables, one like this: "If the first and the second, the third; but not the third; therefore not the first and the second," which is the second indemonstrable, and the other the third, which is like this: "Not the first and the second; but the first; therefore not the second."

(237) Such is the analysis, then, in the case of the mode, and it is analogous in the case of the argument as well. For the third component,[77] "It is not the case that apparent things appear alike to all who are similarly disposed and signs are apparent things," is left out. And it, along with the fact that apparent things do appear alike to all who are similarly disposed,

difficulty. In 232 Sextus himself explains very clearly the construction of the major premise of the compound argument, cites its minor premise, and draws attention to the needed but unstated interim conclusion. These clues are sufficient to restore the argument as shown – as already seen by Kochalsky, whose additions I follow throughout these sections.

[77] As Heintz noticed, this must refer to the third line in the argument if fully spelled out – i.e., the unstated interim conclusion – not to "the third" in the schematic representation of the argument discussed in the previous paragraph.

leads to the <conclusion of the argument>[78] as laid out by the third indemonstrable. So that there is a second indemonstrable like this: "If apparent things appear alike to all who are similarly disposed and signs are apparent things, signs appear alike to all who are similarly disposed; but signs do *not* appear alike to all who are similarly disposed; therefore signs are not apparent things,"[79] (238) and a third indemonstrable like this: "It is not the case that apparent things appear alike to all who are similarly disposed and signs are apparent things; but signs do appear alike to all who are similarly disposed; therefore signs are not apparent things."

vii. Simplified versions of Aenesidemus' argument (239–243)

(239) An argument of the following kind can be put forward with the same conclusive force: if apparent things appear equally to everyone and apparent things are signs of unclear things, unclear things appear equally to everyone; but unclear things do *not* appear equally to everyone, yet apparent things do appear equally to everyone; therefore apparent things are not signs of unclear things. (240) The analysis of this argument is similar – a second indemonstrable overlaps with a third – and the attractiveness of the premises is obvious. For that apparent things appear equally to those who have unimpaired senses is evident; for white does not appear differently to different people, nor does black appear differently to different people, nor does sweet appear differently, but they affect everyone similarly. (241) Well then, if these things appear equally to everyone and have the power of indicating unclear things, then unclear things, too, necessarily strike everyone equally, seeing that the causes are the same and the underlying matter is similar. But this is *not* so; for not everyone recognizes unclear things in the same way, even though they encounter perceptible things equally, but some do not even come to a conception of them, while others do, but are seduced into a variety of shifting and conflicting assertions. It

---

[78] Mutschmann, following Kochalsky, posits a lacuna here. Clearly the general sense is as given above. This sense might just be understood by the words in the transmitted text, but the wording is much less awkward if we supplement with *logou sumperasma*. (Kochalsky also includes an explicit statement of the conclusion, but this seems unnecessary.)

[79] The conclusion should rather be "Therefore it is not the case that apparent things appear alike to all who are similarly disposed and signs are apparent things." Kochalsky supplements the text with the first conjunct. However, as Heintz points out, the words *ara ouk* ("therefore . . . not") in the transmitted text would also have to be deleted to yield the correct sense. Heintz therefore inclines to regard this as an oversight on Sextus' part; with some hesitation I follow him in leaving the text unchanged.

follows, therefore, that we should say signs are not perceptible, in order for this absurdity not to follow.

(242) It is also possible to capture what has previously been said in short order, and to offer arguments as follows. If apparent things appear equally to everyone, and signs do not appear to everyone, signs are not apparent things. But the first; therefore the second.[80] **(243)** And again: if apparent things, in so far as they are apparent things, do not have need of teaching, but signs, in so far as they are signs, do have need of teaching, signs are not apparent things. But the first; therefore the second.

d. Difficulties in supposing that the sign is intelligible (244–274)
i. Exposition of a Stoic view entailing that the sign is intelligible (244–256)
Against those who maintain that the sign is perceptible, let these impasses be enough; **(244)** but let us look into the position opposed to theirs, I mean that of those who have assumed it to be intelligible. But perhaps we will need to preface this with brief remarks about the view that appeals to them, in virtue of which they take the sign to be a proposition, and for this reason intelligible. In sketching it, then, they say that **(245)** a sign is a leading proposition in a sound conditional, capable of uncovering the finisher. And they say that there are many other ways of judging a sound conditional, but that just one out of all of them (and that one not agreed on) is real, namely the one to be explained. Every conditional either begins with a true proposition and finishes with a true one, or begins with a false one and finishes with a false one, or begins with a true one and finishes with a false one, or begins with a false one and finishes with a true one. **(246)** "If there are gods, the universe is administered by the providence of the gods" begins with a true one and finishes with a true one; "If the earth flies, the earth has wings" begins with a false one and finishes with a false one; "If the earth flies, the earth is" begins with a false one and finishes with a true one; "If this person is moving, this person is walking" begins with a true one and finishes with a false one, when he is not walking but is moving. **(247)** So, since there are four combinations of the conditional – when it begins with true and finishes with true, when it begins with false and finishes with false, when it begins with false and finishes with true, or conversely when it begins with true and finishes with false – they say that

---

[80] Here Sextus switches, after the first premise, to representing the argument by its "mode" (cf. 227, 235–236). The Stoics originated this device of abbreviation; see Diogenes Laertius 7.77.

in the first three modes it is true (for if it begins with true and finishes with true it is true, and if it begins with false and finishes with false it is again true; similarly if it begins with false and finishes with true), and that it is false in only one mode, when it begins with true and finishes with false.

(248) And since this is so, they say, one should search for the sign not in this bad conditional but in the sound one; for it was called a proposition that was the leader in a sound conditional. But since there is not one sound conditional, but three – namely, the one that begins with true and finishes with true, the one that begins with false and finishes with false, and the one that begins with false and finishes with true – one must inquire whether the sign is to be sought in all sound conditionals, or in some, or in one. (249) If, then, the sign has to be true and capable of displaying what is true, it will not belong in the one that begins with false and finishes with false, nor in the one that begins with false and finishes with true. So it remains for it to be only in the one that begins with true and finishes with true, seeing that it is itself real and the thing signified ought to be real alongside it.

(250) So when it is said that the sign is a leading proposition in a sound conditional, we need to understand it as a leader in only the conditional that begins with true and ends with true. Yet not *any* proposition that leads in a sound conditional beginning with true and finishing with true is a sign. (251) For example, a conditional such as "If it is day, it is light" begins with the true "It is day" and finishes with the true "It is light," but it does not have within it any leading proposition that is a sign of the finisher. For "It is day" is not capable of uncovering "It is light"; rather, just as the first one struck us all by itself, so "It is light" was grasped by means of its own manifest character. (252) Therefore the sign has to be not just a leader in a sound conditional – that is, the one that begins with true and finishes with true – but it also has to have a nature that is capable of uncovering the finisher, as is the case in conditionals like these: "If she has milk in her breasts, she has conceived" and "If this person has thrown up bronchial matter, he has a wound in his lungs." (253) For this is a sound conditional, beginning with the true "This person has thrown up bronchial matter," and finishing with the true "He has a wound in his lungs," together with the fact that the first is capable of uncovering the second. For by paying attention to the former we create an apprehension of the latter.

(254) In addition, they say, the sign has to be a present sign of a present thing. Some people are misled into holding that a present thing can be a sign of a past thing, as in the case of "If this person has a scar, he has had a wound." For if[81] he has a scar it is a present thing – for it appears – but his having had a wound is a past thing, for there is no longer a wound. And they also hold that a present thing can be a sign of a future thing, such as what is contained in a conditional such as "If this person has been wounded in the heart, he will die"; for they say that the wound to the heart is already there, but the death is to come. (255) But the people who say such things fail to understand that while past things and future things are different, the sign and the thing signified are, even in these cases, a present thing in relation to a present thing. For in the first case, "If this person has a scar, he has had a wound," the wound has occurred already and is gone, but this person's *having had* a wound, which is a proposition, is present, being said about something that has occurred. And in the case of "If this person has been wounded in the heart, he will die," while the death is to come, the proposition that he will die, being said about a thing that is to come, is present, in so far as it is true even now. (256) So that the sign is a proposition, and it leads in a sound conditional that begins with true and finishes with true, and it is capable of uncovering the finisher, and in every case it is a present sign of a present thing.

ii. Difficulties stemming from disagreement about whether the sign is perceptible or intelligible (257)
(257) Now that these things have been pointed out, following their very own technicalities, it is appropriate, first, to say this to them. If the sign is perceptible according to some people and intelligible according to others, and the disagreement about this is undecided up to now, it has to be said that the sign is at this point unclear. And if it is unclear it needs things to uncover it, and must not be itself capable of uncovering other things.

iii. Difficulties over the reality of sayables (258–261)
(258) In addition, if the sign has its subsistence, according to them, in a sayable, and if it is a matter of investigation whether there are sayables, it

---

[81] I retain the mss. *ei*; Mutschmann, following Kochalsky, alters to *to*.

is absurd to take the species as secure before the genus has been agreed on. And we see that there are some who have done away with the reality of sayables – and not only people of other opinions, such as the Epicureans, but even Stoics like Basilides,[82] whose view was that there is nothing incorporeal.[83] The sign, then, is to be kept in suspension of judgment. (259) But, they say, when we have demonstrated the reality of sayables we will have the nature of the sign secure as well. Then someone will say "When you have demonstrated it, *then* take it that the reality of the sign is also reliable; but while you remain with a bare promise, it is also necessary that we remain in suspension of judgment." (260) Then again, how is it possible to demonstrate the reality of propositions? One will have to do this either through a sign or through a demonstration. But it is not possible to do this either through any sign or through a demonstration. For since these are themselves sayables, they are under investigation like the other sayables, (261) and are so far from being able to establish something securely that, on the contrary, they themselves need something to establish them. And the Stoics have failed to notice that they fall into the reciprocal mode. For in order for sayables to be agreed upon, there have to be demonstration and sign; but in order for demonstration and sign to subsist beforehand, it is necessary that the nature of sayables be previously guaranteed. So since they point toward one another and are waiting for trustworthiness from one another, they are equally untrustworthy.

iv. Difficulties in supposing that sayables are either bodily or incorporeal (262–268)

(262) But let it be the case that sayables do occur in reality (even though the conflict about them is not coming to an end); let us allow this as an added bonus, for the sake of the investigation moving forward. Then, if there are these things, they will say that they are either bodies or incorporeal. And they cannot say that they are bodies; but if they are incorporeal,

---

[82] A Stoic of this name is attested as a teacher of the emperor Marcus Aurelius; if this is who Sextus is talking about, he would be by far the latest named figure referred to in Sextus' works. But there is also a Stoic of this name attested in the second century BCE, and there is no way to tell which of them Sextus intends.

[83] It was in fact the *standard* Stoic view that there is nothing incorporeal; sayables, like other incorporeals, are described not as *being* but as merely subsisting (cf. n. 30). Presumably Sextus is speaking loosely, and his point is that certain Stoics do not recognize incorporeals in their ontology at all.

either they do something, according to them, or they do nothing. And they cannot maintain that they do anything; (263) for the incorporeal, according to them, is not of a nature to do anything or to be affected. But if they do nothing, they will not even indicate and make clear the thing of which they are signs; for indicating something and making it clear is doing something. (264) But it is absurd for the sign not to indicate anything or make it clear. Therefore the sign is not intelligible, nor is it a proposition. Besides, as we have often pointed out in many places, some things signify, others are signified. Utterances signify, and sayables, among which are propositions, are signified. But if all propositions are signified, and other things signify, the sign cannot be a proposition. (265) Again, let it be granted that sayables have an incorporeal nature. But since they say that the sign leads in a sound conditional, the sound conditional will need to be judged on and examined beforehand, to see whether it is as Philo sees it, or as Diodorus sees it, or judged in terms of connectedness[84] or in some other way. For since there are lots of differences about this, it is not possible to grasp the sign securely while the disagreement turns out to be undecided.

(266) Moreover, in addition to what has been said, even if we concede that the sound criterion is agreed upon, and that it is of the kind they want – no dispute about it – one is no less forced to agree that what contains the sign is undecided. For they claim that the signified is either clear or unclear. (267) And if it is clear it will not be a thing signified, nor will it be *signified by* something, but will strike us all by itself. But if it is unclear, it will undoubtedly be unknown whether this thing is true or false, since when it is known which of these it is, it will become clear. (268) The conditional that contains the sign and the thing signified, then, is necessarily undecided, since it finishes with something unclear. For that it begins with something true is known, but it finishes with something unknown. But to make a judgment on it we must first of all know what it finishes with. If it finishes with something true, we will regard it as true, given that it begins with something true and finishes with something true;

---

[84] I.e., connectedness of subject-matter between the components of the conditional. On this approach to conditionals (probably due to Chrysippus), cf. *PH* 2.111 and Diogenes Laertius 7.73; also S. Bobzien in K. Algra, J. Barnes, J. Mansfeld, and M. Schofield, eds., *The Cambridge History of Hellenistic Philosophy* (Cambridge University Press, 1999), 106–108. It is not elsewhere mentioned in *Against the Logicians* (though cf. 430 for a related use of the term). On the approaches of Philo and Diodorus see 113–117 above.

but if it finishes with something false, then conversely we will say that it is false, given that it begins with something true and finishes with something false. We should not, therefore, say that the sign is a proposition, nor a leader in a sound conditional.

v. Difficulties stemming from the accessibility of sign-inference to non-philosophers and non-humans (269–271)

(269) To these points it should be added that the proponents of this opinion are in conflict with plain experience. For if the sign is a proposition and leads in a sound conditional, then those who have no conception whatever of a proposition, and have not gone into the technicalities of the dialecticians, should have no part in the use of signs. (270) But this is *not* so. For often illiterate helmsmen and farmers with no experience of dialectical principles are expert judges of signs – the former on the sea, judging winds and calms, storms and still seas, and the latter on the farm, judging good and bad crops, droughts and heavy rains. In fact, why are we talking about human beings, when some of them have even attributed some concept of the sign to non-rational animals? (271) For the dog, when it tracks an animal by its footprints, is actually using signs; but it does not for that reason take in an appearance of the proposition "If this is a footprint, an animal is here." And the horse leaps forward and rushes on to the course at the impact of a spur or the wielding of a whip; but it does not make a dialectical judgment upon a conditional of the form "If a whip has been wielded, I had better run." Therefore the sign is not a proposition that is the leader in a sound conditional.

vi. Miscellaneous difficulties drawing on previous ideas (272–274)

(272) These will suffice as specific arguments against those who maintain that the sign is intelligible; but it will also be possible, in a more general way, to raise against them the ones that were used against those who say that it is perceptible. For if the sign is a proposition that is the leader in a sound conditional, and in every conditional the finisher follows from the leader, and the "followings" are of objects that are present, then necessarily the sign and the thing signified, being present on a single occasion, will coexist with one another, and neither one will become revelatory of the other, but they will both get to be known all by themselves. (273) Besides, the sign

is capable of uncovering the thing signified, and the thing signified is uncovered by the sign. And these are not absolutes, but things in relation to something; for the thing being uncovered is conceived in relation to the thing uncovering it, and the thing that uncovers is conceived in relation to the thing being uncovered. But if both of them, being things in relation to something, are present at the same time, they both subsist together with one another. But if they subsist together, each one is apprehended all by itself – neither one by means of the other. (274) And the following should be said: that whatever the sign may be like, either it itself has a nature suitable for indicating and revealing what is unclear, or we are capable of remembering the things that have been exposed together with it. But it does not have a nature indicative of unclear things, since in that case it ought to indicate unclear things to everyone equally. Therefore the way we go with regard to the subsistence of objects parallels how we are doing in terms of our memory.

e. Dogmatic counter-arguments (275–284)
(275) But if the sign is neither perceptible, as we have shown, nor intelligible, as we have established, and there is no third option besides these, it has to be said that there is no sign. Now, as far as each of these attacks is concerned, the dogmatists have been muzzled. But in constructing the opposite case they say that a human being does not differ from non-rational animals in uttered discourse[85] (for crows and parrots and jays also utter articulate sounds), but in discourse within the mind, (276) and not in the merely simple appearance (for those animals have appearances), but in the one that involves transitions and combinations. Because of this, since he has a conception of following, he immediately grasps the concept of a sign as well, because of following; for the sign, of course, is of the form "If this, this." Therefore from the nature and constitution of the human being it follows that the sign is real.

(277) And demonstration is agreed to belong to the genus sign. For it is capable of showing the conclusion, and the conjunction of its premises will be a sign of the conclusion being so. For example, in a case such as "If there is motion, there is void; but there is motion; therefore there is

---

[85] *Logos*, elsewhere translated both "speech" and "reason" (among other things); here the context demands a word that will straddle both concepts.

void," the conjunction "<There is motion, and>[86] if there is motion, there is void," being a conjunction of the premises, is also immediately a sign of the conclusion "There is void." **(278)** Well then, they say, the arguments produced against the sign by the bringers of impasse are either demonstrative or non-demonstrative. And if they are non-demonstrative, they are untrustworthy – given that they would hardly have been trusted even if they turned out to be demonstrative. And if they are demonstrative, it is clear that there is some sign; for demonstration is, generically speaking, a sign. **(279)** And if nothing is a sign of anything, either the sounds uttered against the sign signify something or they signify nothing. And if they signify nothing, they will not do away with the reality of the sign, either; for how could sounds signifying nothing be trusted concerning there being no sign? But if they do signify, the skeptics emerge as empty-headed, since they toss out the sign in their words but accept it in fact. **(280)** Then again, if there is no rule peculiar to a skill, skill will not differ from lack of skill. But if there is a rule peculiar to a skill, it is either apparent or unclear. But it could not be apparent; for apparent things appear equally to everyone, without teaching. But if it is unclear, it will be observed through a sign. But if there is something observed through a sign, there will also be a sign.

(281) Some people also put forward an argument like this: "If there is any sign, there is a sign; if there is not a sign, there is a sign. But either there is no sign or there is one; therefore there is one." Such is the argument, and they say that its first premise is sound. For it is a differentiated proposition,[87] and there being a sign follows from there being a sign, in so far as if the first is so, the second will also be so, since it is no different from the first. As for "If there is not a sign, there is a sign," it too is sound; for when one says that there is no sign, it follows that one is saying that there is some sign. For if there is no sign, there will be some sign of the very fact that there is no sign. And reasonably so; for the person who says that there is no sign maintains this either by mere assertion or by demonstration. And if he maintains it by assertion, he will face the opposite assertion; **(282)** but if he demonstrates that what he says is true,

---

[86] With Heintz, I retain the mss. *sumpeplegmenon* (Mutschmann, following Bekker, alters to *sunēmmenon*, "conditional") and add <*esti kinēsis kai*>. For the procedure of combining the premises of an argument into a conjunction (as part of an assessment of the argument's validity), cf. 415–417, 421, *PH* 2.137. (However, the procedure described in those passages is Stoic, whereas this argument for the existence of void is Epicurean in origin – cf. 329.)

[87] Cf. 108–109 and n. 49.

then through the argument that shows that there is no sign he will *signify* that there is no sign – but in doing this he will agree that there *is* some sign. The first two premises are true, then, they say. And the third one is also true; for it is a disjunction of contradictories (that there is a sign and that there is not)[88] – since if every disjunction is true when it has one of its components true, and it is also[89] observed that one of a pair of contradictories is true, it has to be said that a proposition constructed like this is straightforwardly true. So that on the basis of the premises, which are agreed upon, the consequence "Therefore there is a sign" is also drawn.

(283) It will also be possible, they say, to proceed this way: in the argument there are two conditionals and one disjunction; and of these the conditionals promise that their finishers follow from their leaders, while the disjunction has one of its components true, since if both of them are true or both false, the whole proposition will be false.[90] (284) Such being the force of the premises, then supposing one of the components of the disjunction true, let us see how the consequence is drawn. And first let us take it that "there is some sign" is true. Then, since this is the leader in the first conditional, it will have the finisher in that conditional following from it.[91] But it finished with there being a sign, which is the same as the consequence. The consequence will be drawn, therefore, supposing there being some sign to be the component in the disjunction that is true. And now, conversely, let us take it that the other component, there not being a sign, is true. Then since this is the leader in the second conditional, it will have the finisher in the second conditional following from it. But what followed from it was there being some sign, which is also the consequence. By this means, too, therefore, the consequence is drawn.

f. Responses to dogmatic counter-arguments (285–297)

(285) This is what the dogmatists say. But (to proceed in order) against the first point, where they conclude that there is a sign from the constitution of the human being, it should be said that they want to teach about what is less under examination by means of what is more under examination.

---

[88] Mutschmann posits a lacuna at this point. But the sense seems acceptable with the text as it stands.
[89] I retain the mss. *kai*, rather than following Mutschmann's alteration to *aei*.
[90] This differs, then, from disjunction as understood in modern logic, where the disjunction is true if both disjuncts are true.
[91] Following Kochalsky I delete *to* before *akolouthon*.

For that there is a sign, even if it is denied by some, such as the skeptics, is still common ground among all the dogmatists; (286) but that the human being is constituted with forethought is disputed by no small number of them. And it is very forced to want to use what is more a matter of disagreement to teach about things that are not in that state.[92] And in fact, Heraclitus says in so many words that "The human being is not rational; only what encompasses us is endowed with mind." And Empedocles, even more paradoxically, maintained that everything is rational – not just animals but even plants, writing in so many words

> You know that all things have insight and a share of understanding.

(287) Along with this, there is a persuasive argument for the non-rational animals being not without insight. For if uttered discourse belongs to them, discourse within the mind must necessarily belong to them too; for without this kind the uttered kind is non-subsistent. (288) But even if we allow that the human being differs from other animals in discourse, and appearance that involves transitions, and a conception of following, we will *not* agree that he is this way when it comes to unclear things and things that are matters of undecided disagreement. Rather, when it comes to apparent things, he has an awareness of following based on watching, in virtue of which he remembers which things were observed with which, which before which, and which after which, and so from his encounters with earlier things renews[93] the rest.

(289) But if it is agreed, they say, that demonstration is, generically speaking, a sign, then if they are not demonstrations, the arguments produced against the sign are untrustworthy, but if they are demonstrations, there is some sign. But since we said before that we do not stand in the way of the recollective sign but the indicative sign, we can concede that the arguments produced against the sign signify something – just not indicatively, but recollectively; for we are affected by them and retrieve in our memories the things that can be said against the indicative sign. (290) And the same things can be said about the next suggestion – the one where they ask whether the sounds uttered against the sign signify something or signify nothing. For if we were doing away with every sign, it would necessarily have to be the case either that the sounds uttered in our case against the sign signified nothing, or that if they did signify, it would be

---

[92] I.e., things that are not so much a matter of disagreement.   [93] Cf. 143, 152–153.

granted that there is some sign. But in fact, since we make a distinction and do away with one but posit the other, the reality of an indicative sign is not conceded even if we take account of the fact that the sounds uttered against the indicative sign signify something. **(291)** It was also said that if there is a rule peculiar to a skill, this will have to be not clear, but unclear and grasped through a sign. But they do not recognize that whereas there is no rule for the skill that reflects on unclear things[94] – as we will explain later[95] – there is a rule peculiar to the one that is involved with apparent things. For it brings about the construction of rules on the basis of things often watched or examined; and the things often watched and examined are peculiar to the people who have most often been watching – they are not common to everyone.

(292) The argument they put forward at the end, in the following mode – "If the first, the first; if not the first, the first; either the first or not the first; therefore the first" – is perhaps bad because of the redundancy in the premises as well, but it undoubtedly seems to bother even them. **(293)** To proceed in order, we should speak about the first point – that is, the redundancy. If the disjunction in the argument is true, it ought to have one component true, as they themselves said before. But if it has one component true it exposes one of the conditionals as redundant. **(294)** For if the component "There is a sign" is taken as true, then in order to get to the conclusion of this argument, the differentiated conditional "If there is a sign, there is a sign" becomes necessary, but the other one, "If there is no sign, there is a sign," becomes redundant. And if the component that there is no sign is taken as true, then the differentiated proposition is redundant for this argument's construction, while "If there is no sign, there is a sign" becomes necessary. The argument is bad, then, on account of redundancy.

(295) But to avoid going with our opponents into the fine details, it is possible to put forward another argument of this kind. If the person who says that there is no sign is turned around into saying that there is some sign, the person who says that there is a sign is also turned around into saying that there is no sign. But the person who said skeptically that there was no sign was turned around, according to them, into saying that there is a sign; therefore the person who says dogmatically that there is

---

[94] Reading *adēlōn* with Kayser, instead of the mss. *allōn*.
[95] It is not clear what this forward reference is pointing to.

a sign will be turned around into saying that there is no sign, as we will establish. (296) For, to begin with, the person who says that there is a sign has to confirm his assertion by a sign. But if there being a sign is not agreed upon, how can this person use the sign for confirmation of there being a sign? But if he is not able to demonstrate by a sign that there is a sign, he is turned around into agreeing that there is no sign. But let us agree, as an added bonus, that there is this one sign, namely the one capable of revealing that there is a sign; what help is this to them, when they have no way of speaking of any sign of their own doctrines? (297) So that this is useless to them – I mean, its being agreed in general that there is some sign; maybe it is necessary to append to "There is some sign," which is indefinite, "*This* is a sign," which is expressed in definite terms. But it is not possible for them to do this. For every sign, just as much as the thing signified, is a matter of opinion and undecided disagreement. For just as "Someone is sailing through rocks" is false, since it is not possible to append to it the definite and true statement "This person is sailing through rocks," so too, since we are unable to append to the indefinite "There is some sign" any definite and true statement "This is a sign," "There is some sign" therefore becomes false and its contradictory, "There is no sign," true.

g. Conclusion: statement of skeptical outcome; transition
to C (298–299)
(298) However, let us suppose both that the arguments produced by them are powerful and that those of the skeptics have remained impossible to oppose. What is left, given the circumstance of equal strength on either side, except to suspend judgment and make no determination about the matter under examination, saying neither that there is a sign or that there is not, but offering the safe comment that there no more is than there is not?[96]

(299) But since demonstration seems to be, generically speaking, a sign, and to uncover the conclusion, which is unclear, through agreed-upon premises, I dare say it is appropriate to append an investigation of it to the inquiry into the sign.

[96] An example of the special skeptical usage of "no more" described by Sextus at *PH* 1.188–191; rather than asserting that each of the alternatives holds to an equal degree (as the words in their natural meaning might suggest), the phrase expresses suspension of judgment as between the two (cf. 328).

C. Demonstration (300–481)

1. The conception of demonstration (300–315)

On demonstration[97]

(300) The purpose of investigating demonstration at present has been pointed out earlier, when we were inquiring into the criterion and the sign.[98] But for the survey not to be unmethodical, and for the suspension of judgment and the rebuttal of the dogmatists to go ahead more safely, we should point out the conception of demonstration. **(301)** Demonstration, then, is generically speaking an argument; for it is obviously not a perceptible object, but a certain motion and assent of thought – and these are rational. And an argument is (simplifying somewhat) what is constituted out of premises and consequence. **(302)** We call "premises" not any posits that we help ourselves to, but ones that the person we are debating with allows and accepts. And a consequence is what is established by means of these premises. For example, this composite whole is an argument: "If it is day, it is light; but it *is* day; therefore it is light"; its premises are "If it is day, it is light" and "But it *is* day," and the consequence is "Therefore it is light." **(303)** Of arguments some are conclusive while others are not. And the conclusive ones are those in which, when the premises have been agreed to be so, the consequence appears to follow in virtue of this agreement, as was so in the case of the one set out just before. For since it consists of the conditional "If it is day, it is light," which promises that if its first component is true its second component will also be true, **(304)** and also of "It is day," which is the leader in the conditional, I am saying that if the conditional is allowed to be true, so that its finisher follows from its leader, and if it is also allowed that its first component, "It is day," is so, then necessarily, because of these things being so, its second component – that is, "It is light" – will be arrived at, and this is the consequence.

(305) Well then, conclusive arguments have a character something like this, and the ones that are not like this are inconclusive. Of the conclusive ones some reach as a conclusion something clear, others something

---

[97] This title and the next (316) are preceded by numerals; for the sake of consistency I omit these. (The presentation of titles in this work, or at least in the surviving manuscripts, is in general haphazard.)

[98] The reference is not entirely clear, but probably 142 is meant. (Bury points to 1.27, but this mentioned neither sign nor demonstration.)

unclear – clear, as in the one that was laid out, as follows: "If it is day, it is light; but it *is* day; therefore it is light." For "It is light" is apparent just as much as "It is day." Or again, in one such as "If Dion is walking, Dion is moving; but Dion is walking; therefore Dion is moving"; for "Dion is moving," which is the conclusion, is discovered by itself. (306) But an argument like this one, for example, reaches an unclear conclusion: "If sweat flows through the body's surface, there are intelligible pores in the flesh; but the first; therefore the second"; for there being intelligible pores in the flesh is something unclear. Again, so does "That upon whose separation from the body human beings die is the soul; but upon the separation of blood from the body human beings die; therefore the soul is blood"; for that the substance of the soul lies in the blood is not plain.

(307) And of these arguments that reach as a conclusion something unclear, some lead us on from the premises to the conclusion in a way that is just progressive, others in a way that is both progressive and that involves uncovering. (308) The ones that lead us on in a way that is just progressive are those that seem to depend on belief and memory – one like this, for example: "If one of the gods said to you that this person will be rich, this person will be rich; but this god (let us suppose I am pointing to Zeus) said to you that this person will be rich; therefore this person will be rich." For here we accept the conclusion, that this person will be rich, not through its being established by the force of the argument set out, but by our believing the assertion of the god. (309) But an example of an argument that leads us on from the premises to the conclusion in a way that is both progressive and involves uncovering is the one put forward on the subject of intelligible pores. For "If sweat flows through the body's surface, there are intelligible pores in the flesh," and the fact that sweat does flow through the body's surface, teach us from their own nature to put together the fact that there are intelligible pores in the flesh, by way of a progression like this: "It is impossible for liquid to flow through a solid body not provided with pores; but sweat does flow through the body; the body cannot, then, be solid, but must be provided with pores."

(310) Well then, since this is so, demonstration has to be first of all an argument; second, conclusive; third, also true; fourth, also having an unclear conclusion; and fifth, having this conclusion uncovered by means of the force of the premises. (311) At any rate, if it is day, an argument such as "If it is night, it is dark; but it *is* night; therefore it is dark" is conclusive (for if its premises are granted the consequence is also concluded

to be so), but it is of course not true (for it includes the false premise "It is night"); for this reason it is not demonstrative either. (312) Again, one like this: "If it is day, it is light; but it is day; therefore it is light," in addition to being conclusive is also true, seeing that if its premises are granted its consequence is also granted, and it shows something true by true premises. But although this is so, it is again not a demonstration given that it has a conclusion, "It is light," that is clear and not unclear. (313) By the same token, too, one of this form: "If one of the gods said to you that this person will be rich, this person will be rich; but this god said to you that this person will be rich; therefore this person will be rich," does have a conclusion (the fact that this person will be rich) that is unclear, but it is not demonstrative because it is not uncovered by means of the force of the premises, but gets its acceptance by means of trust in the god. (314) When all these things come together, then – the argument's being conclusive and true and capable of displaying something unclear, demonstration subsists. Hence they delineate it as follows: "A demonstration is an argument that by means of agreed-upon premises uncovers by way of conclusive reasoning a consequence that is unclear." For example: "If there is motion, there is void; but there *is* motion; therefore there is void." For there being void is unclear, and seems to be uncovered by means of true premises – "If there is motion, there is void" and "There is motion" – by way of conclusive reasoning.

(315) These, then, are the things that it was appropriate to start with concerning the conception of the matter being investigated; next in order we should point out what it is made of.

2. Initial arguments to the effect that demonstration is unclear (316–336)

What demonstration is made of [99]

(316) As we have often said before, some objects are believed to be clear and others unclear. The clear ones are those that are grasped through no will of our own, by appearance and by means of an effect on us, such as (right now) "It is day" and "This is a human being" and everything like that, while the unclear ones are those that are not like this. (317) And of the unclear ones (as some people say who draw a distinction), some are by nature

---

[99] Literally, "What material (*hulēs*) demonstration comes from."

unclear, while others are called unclear "homonymously with the genus." And by nature unclear are those that have neither been apprehended before nor are being apprehended now nor will be apprehended later, but keep their unknown status for all time, such as the number of stars being even or odd. (318) In view of this, they are called by nature unclear not because *they* have an unclear nature considered in themselves – since then we will be saying something inconsistent (that is, at the same time both saying that we do not know them and agreeing on what nature they have) – but because they are unclear to *our* nature. (319) The ones called unclear "homonymously with the genus" are those that are hidden in terms of their own nature, but are held to become known through signs and demonstrations – for example, that there are indivisible elements moving around in an unlimited void. (320) However, if there is such a difference in the things, we say that demonstration is neither clear (for it does not become known all by itself and by means of a necessitated effect on us), nor by nature unclear (for the apprehension of it is not hopeless), but falls into the remaining side of the distinction among unclear things, which have their nature down in the depths and obscure to us, but seem to be apprehended by philosophical reasoning.[100]

(321) But we do not say this firmly, since it would be laughable to be still investigating it if we have accepted its reality; rather, we say that it turns out to be like this in terms of its conception. For in this way, from a conception and prior notion[101] of this kind, the argument about its reality will crop up. (322) That demonstration is, then, in terms of its conception, among the unclear things and cannot become known by means of itself is to be argued in the following way.

What is clear and plain is clear and plain in every way, and is agreed to by everyone and allows for no dissension; what is unclear, on the other hand, is a matter of disagreement and is of a nature to fall into dissension. (323) And reasonably so; for every statement is judged to be true or false according to its reference to the subject-matter about which it has been

---

[100] This classification differs from the one at the opening of the section on the sign (145–150). "Unclear by nature" in the present passage corresponds with "unclear pure and simple" in the earlier discussion; "unclear by nature" in the earlier passage corresponds with "unclear 'homonymously with the genus'" here.

[101] *Prolēpsis*, elsewhere translated "preconception." Here and at 337ff. I use "prior notion" in places where *prolēpsis* is juxtaposed with one of the words regularly translated "conception," simply to avoid the awkwardness of "conception and preconception"; "preconception" and "prior notion" should be understood as semantically equivalent.

produced. If it is found to be in agreement with the subject-matter about which it has been produced, it is thought to be true, and if in disagreement, false. For example, someone declares that it is day. Then after referring what is stated to the subject-matter, and recognizing the reality of this as testifying in favor of the statement, we say that what is stated is true. (324) For this reason, when the subject-matter about which the statement is produced is plain and clear, it is easy, after referring what is stated to it, to say in this way either that the statement is true (if it testifies in favor of the subject-matter) or false (if it testifies against it). But when the subject-matter is unclear and hidden away from us, then, since the reference of the statement to this can no longer be secure, it is left for thought to deal in persuasiveness and be drawn into assent by what is likely. But since different people make different judgments of likelihood and persuasiveness, disagreement arises, with neither the person who has missed the target knowing that he has missed it, nor the one who has hit it knowing he has hit it.

(325) This is why the skeptics very aptly compare those who are investigating unclear things with people shooting at some target in the dark. For just as it is likely that one of these people hits the target and another misses it, but who has hit it and who has missed it are unknown, so, as the truth is hidden away in pretty deep darkness, many arguments are launched at it, but which of them is in agreement with it and which in disagreement is not possible to know, since what is being investigated is removed from plain experience. (326) And Xenophanes said this first:

> And as for what is clear, no man has seen it, nor will there be anyone
> Who knows about the gods and what I say about all things;
> For even if one should happen to say what has absolutely come to pass
> Nonetheless one does not oneself know; but opinion has been
>   constructed in all cases.[102]

(327) So that if what is clear is a matter of agreement, for the reason mentioned before, while what is unclear is a matter of disagreement, demonstration too, if it is a matter of disagreement, has to be unclear. And that it is in fact a matter of disagreement does not require many arguments from us – just a brief and readily available reminder – if indeed the dogmatic philosophers and the rationalist doctors posit it, while the

---

[102] Cf. 1.49, 1.110.

Empiricists do away with it, and perhaps also Democritus (for he spoke strongly against it in his *Rules*), (328) and the skeptics have kept it in suspension of judgment, using the "no more" assertion. And again, there is enough disagreement among those who posit it, as we will show as the discussion moves forward. Demonstration, then, is something unclear.

(329) Moreover, if every demonstration that contains a doctrine in its premises is thereby a doctrine, and every doctrine is a matter of disagreement, then necessarily every demonstration is a matter of disagreement and is among the matters under investigation. For example, Epicurus is of the opinion that he has put forward a very strong demonstration of there being void, like this: "If there is motion, there is void; but there is motion; therefore there is void." (330) But if the premises of this demonstration were agreed upon by everyone, it would necessarily have the consequence that follows from them accepted by everyone as well. (331) But in fact some have resisted this (I mean, the consequence's being drawn from the premises) not on account of its not following from them, but on account of their being false and not agreed to. (332) For – not to rush over a lot of judgments about the conditional, but to say right away that a sound conditional is one that does not begin with a true proposition and finish with a false one – "If there is motion, there is void" will be true according to Epicurus, since it begins with the true "There is motion" and finishes with a true one. But it will be false according to the Peripatetics, since it begins with the true "There is motion" and finishes with the false "There is void." (333) And according to Diodorus, since it begins with the false "There is motion" and finishes with the false "There is void," it will itself be true, but he discredits the minor premise, "There is motion," as false. (334) According to the skeptics, however, since it finishes with one that is unclear, it will be unclear – for according to them "There is void" belongs among the things that are unknown. It is apparent from this, then, that the premises of the demonstration are a matter of disagreement. But since they are a matter of disagreement they are unclear,[103] so that the demonstration using them is also entirely unclear.

(335) Then again, demonstration is among the things in relation to something; for it does not appear by itself but is observed alongside the thing being demonstrated. But whether there are things in relation to something is under investigation, and many a person says that there

---

[103] With Bury I read *onta* for the mss. *kai ta*, accepted by Mutschmann.

are not. But what involves dissension is unclear. In this way too, then, demonstration is unclear. (336) In addition to this, demonstration either consists of sound, as is said by the Epicureans, or of incorporeal sayables, as is said by the Stoics. But which of them it consists of is open to a lot of investigation; for whether sayables subsist is a matter of investigation, and there is a lot of argument about this, and whether sounds signify anything is a matter of impasse. But if it is a matter of investigation which of them demonstration is made of, and what is under investigation is unclear, undoubtedly demonstration is unclear.

Let this be laid down, then, as a sort of starting-point for the rebuttal to come; moving on, let us next look into whether *there is* demonstration.

3. *Difficulties concerning demonstration (337–481)*

a. Rebuttal of Epicurean argument based on the conception of demonstration (337–336a)

Whether there is demonstration

(337) Having described what demonstration is made of, we will follow this by trying to get a grip on the arguments that make it shaky, inquiring whether its reality follows from its conception and prior notion or not. Indeed some people, especially those of the Epicurean school, tend to resist us in a rather crude way, saying "Either you understand what demonstration is, or you do not. And if you understand it and have a conception of it, there is demonstration; but if you do not understand it, how can you investigate what you have not the slightest understanding of?" (331a) For in saying this they are virtually turned about by themselves, since it is agreed that, when anything is being investigated, a prior notion and conception has to come first. For how can anyone investigate if he has no conception of the object being investigated? For neither will he know that he has hit the target when he has hit it, nor that he has missed it when he has missed it. (332a) So that we give them this point. Actually, we are so far from saying that we do not have a conception of the entire object being investigated, that on the contrary we maintain that we have many conceptions and prior notions of it, and thanks to our being unable to discriminate these and to find the one with the most authority we come round to suspension of judgment and equilibrium. (333a) For if we had just one preconception of the object being investigated, then

sticking closely to this we would believe that the matter was such as it struck us in virtue of that one conception; but in fact, since we have many conceptions of this one thing, which are also varied and conflicting and equally trustworthy (both on account of their own persuasiveness and on account of the trustworthiness of the men who support them), being unable either to trust all of them because of the conflict, or to distrust all of them because of having none other that is more trustworthy than them, or to trust one and distrust another because of their equality, we necessarily arrive at suspension of judgment.

(334a) But now, we have preconceptions of objects in the manner that has been pointed out. And for this reason, if preconception was apprehension, then in allowing that we have a preconception of the object we would perhaps also be confessing apprehension of it. But in fact, since the prior notion and conception of the object is not its reality, we say that we do conceive it, but that we do not in the least apprehend it for the reasons mentioned before – (335a) since after all, if preconceptions are apprehensions, we in turn will demand of them whether Epicurus has or does not have a prior notion and conception of the four elements. And if he does not, how will he grasp the object being investigated, and investigate this thing of which he does not even have a conception? But if he does have it, how has he not apprehended that there are four elements? (336a) But I think that they will say in defense that Epicurus does conceive the four elements, but has absolutely not apprehended them; for conception is a mere movement of thought, which he holds onto in his opposition to there being four elements. So we too have a conception of demonstration, and on the basis of this we will examine whether or not it is; but in having this we do not also agree to the apprehension.

b. Difficulties turning on the distinction between generic and specific demonstration (337a–356)

(337a) But we will address these people again at some point.[104] However, since it is appropriate to be methodical in making our rebuttals, we should ask which demonstration we must oppose the most. Now, if we want to oppose particular demonstrations applying to each skill, we will be unmethodical in making our opposition, since such demonstrations are endless. (338) But if we do away with generic demonstration, which seems

---

[104] Epicureans are mentioned at 348ff.; otherwise they do not again figure in the discussion.

to be inclusive of all the specific ones, it is clear that in this way we will have them all done away with. For just as, if there is not animal, neither is there human being, and if human being is not real, neither does Socrates subsist, the specific instances being done away with along with the genera, so if there is no generic demonstration every specific demonstration is also gone. (339) For whereas the genus is not entirely done away with along with the specific instance (such as the human being along with Socrates), the specific instance is, as I said, canceled along with the genus. It is not necessary, then, for those who are putting demonstration in a shaky position to dislodge any other kind than the generic, which the rest of them turn out to follow.

i. Impossibility of establishing either generic or specific demonstration prior to the other (340–347)

(340) So, since demonstration is unclear, as we have argued, it ought to have been demonstrated; for everything unclear, if it is grasped without demonstration, is untrustworthy. That demonstration is something, then, is established either by a generic demonstration or by a specific one. (341) But definitely not by a specific one; for no specific demonstration is yet in place given that generic demonstration is not yet agreed to. For just as, if it is not yet clear whether there is animal, neither is it known whether there is horse, so, if it has not yet been agreed that there is generic demonstration, none of the particular demonstrations can be trustworthy, (342) in addition to the fact that we fall into the reciprocal mode. For in order for generic demonstration to be confirmed, we need to have the specific one trustworthy, but in order for the specific one to be agreed to, we need to have the generic one firm, so that we can neither have the former before the latter nor the latter before the former. It is impossible, then, for generic demonstration to be demonstrated by a specific demonstration. (343) But not by a generic one either; for it is the one being investigated, and if it is unclear and under investigation it cannot be capable of establishing itself – after all, it is what needs things uncovering it. Unless it is said to be capable of establishing something when grasped by hypothesis. But if things are grasped just once by hypothesis and are trustworthy, what need is there still to demonstrate them, since we can grasp them right away and hold them as trustworthy without a demonstration, on account of this hypothesis? (344) In addition, if generic demonstration is capable of displaying generic demonstration, the same one will at the same time

be thoroughly apparent and unclear – thoroughly apparent in so far as it is demonstrating, but unclear in so far as it is being demonstrated. It will also be equally trustworthy and untrustworthy – trustworthy because it is capable of uncovering something, but untrustworthy because it is being uncovered. But it is altogether absurd to say that the same thing is simultaneously clear and unclear, or trustworthy as well as untrustworthy. To maintain, then, that generic demonstration is capable of displaying itself is also absurd.

(345) Furthermore, there is another way in which it is not possible for demonstration, or any other of the things that there are, to be established through generic demonstration. For generic demonstration either has certain premises and a certain consequence, or it does not. But if it has certain premises and a certain consequence, it is one of the specific demonstrations. But if it does not have premises and a consequence, then since demonstration does not reach a conclusion without premises and a consequence, generic demonstration will not reach any conclusion – and if it does not reach any conclusion, neither will it reach as a conclusion its own being. (346) If it is agreed, then, that demonstration has to be demonstrated, but it cannot be demonstrated either by generic or by specific demonstration, it is clear that, since nothing else is found besides these ones, we ought to keep the examination of demonstration in suspension of judgment. (347) Then again, even if the first demonstration is demonstrated, it is demonstrated either by a demonstration that is under examination or by one that is not under examination. But not by one that is not under examination; for when the first one has fallen into dispute, every demonstration is under examination. Nor by one that is under examination; for again, if that one is under examination, it ought to be established by another demonstration, and the third one by a fourth, and the fourth by a fifth, and so *ad infinitum*. So it is not possible for demonstration to be secure.

ii. Demetrius' response to this, and a rebuttal of it (348–356)

(348) Demetrios of Laconia, a prominent member of the Epicurean school, used to say that this sort of opposition is easily dismissed. For, he says, if we have established a single specific demonstration (for example, the one that draws the conclusion that there are indivisible elements, or that there is void) and shown that it is secure, in this we will right away also

have generic demonstration as trustworthy. For where there is the specific instance of a certain genus, the genus of which it is the specific instance is undoubtedly found there as well, as we pointed out above. (349) But this, while it seems to be persuasive, is impossible. For, first, no one will let the Laconian establish the specific demonstration if generic demonstration does not subsist first; and just as he himself maintains that if he has the specific demonstration, he immediately has the generic kind as well, so too the skeptics will maintain the need for its genus to be demonstrated first, in order for the specific instance to be trusted. (350) But anyway, even if they permit him this (I mean, establishing some specific demonstration as a way of confirming the generic), some of the schools of the same kind[105] will not keep quiet, but whatever demonstration he offers as trustworthy, they will overturn it, and he will have a large mob of people not letting it be posited. For example, if he takes the demonstration about atoms, an untold number will speak against him; if he takes the one about void, an enormous group will oppose him; and likewise if he takes the one about images. (351) So even if the skeptics go along completely with his choice, he will not be able to make trustworthy a single particular demonstration on account of the conflict among the dogmatists.

Besides, whatever is the firm specific demonstration that he says he will have? It will be either the one that, out of all of them, is acceptable to him in itself, or any one whatever, or the one that is being demonstrated. But to take the one that, out of all of them, is acceptable to him is self-willed and more like a lottery. (352) And if he takes any one whatever, he will be positing all demonstrations – those of the Epicureans on the one side, those of the Stoics and also the Peripatetics on the other – which is absurd. But if he takes the one that is being demonstrated, it is not a demonstration; for if it is being demonstrated, it is under examination, and since it is under examination it cannot be trustworthy, but in need of things to confirm it. Therefore it is not possible to have one of the particular demonstrations as trustworthy.

(353) Then again, the premises of the demonstration of which the Laconian speaks are either disputed and untrustworthy or undisputed and trustworthy. But if they are disputed and untrustworthy, undoubtedly the

---

[105] I.e., other dogmatic schools (see 351).

demonstration made out of them will be untrustworthy for establishing anything. And that they are trustworthy and undisputed is wishful thinking rather than the truth. (354) For if all the things there are are either perceptible or intelligible, the premises of the demonstration should also be either perceptible or intelligible. And whether they are perceptible or intelligible, they are under examination. For perceptible things either exist just as they appear, or are empty effects and figments of thought, or some of them in addition to appearing also are, while others merely appear and do not also exist. And it is possible to see distinguished supporters of each position, (355) seeing that Democritus has upset all perceptible reality, while Epicurus said that every perceptible thing is secure, and the Stoic Zeno made use of a distinction – so that if the premises are perceptible, they are matters of disagreement. Similarly if they turn out to be intelligible; for about these too it is possible to see a great deal of conflict, both in ordinary life and in philosophy, different things being acceptable to different people. (356) Then, in addition to what has been said, if every perceptible thing has its starting-point and source of confirmation from sense-perception, yet the things that we come to know through sense-perception are, as we have argued, matters of disagreement, intelligible things necessarily turn out to be like this as well – so that the premises of the demonstration, whichever side they belong to, are untrustworthy and insecure. And for this reason demonstration is also not trustworthy.

c. Difficulties in supposing that the premises of demonstration are either apparent or unclear (357–366)

(357) And to speak more generally, premises are apparent things, but it is a matter of investigation whether apparent things exist; and things that are under investigation are not premises right away, but need to be confirmed by something. By what, then, are we able to establish the fact that the way what appears does appear is also how it exists? (358) Undoubtedly either through an unclear object or through a clear one. But it is absurd that it should be through an unclear one; for the unclear is so far from being able to uncover anything that, on the contrary, it needs something to display it. (359) But it is much more absurd that it should be through an apparent one; for this is the very thing under investigation, and nothing that is under investigation is capable of confirming itself. It is, therefore, impossible to establish apparent things in order in this way to have demonstration, too,

as trustworthy. (360) But apparent things, say the dogmatists, have to be posited in any case, first because we have nothing more trustworthy than them, and then because the argument that upsets them is turned about by itself. For it does away with them using either an assertion alone, or apparent things, or non-apparent things. But if it uses an assertion, it is untrustworthy; for it is easy to set out the assertion that contradicts it. (361) But if it uses non-apparent things, it is again untrustworthy, wanting to turn about apparent things by means of non-apparent things. But if it upsets apparent things by apparent things, undoubtedly the latter are trustworthy, and so right away apparent things will be trustworthy. So that the argument actually goes against them.[106]

(362) But we argued earlier that apparent things, whether they are perceptible or intelligible, are full of a great deal of conflict both among philosophers and in ordinary life. But for now, against the dilemma laid out the following should be said, that we do not upset apparent things using an assertion or non-apparent things, but by comparing them with themselves. For if perceptible things were found to be in agreement with perceptible things and intelligible with intelligible and perceptible with intelligible, we would perhaps accept that they turn out to be such as they appear. (363) But in fact, since we find undecided conflict in the comparison, in virtue of which some are tossed out by others – given that we cannot posit all of them on account of this conflict, nor can we posit some of them on account of the equal strength of the ones contradicting them, nor can we toss out all of them on account of having nothing more trustworthy than appearing – we have arrived at suspension of judgment. (364) "But the argument that takes its trust from apparent things, in upsetting these tosses itself out as well." But this claim comes from men helping themselves to the point under examination. For the argument is not confirmed by the apparent things; rather, the apparent things get their strength from the argument. (365) And reasonably so; for if they are matters of disagreement (some people saying that they exist, others not), they ought to be established by the argument. And the witnesses to this are none other than the people of a different opinion,[107] <. . .>,[108] but

---

[106] I.e., against the opponents of this argument set out by the dogmatists – namely, the skeptics themselves.

[107] I.e., the proponents of the argument Sextus is attacking.

[108] Mutschmann and others posit a lacuna here; the sense of the missing text would have to be "who do not simply accept" or the like. But Bury's deletion of "but" (*d'*), which would restore the sense without assuming a lacuna, may also be correct.

who want to show by argument, that apparent things are true.[109] (366) Apparent things, therefore, are not more secure than argument; rather, argument is more secure than apparent things, since it makes trustworthy both itself and them.

Of course, if the premises of the demonstration are unclear, and the consequence is also unclear, and again if what consists of unclear things is unclear, then demonstration is unclear and requires something to display its trustworthiness – which is not in the purview of demonstration.

d. Difficulties in supposing that demonstration starts from hypothesis (367–378)

(367) But, they say, one should not ask for a demonstration of everything; one should assume some things by hypothesis, since our argument cannot go forward unless it is granted that something is trustworthy all by itself. But we will say, first of all, that it is not necessary for their dogmatizing arguments to go forward – they are fictitious. (368) Besides, where are they headed? For since apparent things display just that – that they appear – and have no further power to teach us that they also exist, let it be supposed both that the premises of the demonstration appear and similarly that the consequence does. But in this way the conclusion being sought will not be drawn and the truth will not be brought forward, since we remain at the level of mere assertion and an effect on ourselves. And wanting to show that they do not only appear, but also exist, is the mark of men who are not content with what is necessary for normal use, but are eager also to help themselves to whatever possible.

(369) And in general, since it is maintained by the dogmatists that not only demonstration, but virtually the whole of philosophy proceeds from hypothesis, we will try to the extent possible to go through a few points in response to those who assume something by hypothesis. (370) If the things they say they accept by hypothesis are trustworthy because of having been accepted by hypothesis, the opposites of these things will also appear trustworthy when accepted by hypothesis, and in this way we will be positing things that conflict. But if in the latter cases – I mean, the opposites – the hypothesis is weak for the purpose of trust, it will be weak in the former cases as well, so that, again, we will hypothesize neither.

---

[109] With Heintz, I delete as a gloss the words *kai allōs to hoti tois phainomenois dei pisteuein* ("And besides, that one must trust apparent things"); Mutschmann retains them and posits another lacuna immediately after them.

(371) And what someone hypothesizes is either true and such as it is hypothesized to be, or false. And if it is true, the person who hypothesizes it is doing himself an injustice, if indeed, when it was possible for him not to postulate it but to grasp it as true all by itself, he takes refuge in a thing full of suspicion – hypothesis – postulating something that is true all by itself. But if it is false, it is no longer himself, but the nature of things that the person who uses hypothesis is doing an injustice to, expecting what is not so to be conceded to him as if it is so, and forcing us to take what is false as true. (372) Moreover, if one maintains that everything that follows from things assumed by hypothesis is secure, one is putting the whole of philosophical investigation into confusion. For right away we will be hypothesizing that three is four, and drawing the conclusion (as following from it) that six is eight; and this will be true (that is, six being eight).[110] (373) But if they were to say to us that this kind of thing is absurd – for the thing hypothesized has to be firm, in order for what follows from this to be agreed to along with it – they will hear our side as well, as we maintain that nothing ought to be assumed all by itself, but everything posited ought to be posited with accuracy. (374) In addition to this, if the thing hypothesized is firm and secure in so far as it is hypothesized, let the dogmatic philosophers hypothesize not those things from which they conclude what is unclear, but the unclear itself – that is, not the premises of the demonstration but its consequence. But even if they hypothesize this thousands of times, it is not trustworthy, because it is unclear and there is an investigation about it. It is surely clear that if they postulate the premises of the demonstration without demonstration, they are not accomplishing anything for its trustworthiness given the fact that these too are in dispute.

(375) But they typically interrupt, for God's sake, and say that an assurance of the hypothesis' being strong is the fact that the consequence that is drawn from the things assumed by hypothesis is found to be true; for if what follows from these is sound, the things from which it follows are also true and unquestionable. (376) But now, someone will say, by what means are we able to show that what follows from the thing assumed by hypothesis is true? Is it by means of itself or by means of the premises from which it follows? It cannot be by means of itself; for it is unclear. From the premises, then? Not like that either; for it is about these that

---

[110] Following Kochalsky, Mutschmann posits a lacuna at this point; this is unnecessary.

there is the conflict, and they have to be established first. (377) But let us even suppose that what follows from the things assumed by hypothesis actually is true; not even along these lines will the things assumed by hypothesis become true. For if, according to them, true only followed from true, the argument would go forward, so that if what follows from the thing assumed by hypothesis is true, the thing assumed by hypothesis becomes true. (378) But in fact, since they say both that false follows from false and that true follows from false, it is not necessarily the case that if the finisher is true, the leader is also true, but it is possible for the leader to be false while the finisher is true.

e. The reciprocal mode applied to demonstration
and criterion (378–380)
Well then, let this much be said as a "side-task on the journey," as they say,[111] and a parenthetical extra,[112] about how demonstration must not start out from hypothesis.[113] (379) Following this it should be pointed out it also falls into the reciprocal mode, which is even more intractable. For we established earlier that demonstration is an unclear thing, but every unclear thing has to have a judgment upon it, and what has to have a judgment upon it needs a criterion to establish whether it is sound or not. For just as what ought to be measured is not of a nature to be measured without a measure, and nothing that is ruled is ruled without a rule, so what is judged[114] is not scrutinized without a criterion. (380) Since, then, it is a matter of investigation whether there is a criterion, some people saying that there is none, some that there is one, and some keeping this in suspension of judgment, it will again be necessary for the fact that there is a criterion to be demonstrated through some demonstration. But now, in order to have the demonstration as trustworthy, it will be necessary to turn back to the criterion, and so, not having the latter as trustworthy before the former nor the former as secure before the latter, to agree on suspension of judgment about both.

---

[111] See Euripides, *Electra* 509.
[112] With Kochalsky I read *parenthēkē* for the mss. *parenthēkēs*, retained by Mutschmann.
[113] Like the reciprocal mode (mentioned just below), the attack on hypothesis is one of the Five Modes (or standardized ways of inducing suspension of judgment) of the later skeptics, summarized by Sextus at *PH* 1.164–177.
[114] *Krinomenon*, from the verb corresponding to *kritērion*.

f. Difficulties stemmming from the conception
of demonstration (381–390)
(**381**) Along with what has been said, it will be possible to upset demonstration as a result of its conception. Although if it *was* conceived, it
would not definitely be real; for there are many things that are conceived,
as I said, but do not partake of any reality. But in fact, when even the
conception of demonstration is found to be impossible, the hope of its
reality is also undoubtedly cut off. (**382**) Since there are two kinds of
demonstration, then, the generic and the specific, we will right away find
the generic kind inconceivable; for none of us knows generic demonstration nor has ever been able to show anything by this means. (**383**)
And besides, it is worth asking whether this kind of demonstration has
premises and a consequence or not. And if it does not, how can it still be
conceived of as a demonstration, seeing that the concept of any demonstration is not put together apart from its premises and consequence?
But if it has them both – that is, the premises and the consequence –
it is a specific demonstration; (**384**) for if everything that is demonstrated
and everything that demonstrates is a particular, the demonstration too is
necessarily one of the specific ones. But our argument was not about the
specific kind, but about the generic kind; therefore generic demonstration is not conceived. (**385**) Yet neither is the specific kind. For demonstration was said to be an argument that, by means of certain apparent
things, uncovers something unclear by way of conclusive reasoning.[115]
Either, then, the entire compound – that is, what is conceived out of
the premises and the consequence – is a demonstration, or the premises
alone are a demonstration and the consequence is what is demonstrated.
But whichever of these they say, the conception of demonstration is shaky.
(**386**) For if the composite of the premises and the consequence is a demonstration, then necessarily, since it includes something unclear, demonstration must right away be unclear, and being like this it must need some
demonstration, which is absurd. What is constituted out of the premises
and the consequence cannot, then, be a demonstration, seeing that we
conceive demonstration neither as unclear nor as needing demonstration.

(**387**) Besides, demonstration is one of the things in relation to
something; for it does not look toward itself, nor is it conceived

---

[115] Cf. 314.

individually, but it has something of which it is a demonstration. If, then, the consequence is contained within it, and everything that is in relation to something is outside the thing in relation to which it is called "in relation to something," then demonstration is conceived in relation to nothing, since the consequence is included within it. (388) But even if we suppose another consequence outside it, in relation to which the demonstration is conceived, there will then be two consequences in place, first the one that is included in the demonstration, and second the one outside it, in relation to which the demonstration is conceived. But it is absurd to speak of two consequences of one demonstration; it is not the case, therefore, that what is constituted out of premises and consequence is a demonstration. (389) It remains, then, to say that the part consisting just of the premises is a demonstration. Which is silly; for this is not even an argument to begin with, but a deficient object not fit for thought, seeing that no one with any intelligence says that something like "If there is motion, there is void; but there *is* motion" – taken on its own – either is an argument or conveys any thought. (390) If, then, demonstration is conceived neither as the composite of the premises and the consequence nor as the part consisting just of the premises, demonstration is inconceivable.

g. Difficulties in supposing that either demonstration or the thing demonstrated is either clear or unclear (391–395)
(391) In addition, the demonstration that demonstrates is either clear and is a demonstration of a clear thing, or unclear and of an unclear thing, or unclear and of a clear thing, or clear and of an unclear thing. But it is none of these, as we will establish; therefore demonstration is not anything. (392) Now, a demonstration cannot be clear and of a clear thing, since what is clear does not need demonstration, but is known all by itself. Again, a demonstration cannot be unclear and of an unclear thing, in so far as, if it is unclear, it will itself need something to display it, and will not be capable of displaying something else. (393) Likewise neither will it be unclear and of a clear thing. For both impasses will come together; the thing being demonstrated will not need any demonstration, since it is clear, and the demonstration will have need of something to establish it, since it is unclear. So that there could never be a demonstration that is unclear and of a clear thing. (394) It remains to say that it is clear and of an

unclear thing – but that is also something intractable. For if demonstration is not one of the things conceived individually and absolutely, but one of the things in relation to something, and things in relation to something, as we showed in our examination of the sign,[116] are apprehended together with one another, and things apprehended together are not uncovered by one another but are clear by themselves, demonstration will not be a clear demonstration of an unclear thing given that the latter, being apprehended together with it, strikes us by means of itself. **(395)** If, then, demonstration comes out neither as apparent and demonstrative of an apparent thing, nor as unclear and of an unclear thing, nor as unclear and of an apparent thing, nor as apparent and of an unclear thing, and besides these there is nothing, it has to be said that demonstration is nothing.

h. Difficulties stemming from Stoic theories (396–447)
(396) Following what has been said, since the Stoics seem to have worked out the modes of demonstration with the most precision, all right: let us go through a few points in reply to them, establishing the fact that, as far as their hypotheses go, everything is probably inapprehensible, but more specifically, demonstration is inapprehensible.

i. Stoic account of apprehension in terms of appearance (397–399)
(397) Well then, apprehension is, as one can learn from them, assent to an apprehensive appearance – which seems to be a twofold affair, and to have one part that is involuntary, another that is voluntary and lies in the power of our own judgment. For having appearances is unwilled, and it does not lie in the power of the person affected, but in the power of the thing producing the appearances, that he is so disposed – for example, whitely when the color white impinges on him, or sweetly when something sweet is brought to his sense of taste; but assenting to this movement does lie in the power of the person receiving the appearance. **(398)** So that apprehension is preceded by apprehensive appearance, to which it is the assent. And apprehensive appearance is preceded by appearance, of which it is a species. For if there is not appearance, neither is there apprehensive appearance, in so far as, if there is not the genus, neither is there the species;

[116] Cf. 174.

and if there is not apprehensive appearance, neither is there assent to it. And if assent to the apprehensive appearance is taken away, apprehension is also taken away. **(399)** Hence if it is shown that there cannot come to be an appearance of demonstration, according to the Stoics, it will be clear that neither will any apprehensive appearance of demonstration subsist – and if there is not this, nor is there assent to it, which is apprehension.

ii. Difficulties in supposing that there can be an appearance (and therefore, in Stoic terms, an apprehension) of demonstration (400–410)

(400) That there is not, according to the Stoics, an appearance of demonstration is shown first by the rather common disagreement among them on what appearance is. For while they have agreed to the extent of saying that it is an imprinting on the leading part, they disagree about this very imprinting, Cleanthes understanding it in the strict sense as the kind conceived with hollows and projections, Chrysippus more loosely as standing for alteration.[117] **(401)** Now, if there is up to now no agreement about imprinting even among themselves, necessarily appearance too, being up to this point a matter of disagreement, should be kept in suspension of judgment – and so should demonstration, which depends on it. **(402)** Then again, let appearance be allowed to be whatever they want, whether an imprinting in the strict sense with hollows and projections or an alteration; how this becomes an appearance of demonstration is a most intractable question. For it is clear that the thing that appears ought to act, and the leading part that has the appearances ought to be affected, in order for the former to imprint and the latter to be imprinted on; it is not likely that appearance happens in another way. **(403)** Well, perhaps someone will agree that the leading part can be affected, although it should not be agreed to; but how is demonstration likely to act? For it is either a body, according to them, or incorporeal. **(404)** It is not a body, for it consists of incorporeal sayables. But if it is incorporeal, then since incorporeals, according to them, are of a nature neither to do anything nor to be affected, demonstration too, being incorporeal, will not be able to do anything. And if it does not do anything, neither will it imprint on the leading part, and if it does not imprint on it, neither will it make an appearance of itself on it – **(405)** and if this is so, not an apprehensive appearance either. But if there is no apprehensive appearance of it in the

[117] Cf. 1.228–231.

leading part, nor will there be apprehension of it. (406) According to the Stoics' technicalities, therefore, demonstration is inapprehensible.

Furthermore, it is not possible to say that incorporeals do not do anything or cause appearances in us, but that we are the ones who get appearances on the basis of them. For if it is agreed that no end result is brought about without an agent and a thing affected, then the appearance of demonstration, being an end result, ought not to be conceived without both the agent and the thing affected. (407) Now, that the leading part is the thing affected, the Stoic philosophers have admitted; but what it might be that imprints and does something, according to them, is worth learning. For either demonstration is what imprints on the leading part and activates the appearance of itself, or the leading part imprints on and causes appearances in itself. But demonstration cannot be capable of imprinting on the leading part; for it is incorporeal, and what is incorporeal, according to them, neither does anything nor is affected. (408) But if the leading part imprints on itself, either what imprints is of the same kind as the imprint, or the imprint is one kind of thing, and what imprints is something unlike it. And if it is unlike, then the underlying objects will be one thing and the things the appearances are of will be another[118] – which again closes the Stoics off in the inapprehensibility of everything. But if the imprint is like the thing that imprints, then since the leading part imprints on itself, it will grasp an appearance not of demonstration but of itself – which is again absurd.

(409) But they try to make us comfortable with their claim by means of examples. For, they say, just as the gym teacher or the drill sergeant sometimes takes the boy's hands to get him in order and teach him to go through certain motions, and at other times he stands off and goes through some kind of orderly motion, presenting himself for the boy to

---

[118] This must be the sense of the Greek. But it is hard to understand the reasoning. "What imprints" is (*ex hypothesi*) the leading part of the soul, and "the imprint" is the appearance of demonstration. We might understand "the underlying objects" to be leading parts of the soul (in different people) – that is, what the imprints are imprinted on – and "the things the appearances are of" are naturally taken to be demonstrations. But why would the distinctness of these two necessarily result in inapprehensibility? Perhaps because if the medium in which the imprints are made is different in kind from the things of which they are the imprints, the imprints cannot be assumed to be reliable guides to the character of these things. Alternatively, we might understand "the underlying objects" to refer to the actual objects of the appearances – that is, demonstrations – and "the things the appearances are of" as the *content* of those appearances. But that is a more forced reading of the latter phrase; and in any case, it is not clear why the distinctness of the imprint and what imprints would show that the content of the appearances was distinct from their objects.

imitate, so too some of the things that appear, like white and black and generally body, create their imprint in the leading part by, as it were, touching and handling it, while others, such as incorporeal sayables, <do not>[119] have a nature like this – the leading part gets appearances on the basis of them but not by them. (410) The people who say this do use a persuasive example, but they are not conclusive on the matter at hand. For the gym teacher and the drill sergeant are corporeal, and in virtue of this can create an appearance in the boy; but demonstration is incorporeal, and this is how there arose an investigation as to whether it can imprint on the leading part with an appearance. So that the point originally under investigation has not been demonstrated by them.

iii. Stoic interrelations among conclusive, true, and demonstrative arguments (411–423)

(411) So, now that these points have been brought forward, let us move on and look at whether the promise of demonstration (as they see it) can be preserved in terms of dialectical theory. They say that three kinds of argument are interconnected – the conclusive and the true and the demonstrative. (412) The demonstrative is always both true and conclusive; the true is always conclusive but not necessarily also demonstrative; and the conclusive is neither always true nor always demonstrative. (413) An argument (when it is day) such as "If it is night, it is dark; but it *is* night; therefore it is dark" does reach its conclusion, because it is put forward in a sound pattern, but it is not true, since it has a false second premise, the minor premise "But it *is* night." (414) But one like this (when it is day): "If it is day, it is light; but it *is* day; therefore it is light," is both conclusive and true because it both is put forward in a sound pattern and reaches a true conclusion by means of true premises.

(415) And they say that the conclusive argument is judged to be conclusive when the conclusion follows from the conjunction of the premises, like this kind of argument (when it is day): "If it is night, it is dark; but it *is* night; therefore it is dark"; although it is not true because it leads to a falsehood, we say that it is conclusive. (416) For if we make a conjunction of the premises, as follows: "It is night, and if it is night, it is dark," we create a conditional that begins with a conjunction like this and finishes

---

[119] With Bury I add *ou*. Mutschmann, following Kochalsky, instead posits a lacuna after "have a nature like this" (where the nature in question was specified).

with the conclusion – <namely, the> following: "<If> it is night, and if it is night it is dark, <it is dark>."[120] For this conditional is true because it never begins with something true and finishes with something false. For when it is day it will begin with the false "It is night, and if it is night, it is dark," and will finish with the false "It is dark," and so will be true; and if it is night it will begin with something true and finish with something true, and will for this very reason be true. (417) The conclusive argument is sound, then, when after we conjoin the premises and create a conditional that begins with the conjunction of the premises and finishes with the conclusion, this conditional is itself found to be true.

(418) And the true argument is judged to be true not from the mere fact that the conditional that begins with the conjunction of the premises and finishes with the conclusion is true, but also from the fact that the conjunction made by means of the premises is sound – as, if one of these is found to be false, the argument necessarily becomes false. For example (when it is night), one such as "If it is day, it is light; but it *is* day; therefore it is light" is false because of having the false premise "It is day." (419) But, while the conjunction made by means of the premises that has one of those premises ("It is day") false is false, the conditional that begins with the conjunction of the premises and finishes with the conclusion will be true. For it never begins with a true proposition and finishes with a false one, but at night it begins with a conjunction that is false, while in the day time it finishes with a true proposition just as it begins with a true one. (420) And again, an argument such as "If it is day, it is light; but it *is* light; therefore it is day" is false, since it can lead us by means of true premises to falsehood. (421) But now, if we examine it, it is possible for the conjunction made by means of the premises to be true – namely, the following: "It is light, and if it is day, it is light" – but for the conditional that begins with the conjunction of the premises and finishes with the conclusion to be false – namely, the following: "If it is light, and if it is day, it is light, <it is day>."[121] For this conditional, when it is night, can

<hr/>

[120] I follow Heintz's restoration of the text (borrowing from von Arnim): *to sumperasma, <hoion to> toiouton, <ei> nux esti kai ei nux esti, skotos esti, <skotos esti>*. Mutschmann (following Kochalsky) deletes *nux esti kai ei nux esti* and leaves the remaining text unchanged. But the following sentences specify the antecedent and the consequent of this more complicated conditional (416), and explain how to construct the conditional corresponding to the argument (417). For a similar case, cf. n. 76.

[121] With Heintz (following Kochalsky), I add *hēmera estin* to the end of this sentence. I do not, however, follow Heintz and Mutschmann in adding *<estin>* after *pseudos*. This latter addition

begin with a conjunction that is true but finish with the false "It is day," and for this reason be false. So that the argument becomes true not just when the conjunction is true, nor when the conditional is true, but when both of them are true.

(**422**) But the demonstrative argument differs from the true one, because the true one can have all its components plain (I mean, the premises and the consequence), but the demonstrative one professes to have something more – I mean, the fact that the consequence, which is unclear, is uncovered by the premises. (**423**) Hence one such as "If it is day, it is light; but it *is* day; therefore it is light," since it has premises and a consequence that are plain, is true and not demonstrative, whereas one such as "If she has milk in her breasts, she has conceived; but she does have milk in her breasts; therefore she has conceived," in addition to being true is also demonstrative. For it has a conclusion ("Therefore she has conceived") that is unclear, and uncovers this by means of the premises.

iv. Difficulties with conclusive argument, and therefore (in Stoic terms) with demonstrative argument (424–428)

(**424**) There are, then, three types of argument, the conclusive and the true and the demonstrative. If some argument is demonstrative, it is, as a precondition, true and conclusive; if an argument is true, it is not necessarily demonstrative, but it is definitely conclusive; but if one is conclusive, it is not definitely true nor definitely demonstrative. (**425**) Since, then, the property of being conclusive has to be an attribute of all of them in common, if we show that the conclusive argument is undiscoverable by the Stoics, we will have shown that the true and the demonstrative arguments cannot be found either. (**426**) And that there is no conclusive argument is easy to recognize. For if they say that there is a conclusive argument whenever the conditional that begins with the conjunction of its premises and finishes with its consequence is true, the true conditional will have to have been judged upon beforehand, and then the conclusive argument that is thought to depend on this will have to be firmly grasped.

would have Sextus saying that the conditional *is* false (rather than that it is possible for it be false). On the Diodoran view of the truth-conditions for conditionals that seems to be presupposed in this passage (cf. 115–117), this is indeed what he should say. But it is clear from the Greek that this part of the sentence is still governed by "it is possible." See also the next sentence, where it is again said that the conditional *can* be false.

(427) But the sound conditional is undecided up to now; hence neither can the conclusive argument be known. For just as, when a measure does not stay put but shifts sometimes one way and sometimes another, the thing being measured does not stay put either, so, since the sound conditional is as it were the measure of the argument's reaching its conclusion, it will follow that, if the former is undecided, the latter is not clear either. (428) But the Stoics' introductory works teach us that the sound conditional is undecided; in these they put forward many judgments about it that are in disagreement and up to now undecided. Hence, if this is how the conclusive argument turns out to be, the true argument is undoubtedly like this as well, and for this reason the demonstrative argument also should be kept in suspension of judgment.

v. Stoic distinction between "terminating" and "non-terminating" arguments; the varieties of non-terminating arguments (428–434)

But even if we back off from this objection and go to the technicalities about terminating and non-terminating arguments,[122] putting together the demonstrative argument will be found to be impossible. (429) It is not necessary now to go through the terminating ones, about which there is a lot of precise investigation, but about the non-terminating arguments a certain amount should be pointed out. They say, then, that the non-terminating argument comes about in four ways, either by disconnectedness or by redundancy or by being put forward in a bad pattern or by deficiency. (430) By disconnectedness, when the premises have no common ground or connectedness with one another or with the consequence, as in the case of an argument such as "If it is day, it is light; but wheat *is* being sold in the market; therefore it is light." For we see that in this case neither does "It is day" have any common spirit or conjunction with "Wheat is being sold in the market," nor does either of them with "Therefore it is light," but each is disconnected from the others.[123]

(431) The argument becomes non-terminating by redundancy, when something extraneous and superfluous is admitted into the premises, as in the following case: "If it is day, it is light; but it *is* day, and virtue is

---

[122] Cf. n. 52.

[123] It seems very odd to claim that "It is day" and "It is light" have no connection, especially given the prevalence of illustrative arguments using these two elements. The parallel passage of *PH* (2.146) has "Dion is walking" as the conclusion, which is much more appropriate to the context. But there is no sign of any textual difficulty in the present passage (and cf. 435).

also beneficial; therefore it is light." For the fact that virtue is beneficial is admitted superfluously along with the other premises, given that, when it is taken away, it is possible for the consequence "Therefore it is light" to be reached by means of the remaining ones, "If it is day, it is light" and "But it *is* day."

(**432**) The argument becomes non-terminating because of being put forward in a bad pattern, when it is put forward in some pattern that is viewed as violating the sound patterns. For example, since a pattern such as "If the first, the second; but the first; therefore the second" is sound, (**433**) and so is one such as "If the first, the second; but not the second; therefore not the first," we say that one put forward in a pattern such as "If the first, the second; but not the first; therefore not the second" is non-terminating, not because it is impossible for an argument that reaches a true conclusion by means of true premises to be put forward in such a pattern (for it *is* possible – for example, one such as "If three is four, six is eight; but three is *not* four; therefore six is not eight"), but because some bad arguments can be devised using it – for example, one like this: "If it is day, it is light; but it is *not* day; therefore is it not light."

(**434**) And the argument becomes non-terminating by deficiency, when one of the conclusive premises is missing something. For example, "Either wealth is a bad thing or wealth is a good thing; but wealth is not a bad thing; therefore wealth is a good thing." For wealth's being an indifferent thing is missing in the disjunction, so that the sound version is, rather, like this: "Either wealth is a good thing or a bad thing or an indifferent thing; but wealth is neither a good thing nor a bad thing; therefore it is an indifferent thing."

vi. Difficulties with all forms of non-terminating argument; inference that terminating and therefore demonstrative arguments are also unknown (435–447)

(**435**) Well, such are the technicalities in place among the Stoics. But it may be that, as far as they are concerned, an argument cannot be judged non-terminating – even, for instance, the one with disconnectedness, as follows: "If it is day, it is light; but wheat *is* being sold in the market; therefore it is light." For that the premises are disconnected, and have no common ground either with one another or with the consequence, they say either in a bare assertion or establishing the point through some technical and teacherly approach. (**436**) But if it by an undemonstrated assertion, it is easy to oppose them with an assertion, which asserts that every argument said to be non-terminating by way of disconnectedness does terminate; for if they can be trusted on the basis of a bare assertion, the people who say the opposite can also be trustworthy when they bring forward their equally strong assertion. But if it is by teaching this by a method, let us investigate what this method may be. (437) And if they say that an indication of the argument that is non-terminating by way of disconnectedness is the fact that its conclusion does not follow in every case from the conjunction of its premises, and that the conditional that begins with the conjunction of the premises and finishes with the conclusion is not sound, we will say that they again fall into the original impasse. For if, in order for us to learn the argument that is non-terminating by way of disconnectedness, we need to have the sound conditional decided, but we do not have this decided up to now, we definitely cannot come to know the argument that is non-terminating by way of disconnectedness either.

(438) But there is a second mode of non-terminating argument, the one by way of redundancy, when something extraneous is admitted into the premises, which is redundant for getting to the conclusion. But as far as this is concerned, the argument put forward in the first mode[124] will have to be non-terminating by way of redundancy, since the turning premise[125] in it is redundant. And we will know this when we have put the arguments side by side. (439) For they say that one like this is non-terminating – "If it is day, it is light; but it *is* day, and virtue is also beneficial; therefore it is light." For in this case "virtue is beneficial" is redundant for getting to the conclusion, because when it is taken away the consequence can be reached without deficiency from the two remaining premises. (440) In reply, then, the skeptics will say that, if an argument is non-terminating by way of redundancy in which, when one premise is taken away, the consequence is reached from the remaining ones, it has to be said that the argument put forward in the first mode, as follows: "If it is day, it is light; but it *is* day; therefore it is light," is also non-terminating. For its turning premise, "If it is day, it is light," is redundant for getting to its conclusion, and "Therefore it is light" can be reached from "It is day" alone.

---

[124] Here Sextus is referring to the first indemonstrable (i.e., in our terms, modus ponens); cf. 224, 227. This is confusing given that he is currently enumerating modes of non-terminating argument.

[125] *Tropikon*, a Stoic term for conditionals (or, on one account, conditionals and disjunctions). See [Ammonius], *On Aristotle's Prior Analytics* p. 68, 4ff. (= *SVF* 2.236), Philoponus, *On Aristotle's Prior Analytics* p. 243, 6–7.

(441) This conclusion is both clear all by itself, and can be supported from its following in relation to the latter point.[126] For either they will say that its being light follows from its being day, or that it does not follow. And if it follows, then if "It is day" has been agreed to be true, "It is light" is reached right away, since it follows necessarily from it – and this is the conclusion. (442) But if it does not follow, it will not follow in the case of the conditional either, and for this reason the conditional will be false, since its finisher does not follow from its leader. So that, as far as the aforementioned technicalities are concerned, we have one of two things: the argument put forward in the first mode is found to be either non-terminating, since its turning premise is redundant, or absolutely false because of its turning premise being false. (443) For to say that single-premised arguments are not acceptable to Chrysippus (which perhaps some people will say against this objection) is completely silly. For it is not necessary either to trust Chrysippus' utterances like deliverances of the Delphic oracle, nor to pay attention to the testimony of men . . . from a witness who says the opposite;[127] for Antipater, one of the most prominent men in the Stoic school, said that it was possible to put together single-premised arguments.

(444) In addition, an argument was said to be non-terminating in a third mode through being put forward in a bad pattern. Again, then, either they will satisfy themselves with a mere assertion when they say that an argument is put forward in a bad pattern, or they will make a case for this. And if they satisfy themselves with an assertion, we too will put an assertion up against it, one that says that it was *not* put forward in a bad pattern. (445) And if they make use of an argument, it is surely a true one. But by what means is it shown that this argument (I mean, the one that shows that some argument is put forward in a bad pattern) is true? Clearly, from its being put forward in a sound pattern. So in order for the argument put forward in a bad pattern to be recognized as having been put forward in a bad pattern, a sound argument has to be made use of; and in order for this to be sound, it has to be put forward in a sound pattern. And for this reason, since neither can the sound argument be guaranteed

---

[126] With Heintz I read *ekeino* for the mss. reading *ekeinous*.

[127] The gap in this sentence is filled in the mss. by *eis oikeian aporēsin*, "into an impasse of their own." Clearly the text is corrupt – the sentence as it stands yields no coherent sense – and minor alterations do not seem to improve it (*pace* LS vol. 1, p. 216). At the same time, the general point is clear enough: why trust Chrysippus on this point any more than another member of his own school who says the opposite?

as sound before its pattern, nor can the pattern be guaranteed as being a sound pattern before the argument that judges upon it, the reciprocal mode arises, which is most intractable.

(446) Against the remaining class of non-terminating arguments – that is, the one due to deficiency – we have more or less spoken already. For if the completed argument is undiscoverable, as we pointed out above, the deficient one must also be unknowable. But the completed argument *is* undiscoverable, as we showed; therefore the deficient one will also be unknowable.

(447) If, however, there are four modes in which, according to the Stoics, an argument becomes non-terminating, and we have shown in each of these cases that the non-terminating arguments are not known, it will follow that the terminating argument, too, is unknown. And if this is not known, the demonstrative argument will also be undiscoverable.

i. Difficulties stemming from the unclarity of the conditional premises of demonstrations (448–452)

(448) In addition to this, in the case of every true argument the premises have to be decided on (for when these are agreed, the consequence is accepted as following from them), but in the case of demonstration the premises are undecided, as we will establish;[128] therefore demonstration will not be able to be a true argument. (449) For, as we showed earlier, they maintain that the conditional is sound when it begins with a true proposition and finishes with a true one, or when it begins with a false one and finishes with a false one, or when it begins with a false one and finishes with a true one, and is false in one way, when it begins with a true one and finishes with a false one. And since this is so, the conditional will be found undecided in the case of demonstration. (450) For in every case it begins with the minor premise and finishes with the consequence, as is the case for arguments such as "If there is motion, there is void; but there *is* motion; therefore there is void." For there the conditional begins with the minor premise "There is motion" and finishes with the consequence "There is void." (451) Either, then, the consequence is a matter that is clear and known to us, or unclear and unknown. And if it is clear and known, the argument is no longer demonstrative, since it consists of components that are all clear – both the premises and the consequence. But if it is

---

[128] With Heintz I read *parastēsomen* for the mss. *parestēsamen*.

unclear, necessarily the conditional becomes undecided. (**452**) For, on the one side, what it begins with is known to us (for it is clear), and on the other, what it finishes with is not known because of its unclarity. But if we do not know whether something like this is true or false, we cannot decide on the conditional. And if this is undecided the argument, too, becomes bad.

j. Difficulties stemming from the relative status
of demonstration (453–462)
(**453**) Moreover, demonstration is among the things in relation to something. But things in relation to something are only conceived – they are not also real; so demonstration too is only in conception and not in reality. And that things in a certain state in relation to something are in fact held only in conception, and do not also have reality, it is possible to explain from the dogmatists' confession. (**454**) For in sketching the "in relation to something" they are in agreement in saying "In relation to something is what is conceived in relation to another thing." But if it had a share in reality, they would not have presented it like that, but rather like this: "In relation to something is what has reality in relation to another thing." Therefore the "in relation to something" does not exist at all in the things that there are.[129]

(**455**) Besides, nothing that is real can undergo any change or alteration without an effect on it. For example, the color white cannot become black without being turned around and changing, and black cannot change into another color while remaining black, and likewise sweet cannot become bitter while lying unaffected and unaltered. (**456**) So that nothing that is real undergoes change into something else without an effect on it. But the "in relation to something" changes without an effect on it or any alteration occurring in it. For example, when a cubit-long piece of wood is put up against another cubit-long piece, it is said to be equal to it, but if the other one is two cubits long it is no longer equal but unequal, even though no turning or alteration occurred in it. And if we were to conceive someone pouring water from a pitcher, this person will be said to be pouring in if another pitcher has been placed below it, but pouring out if it has not been, although it has itself undergone no turning or alteration. (**457**) So that if it is an attribute of what is real not to submit to a change without

---

[129] I retain the mss. *to*; Mutschmann (following Heintz) alters to *tōn*.

being affected, but the "in relation to something" has no such attribute, it has to be said that the "in relation to something" is not real.[130] (459) But if the "in relation to something" is real and does not have mere conception, a single thing will be opposites. But it is absurd to say that one thing is opposites; therefore the "in relation to something" is not real, but is only conceived. For again, the cubit-long body is called greater if juxtaposed with one half a cubit long, but smaller if juxtaposed with one two cubits long. But for the same thing at the same time to be both greater and smaller – that is, opposites – is something impossible. For it can perhaps be conceived, in terms of the comparison to one thing and to another, but it is not possible for it to be and to be real. Therefore things in relation to something are not real.

(460) Anyway, if there are things in relation to something, there is something that is the same and opposite to itself. But this is *not* the case; therefore it has to be said that in this way, too, the "in relation to something" is not real. Besides, if the "in relation to something" is real, there will be something opposite to itself. But it is not reasonable that there should be anything that is opposite to itself; neither is it reasonable, then, that the "in relation to something" is real. (461) For above is opposite to below, and the same thing is above in relation to what lies under it and below in relation to what lies over it. And if there are going to be three things, above and below and in the middle of above and below, the middle will be above in relation to what lies under it, but below in relation to what lies over it, and the same thing will be above and below – which is impossible. Therefore the "in relation to something" is not real. But if the "in relation to something" is real, the same thing will be above and below. And for this reason, even if there is such a thing, the same thing is called above and below in terms of its state in relation to one thing or another. (458) Along with this, the "in relation to something" is separate from itself; for above is separate from below.[131] The same thing, therefore, will be separate from itself, which is the most absurd thing of all.

(462) But if things in relation to something are unreal, demonstration, which is a thing in relation to something, will definitely be unreal as

[130] I transpose section 458; see below, n. 131.
[131] With Kochalsky I transpose this short section (consisting of just this sentence – the next sentence continues section 461) from its place in the mss., and alter *tou* to *heautou*. The sentence makes no sense in its original context, but clearly belongs to the topic in this context. Admittedly it makes for a certain repetitiveness; but this paragraph is already full of glaring repetitions (see especially 460), probably a result of incomplete editing.

well. But things in relation to something *have* been shown to be unreal. Therefore demonstration too will be something unreal.

k. Dogmatic counter-argument to the effect that skeptical arguments are self-refuting (463–469)

(463) Well then, these are the kinds of things said in favor of there being no demonstration; but let us also look at the opposing argument. For the dogmatic philosophers think that the argument[132] maintaining that there is no demonstration is turned about by itself, and determines demonstration[133] by the very means by which it does away with it. Hence, setting themselves against the skeptics, they say: "The person who says that demonstration is nothing says that demonstration is nothing either with the use of a bare and undemonstrated assertion, or by demonstrating this with an argument. (464) And if it is with the use of a bare assertion, none of those receiving the demonstration[134] will believe him, since he is using a bare assertion, but he will be stopped by the opposing assertion, when someone says that there is demonstration. But if it is by demonstrating that there is no demonstration (their words), he has right away agreed that there is demonstration; for the argument that shows that there is no demonstration is a demonstration of there being demonstration. (465) And generally the argument against demonstration either is a demonstration or is not a demonstration; and if it is not a demonstration it is untrustworthy, while if it is a demonstration, there is demonstration."

(466) And some people also put forward the following argument: "If there is demonstration, there is demonstration; if there is not demonstration, there is demonstration. But either there is demonstration or there is not; therefore there is demonstration." And in fact, the attractiveness of the premises of this argument is obvious. For the first conditional – "If there is demonstration, there is demonstration" – being a differentiated proposition,[135] is true; for its second component follows from its first, since it is not distinct from it. And the second conditional – "If there is not demonstration, there is demonstration" – is again sound. For from

---

[132] With Heintz I retain *logon* (present in one manuscript – the others have *logoi*, bracketed by Mutschmann) but transpose it to after *ton axiounta mē einai apodeixin.*

[133] I.e., establishes (contrary to the argument's proponents) that there *is* such a thing.

[134] A misleading choice of term, since the argument presents demonstration and bare assertion as alternatives.

[135] Cf. 108–109 and n. 49.

there not being demonstration, which is the leader, there being demonstration follows; (**467**) for the very argument showing that there is not demonstration, since it is demonstrative, confirms that there is demonstration. And the disjunction "Either there is demonstration or there is not demonstration," since it is a disjunction of contradictories – there being demonstration or there not being – ought to have one component true and for this reason be true. So that since the premises are true, the consequence is also drawn. (**468**) It is also possible to teach in another way that it follows from them. For if the disjunction is true when it has one of its components true, whichever of these we suppose is true, the consequence will be drawn. Let us suppose first that the component that is true is there being demonstration. Then, since this is the leader in the first conditional, the finisher in the first conditional will follow from it; but it finished with "There is demonstration," which is also the consequence. Therefore if it is a given that there being demonstration is true in the disjunction, the consequence of the argument will follow. (**469**) And the same mode of persuasion applies in the case of the remaining proposition, there not being demonstration; for it led in the second conditional <and>[136] had the consequence of the argument following from it.

l. Skeptical replies to the counter-argument (470–481)
(**470**) This is what the dogmatists' opposition is like; and the skeptics' way of meeting it is brief. For they will say: if it is not possible to answer the question in which they asked whether the argument against demonstration is a demonstration or not a demonstration, they ought to be considerate if they are not in a position to answer such an intractable question. (**471**) But if what they are ordering the skeptics to do is easy, let them do this thing that they treat as easy, and answer as to whether they say that the argument against demonstration is a demonstration or not a demonstration. For if it is not a demonstration, it is not possible to teach from it that there is demonstration, nor to say that, because this argument is a demonstration, there will be demonstration; for they have agreed that it is not a demonstration. (**472**) But if it is a demonstration, undoubtedly it has its premises and consequence true; for it is with the truth of these that demonstration is conceived. But its consequence is that there

---

[136] With Kochalsky I add the supplement *kai*, which is the minimum needed to complete the sense. But Mutschmann may be right that a longer passage has been lost. In any case the general purport of this section is clear.

is no demonstration; therefore it is *true* that there is no demonstration, and its contradictory, that there is demonstration, is false. For wanting in this way to demonstrate that the argument against demonstration is demonstrative, they no more posit it[137] than do away with it.

(473) However, if the skeptics have to answer for themselves, they will answer in a safe way. For they will say that the argument against demonstration is merely persuasive, and that for the moment it persuades them and induces assent, but that they do not know whether it will also be like this in the future given the fickle character of human thought. For when the answer comes in this way the dogmatist will have nothing further to say. For either he will teach that the argument produced against demonstration is not true, or he will establish the following: that he does not persuade the skeptic. (474) But if he shows the first, he is not in conflict with the skeptic, since the latter does not take a firm stand, either, on the truth of this argument, but merely says that it is persuasive. (475) And if he does the second he will be rash, wanting to overthrow by argument an effect on another person. For just as no one can persuade the person who is glad with an argument that he is not glad, or the person who is grieving that he is not grieving, neither can one persuade the person who is persuaded that he is not persuaded. (476) In addition, if the skeptics made a strong statement, with assent, to the effect that demonstration is nothing, perhaps they would be turned away from this position by the person who teaches that there is demonstration. But in fact, since they engage in a bare positing of the arguments against demonstration, without assenting to them, they are so far from being damaged by those who construct the opposite case that, rather, they are helped. (477) For if the arguments produced against demonstration have remained unrefuted, and the arguments taken up in favor of there being demonstration are also strong, let us attach ourselves neither to one set nor to the other, but agree to suspend judgment. (478) And if the argument against demonstration is agreed to be demonstrative, the dogmatists are not helped on this account toward there being demonstration, as we have already pointed out; for it concludes that there is *not* demonstration, and if this is true it becomes false that there is demonstration.

(479) Yes, they say, but the argument that concludes that there is not demonstration, being demonstrative, tosses itself out. To which it should

[137] I.e., demonstration.

be said that it does not definitely toss itself out. For many things are said that allow for an exception, and just as we say that Zeus is the father of gods and humans, allowing for the exception of himself (for of course he is not his own father), so too, when we say that there is no demonstration, we say this allowing for the exception of the argument showing that there is no demonstration; for this alone is a demonstration. (480) And even if it does toss itself out, that there is demonstration is not thereby ratified. For there are many things that put themselves in the same condition as they put other things. For example, just as fire after consuming the wood destroys itself as well, and just as purgatives after driving the fluids out of bodies eliminate themselves as well, so too the argument against demonstration, after doing away with all demonstration, can cancel itself as well. (481) And again, just as it is not impossible for the person who has climbed to a high place by a ladder to knock over the ladder with his foot after his climb, so it is not unlikely that the skeptic too, having got to the accomplishment of his task by a sort of step-ladder – the argument showing that there is not demonstration – should do away with this argument.

D. *Transition to* Against the Physicists *(481)*

But now, having created so many impasses about the methods used in the area of logic, we will move on to the investigation directed against the physicists.

Glossary

This Glossary includes recurring and philosophically significant terms in the translation. In most cases only one member of a group of cognate terms is included. The correspondences listed here are not absolutely invariable. In some cases a Greek word will occasionally be translated by something other than the English equivalent(s) listed here; and occasionally an English word will be used to to render a Greek word other than (and not cognate with) the Greek equivalent(s) listed here. Divergences from Annas and Barnes' translation of *PH* are noted in parentheses by "A/B," followed by their preferred alternative(s). They are not always included, however, when the word in question is rare in *PH* or its usage or context is significantly different in the two works. When no Annas and Barnes translation is noted, the reason is sometimes because the word does not appear at all in *PH*. (Differences in vocabulary between the two works are sometimes of considerable interest.)

1. English–Greek

apparent (thing)	*phainomenon*
appearance	*phantasia*
apprehension	*antilēpsis, katalēpsis*
argument	*logos*
assent	*sugkatathesis*
assertion	*apophasis*
attribute	*sumbebēkos*
bad	*mochthēros*

be	*eimi, huparchō*
being	*ousia*
be real	*huparchō*
clear	*prodēlos*
clever	*sunetos*
composition	*sustasis*
concept	*noēsis*
conception	*ennoia, epinoia*
conclude	*sun(eis)ago*
conclusion	*sumperasma*
conclusive	*sunaktikos*
condition	*diathesis*
conditional	*sunēmmenon*
conjunction (i.e., proposition of the form P & Q)	*sumpeplegmenon, sumplokē*
conjunction (i.e., the part of speech)	*sundesmos*
consequence	*epiphora*
consistency	*akolouthia*
contradict	*antikeimai*
criterion	*kritērion*
deduction	*sullogismos*
demonstration	*apodeixis*
demonstrative reference	*deixis*
disagree	*diaphōnō*
disjunction	*diezeugmenon*
do away with	*anairō*
doctrine	*dogma*
dogmatist	*dogmatikos*
effect (on us)	*pathos*
end	*telos*
equal strength	*isostheneia*
evident	*sumphanēs*
examine	*zētō*
exist	*hupokeimai*

false(hood)	*pseudos*
finisher	*lēgon*
following	*akolouthia*
generic	*genikos*
grasp	*lambanō*
grasping	*antilēpsis*
human being	*anthrōpos*
impasse	*aporia*
imprinting	*tupōsis*
impulse	*hormē*
inapprehensible	*akatalēptos*
inconclusive	*asunaktos*
incorporeal	*asōmatos*
indicative	*endeiktikos*
inferior	*phaulos*
inquire	*skeptomai*
in relation to something	*pros ti*
insight	*phronēsis*
intellect	*nous*
intelligence	*noēsis*
intelligible	*noētos*
intractable	*aporos*
investigate	*zētō*
judge	*krinō*
knowledge	*epistēmē, gnōsis*
leader	*hēgoumenon*
leading part (of the soul)	*hēgemonikon*
look into	*skeptomai*
minor premise	*proslēpsis*
mode	*tropos*

motion	*kinēsis*
movement	*kinēma*
negative	*apophatikos*
non-apparent	*aphanēs*
non-existent	*anuparktos*
non-rational	*alogos*
non-subsistent	*anupostatos*
opinion	*doxa*
peculiarity	*idiōma*
persuasive	*pithanos*
plain experience	*enargeia*
preconception	*prolēpsis*
premise	*lēmma*
principle	*archē*
property	*idiōma*
proposition	*axiōma*
reason	*logos*
reciprocal (mode)	*di'allēlōn (tropos)*
recollective	*hupomnēstikos*
reliable	*pistos*
rule	*kanōn*
ruler	*kanōn*
sayable	*lekton*
skeptic	*skeptikos*
search	*zētō*
sense-perception	*aisthēsis*
sign	*sēmeion*
skill	*technē*
soul	*psuchē*
sound	*hugiēs*
species	*eidos*
specific instance	*eidos*

speech	*logos*
standard	*kanōn*
starting-point	*archē*
state	*schesis*
strike	*prospiptō*
subsist	*huphistēmi*
suspension of judgment	*epochē*
thing that appears	*phantaston*
thinking	*dianoia*
thought	*dianoia*
(what is) true	*(to) alēthes*
trustworthy	*pistos*
(the) truth	*(hē) alētheia*
turning about	*peritropē*
unbelievable	*apistos*
unclear	*adēlos*
undecided	*anepikritos*
underlie	*hupokeimai*
untrustworthy	*apistos*

2. Greek–English

adēlos	unclear
aisthēsis	sensation, sense, sense-perception
akatalēptos	inapprehensible, non-apprehensive
akolouthia	consistency, following
(hē) alētheia	(the) truth
(to) alēthes	(what is) true, (the) true (A/B: truths)
alogos	non-rational (A/B: irrational)
anairō	do away with (A/B: deny)
anepikritos	not judged upon, undecided (A/B: undecidable)
anthrōpos	human being
antikeimai	contradict (A/B: oppose)
antilēpsis	apprehension, grasping

anuparktos	non-existent (A/B: unreal)
anupostatos	non-subsistent (A/B: non-existent)
aphanēs	non-apparent
apistos	untrustworthy, unbelievable (A/B: unconvincing)
apodeixis	demonstration (A/B: proof)
apophasis	assertion
apophatikos	negative
aporia	impasse (A/B: impasse, puzzle)
aporos	intractable
archē	starting-point, principle
asunaktos	inconclusive
asōmatos	incorporeal
axiōma	proposition (A/B: statement)
deixis	demonstrative reference
di'allēlōn (tropos)	reciprocal (mode)
dianoia	thinking, thought (A/B: intellect, thought)
diaphōnō	disagree
diathesis	condition
diezeugmenon	disjunction
dogma	doctrine (A/B: belief)
dogmatikos	dogmatist
doxa	opinion
eidos	species, specific instance
eimi	be
enargeia	plain experience (A/B: evident impression)
endeiktikos	indicative
ennoia	conception (A/B: concept)
epinoia	conception (A/B: concept)
epiphora	consequence
epistēmē	knowledge
epochē	suspension of judgment
genikos	generic

gnōsis	knowledge (A/B: knowledge, recognition)
hēgemonikon	leading part (of the soul) (A/B: ruling part)
hēgoumenon	leader (i.e., antecedent of a conditional) (A/B: antecedent)
hormē	impulse
hugiēs	sound
huparchō	be real, be (so) (A/B: be real)
huphistēmi	subsist
hupokeimai	exist, underlie (A/B: exist)
hupomnēstikos	recollective
idiōma	peculiarity, property
isostheneia	equal strength (A/B: equipollence)
kanōn	standard, rule, ruler
katalēpsis	apprehension
kinēma	movement
kinēsis	motion (A/B: change, motion)
krinō	judge
kritērion	criterion (A/B: standard)
lambanō	grasp
lēgon	finisher (i.e., consequent of a conditional) (A/B: consequent)
lekton	sayable
lēmma	premise (A/B: assumption)
logos	reason, reasoning, argument, speech (A/B: account, argument)
mochthēros	bad (A/B: unsound)
noēsis	concept, intelligence
noētos	intelligible (A/B: object of thought)
nous	intellect

ousia	being (A/B: substance)
pathos	effect (on us) (A/B: feeling)
peritropē	turning about
phainomenon	apparent (thing)
phantasia	appearance
phantaston	thing that appears
phaulos	inferior (A/B: bad)
phronēsis	insight (A/B: intelligence)
pistos	reliable, trustworthy (A/B: convincing)
pithanos	persuasive (A/B: plausible)
prodēlos	clear
prolēpsis	preconception, prior notion
proslēpsis	minor premise (A/B: further assumption)
prospiptō	strike
pros ti	in relation to something (A/B: relative)
pseudos	false(hood)
psuchē	soul
schesis	state
sēmeion	sign
skeptikos	skeptic
skeptomai	inquire, look into
sugkatathesis	assent
sullogismos	deduction
sumbebēkos	attribute
sumpeplegmenon	conjunction (i.e., proposition of the form P & Q)
sumperasma	conclusion
sumphanēs	evident
sumplokē	conjunction (i.e., proposition of the form P & Q)
sunago, suneisago	conclude, draw (a conclusion), reach ([as] a conclusion), be conclusive

sunaktikos	conclusive, capable of concluding
sundesmos	conjunction (i.e., the part of speech)
sunēmmenon	conditional
sunetos	clever
sustasis	composition (A/B: compound, constitution)
technē	skill (A/B: expertise)
telos	end (A/B: aim)
tropos	mode, way, manner, method, process (A/B: mode, way)
tupōsis	imprinting
zētō	search, examine, investigate, seek, ask (A/B: inquire, investigate)

Parallels between *Against the Logicians* and other works of Sextus

Note: Few of these parallels involve any close verbal similarity. Rather, they are parallels at the level of subject-matter and approach, some closer and more detailed than others.

1.2–26	*PH* 2.12–13
1.29–30	*PH* 2.14
1.31–33	*PH* 2.15
1.34–37	*PH* 2.16
1.38–45	*PH* 2.81–83
1.47–54	*PH* 2.18
1.92–93	*M* 1.303
1.94	*M* 4.2–3
1.95–98	*M* 4.6–9, *PH* 3.155
1.99–100	*M* 4.4–5, *PH* 3.154
1.119–121	*M* 1.303
1.159–189	*PH* 1.226–228
1.263	*PH* 2.21–22, *PH* 2.47
1.264	*PH* 2.22
1.265–266	*PH* 2.23
1.267–268	*PH* 2.25
1.269	*PH* 2.26
1.281	*PH* 2.28
1.294–295	*PH* 2.29–30
1.299	*PH* 2.30
1.315–316	*PH* 2.34–36

1.325	*PH* 2.42
1.327–334	*PH* 2.43–44
1.343	*PH* 2.48
1.345–346	*PH* 2.51–52
1.349–350	*PH* 2.58
1.351	*PH* 2.59–60
1.354	*PH* 2.72
1.358	*PH* 2.74–75
1.371–373	*PH* 2.70
1.388–390	*PH* 2.76
2.3–10	*PH* 2.85
2.15–16	*PH* 2.85
2.17–31	*PH* 2.88–94
2.32–36	*PH* 2.86–87
2.58–60	*M* 9.393–395, *M* 11.250–251
2.76–77	*M* 1.157, *PH* 2.107–108
2.81–84	*PH* 2.109
2.113–117	*PH* 2.110–111
2.118–123	*PH* 2.113–114
2.135–136	*PH* 2.109
2.144–147	*PH* 2.97–98
2.148–155	*PH* 2.99–101
2.156–158	*PH* 2.102
2.159–160	*PH* 2.103
2.161	*M* 10.263
2.162	*M* 10.265
2.163–165	*PH* 2.117–120
2.174	*PH* 2.125
2.178	*PH* 2.124
2.179–181	*PH* 2.121–123
2.223–226	*PH* 2.157–158
2.244–253	*PH* 2.104–106
2.258–261	*M* 1.157, *PH* 2.107–108
2.265	*PH* 2.110–112
2.277–278	*PH* 2.131
2.279	*PH* 2.130
2.281–282	*PH* 2.131
2.298	*PH* 2.133

2.299–300	*PH* 2.134–135
2.301–302	*PH* 2.135–136
2.303–305	*PH* 2.137
2.305–306	*PH* 2.140
2.307–309	*PH* 2.141–142
2.310	*PH* 2.143
2.311	*PH* 2.139
2.313	*PH* 2.141
2.314	*PH* 2.143
2.316–320	*PH* 2.97–98
2.327–334	*PH* 2.180–181
2.345	*PH* 2.172
2.367–378	*M* 3.7–17
2.382–390	*PH* 2.171–176
2.391–395	*PH* 2.177–179
2.422–423	*PH* 2.140
2.426–428	*PH* 2.145
2.429–434	*PH* 2.146–150
2.435–437	*PH* 2.152–153
2.438	*PH* 2.156
2.440–442	*PH* 2.159–162
2.443	*PH* 2.166
2.444–445	*PH* 2.154
2.446	*PH* 2.155
2.451–452	*PH* 2.167–168
2.465–467	*PH* 2.185–186
2.473	*PH* 2.187
2.480	*PH* 2.188

Names referred to in *Against the Logicians*

This index includes all historical persons, and all philosophical schools –
except the (Pyrrhonist) skeptics themselves – referred to by name
in *Against the Logicians*, listed by book and section number. It does
not include fictional, mythical, or divine characters, nor place names.
References in parentheses (under Socrates and Plato) indicate names
used purely for exemplary purposes, designating any arbitrary human
being. Cities of origin are included with names in cases where there
might be confusion with others of the same name. For additional (but
still brief) descriptions of the figures and schools listed here, with
further bibliography, see S. Hornblower and A. Spawforth, eds. *The
Oxford Classical Dictionary* (Oxford University Press, 3rd edn., 1996) and
D. J. Zeyl, ed., *Encyclopedia of Classical Philosophy* (Greenwood Press,
1997).

Academics   1.169, 174, 179, 190, 201, 252, 331, 388, 401, 408, 412

   Members of the Academy, the school founded by Plato (in an area on
   the edge of Athens sacred to the hero Academus) and continuing as an
   institution until the early 1st century BCE.

Aenesidemus   1.345, 349, 350; 2.8, 40, 215, 216, 234

   Active early to mid-1st century BCE. Academic who broke away from
   the school to found the Pyrrhonist movement to which Sextus later
   belonged.

Alexander of Aetolia   2.204

Born ca. 315 BCE. Poet; author of *Phainomena*, a poem on constellations, but best known for tragedies.

Alexinus   1.13

Active late 4th to early 3rd century BCE. Belonged to the school of Eubulides; known for attacks on a variety of targets.

Anacharsis   1.48, 55

A largely legendary Scythian prince, to whom various writings were falsely attributed.

Anaxagoras   1.90, 91, 140

ca. 500–428 BCE. Cosmologist. Held a non-particulate theory of matter; postulated Mind as cosmic directing force.

Anaxarchus   1.48, 88

ca. 380–320 BCE. Teacher of Pyrrho; accompanied Alexander the Great to India.

Anaximander   1.5

Died soon after 547 BCE. Early cosmologist, said to have learned from Thales.

Anaximenes   1.5

Active ca. 545–525 BCE. Early cosmologist, learned from Anaximander.

Antiochus of Ascalon   1.162, 201, 202

ca. 130–ca. 68 BCE. Academic who left the school in the waning days of its skeptical period, founding a separate school billed as the "Old Academy" and claiming to represent the true Platonic legacy.

Antipater of Tarsus   2.443

ca. 200–ca. 130 BCE. Leading Stoic philosopher; defended Stoicism against attacks from Carneades.

Aratus   2.204

ca. 315–before 240 BCE. Poet of Stoic leanings; best known as author of *Phainomena*, a poem on astronomical and meteorological topics.

Arcesilaus   1.150, 153, 158, 159

316–241 BCE. Head of the Academy who initiated the school's skeptical turn.

Archelaus   1.14

5th century BCE. Cosmologist; also had ethical/anthropological interests.

Archilochus   1.128

7th century BCE. Lyric poet.

Ariston of Chios   1.12

Active mid-3rd century BCE. Unorthodox and extremist early Stoic.

Aristotle   1.6, 7, 216, 327, 328

384–322 BCE. Studied with Plato, but diverged from him philosophically in important ways. Generally considered (alongside Plato) one of the two greatest Greek philosophers.

Asclepiades   1.91, 202, 323, 380; 2.7, 188, 220

1st century BCE. Physician known for a corpuscular theory of the body.

Basilides   2.258

See Book 2, n. 82.

Bryson   1.13

Active early 4th century BCE. Attempted to square the circle; denied that obscenity was possible.

Carneades   1.159, 166, 173, 175, 184, 402

214–129 BCE. The most important head of the skeptical Academy after Arcesilaus.

Chares   1.107

Active ca. 300 BCE. Sculptor; famous for designing Colossus of Rhodes.

Chrysippus   1.229, 372, 373, 416, 433, 434; 2.223, 400, 443

ca. 280–ca. 208 BCE. The third head of the Stoic school and its foremost systematizer.

Cleanthes   1.228, 372, 433; 2.400

331–230 BCE. Student of Zeno of Citium and his successor as head of the Stoa.

Cyrenaics   1.11, 15, 190, 191, 200, 299

School founded by Aristippus of Cyrene (one of Socrates' associates); emphasized pleasure, denied the possibility of knowledge of external objects.

Demetrius of Laconia   2.348

ca. 150–75 BCE. Epicurean and exegete of Epicureanism.

Democritus   1.53, 116, 117, 118, 135, 140, 265, 321, 349, 369, 389; 2.6, 56, 62, 139, 184, 327, 355

ca. 460–ca. 360 BCE. Leading atomist philosopher; also had epistemo- logical and ethical views.

Dicaearchus   1.349

Active late 4th century BCE. Peripatetic philosopher, student of Aristotle.

Diodorus Cronus   2.115, 116, 117, 265, 333

Died ca. 284 BCE. Logician of great subtlety and versatility; teacher of Zeno of Citium.

Dionysodorus   1.13, 48, 64

See Euthydemus.

Diotimus   1.140

Dates unknown. Probably the Democritean philosopher mentioned by two other late sources.

Empedocles   1.5, 6, 115, 120, 122, 126; 2.286

ca. 492–432 BCE. Cosmologist with Pythagorean tendencies.

Empiricists   2.191, 204, 327

School of medicine founded in the late 3rd century BCE (but drawing on earlier tendencies); based their medical practice on experience rather than on theorizing.

Epicureans   1.22, 205, 267, 327, 331; 2.258, 336, 337, 348, 352

Philosophers in the tradition of Epicurus; persisted well into Roman imperial period.

Epicurus   1.14, 203, 211, 213, 216, 321, 328, 369; 2.8, 9, 13, 63, 65, 139, 177, 185, 329, 332, 335a, 336a, 355

341–270 BCE. Founder of Epicureanism, an atomist philosophy stressing the importance of *ataraxia*, freedom from worry.

Erasistratus   2.188, 220

ca. 315–240 BCE. Physician, known for a comprehensive physiological model centered on the workings of *pneuma* (breath).

Eubulides   1.13

Active mid-4th century BCE. Credited with invention of numerous paradoxes, including the Liar and the Sorites.

Euripides   1.128

ca. 485–406 BCE. The last of the three great tragedians; shows affinity for philosophical trends of his day.

Euthydemus   1.13, 64

Sophist, working in collaboration with his brother Dionysodorus; both presented by Plato as purveyors of devious and fallacious arguments.

Gorgias   1.48, 65, 77, 87

ca. 485–ca. 380 BCE. Theorist and practitioner of rhetoric, generally classified with the Sophists (cf. Protagoras).

Heraclitus   1.5, 7, 126, 129, 131, 135, 349; 2.286

Active ca. 500 BCE. Proposed a conception of the world as stable and unified within constant change.

Herophilus   2.188, 220

ca. 330–260 BCE. Physician, known for numerous anatomical discoveries.

Hippocrates   1.50

Contemporary of Socrates. Renowned but little-known physician, to whom many important medical writings were (in most if not all cases falsely) attributed.

Homer   1.128

8th century BCE.? Allegedly the author of the *Iliad*, *Odyssey*, and other epic poems.

Metrodorus of Chios   1.48, 88

Early 4th century BCE. Student of Democritus; atomist with extreme doubts about knowledge.

Monimus   1.48, 88; 2.5

4th century BCE. Cynic philosopher, often thought to have had skeptical tendencies.

Panthoides   1.13

Active ca. 299–265 BCE. Logician; diverged from Diodorus Cronus on necessity and possibility.

Parmenides   1.5, 7, 111, 112

Late 6th to mid-5th century BCE. Cast doubt on the senses and on cosmology through reasoning about the character of "what is."

Peripatetics   1.16, 216, 222, 226, 331, 369, 388; 2.185, 332, 352
Philosophers in the tradition of Aristotle; named after the "walkways" (*peripatoi*) in the region where they first congregated.

Philo   2.113, 115, 116, 117, 265
Active late 4th to early 3rd century BCE. Logician, student of Diodorus Cronus. (Not the same as Philo of Larissa or Philo of Alexandria.)

Philolaus   1.92
ca. 470–390 BCE. Pythagorean with mathematical and cosmological emphasis.

Plato   1.9, 10, 16, 93, 116, 119, 141, 145, 190, 200, (212), (215), 281, 321, 389; 2.6, 7, 56, 62, 91, 92
423–347 BCE. Learned from Socrates, but transcended him in philosophical breadth; author of philosophical dialogues and founder of the Academy.

Posidonius   1.19, 93
ca. 135–ca. 51 BCE. Stoic with innovative views in several areas.

Protagoras   1.48, 60, 65, 369, 388, 389
ca. 490–420 BCE. The earliest and most famous of the 5th-century Sophists.

Pythagoras   1.94
ca. 570–490 BCE. Founder of Pythagorean school or way of life, around whom many legends collected.

Pythagoreans   1.92, 94, 110
Philosophy claiming descent from Pythagoras and emphasizing (to varying degrees among different sub-groups) transmigration of souls, adherence to religious rituals, and mathematics as the key to cosmic understanding.

Socrates   1.8, 10, 21, (178), 190, (279), (358), (391); (2.59), (80), (81),
(93), (97), (100), (101), (102), (338), (339)

469–399 BCE. Ethical philosopher, executed by the Athenians; inspired
Plato and many others.

Sotion   1.15

Active ca. 200–170 BCE. Peripatetic author of a work classifying philosophers in "successions" within schools.

Speusippus   1.145

ca. 410–339 BCE. Plato's nephew and immediate successor as head of
the Academy.

Stoics   1.15, 16, 22, 38, 150, 151, 153, 155, 156, 214, 227, 233, 239, 241,
252, 253, 261, 327, 331, 369, 388, 401, 402, 408, 409, 422, 433,
434; 2.10, 11, 67, 68, 70, 75, 76, 77, 80, 87, 88, 177, 185, 258,
261, 336, 352, 355, 396, 399, 400, 406, 407, 408, 425, 428, 435,
443, 447

The leading Hellenistic philosophy; flourished well into the Roman
imperial period. Named after the *Stoa poikilē* (painted porch) in Athens,
where Zeno of Citium began teaching shortly before 300 BCE.

Strato   1.350; 2.13

Died ca. 268 BCE. The third head of the Peripatetic school, following
Theophrastus.

Thales   1.5, 89

Active in 585 BCE. Generally considered the first Greek scientific
thinker.

Theophrastus   1.216, 218

372 or 371–288 or 287 BCE. Peripatetic philosopher, colleague of Aristotle and his successor as head of the school.

Timon   1.8, 10, 30

ca. 320–230 BCE. Disciple and biographer of Pyrrho.

Xeniades   1.48, 53, 388, 399; 2.5

Dates unknown (but not later than Democritus); not mentioned except by Sextus.

Xenocrates   1.16, 147

396–314 BCE. The third head of the Academy.

Xenophanes   1.14, 48, 49, 53, 110; 2.326

Mid-6th to early 5th century BCE. Philosophical poet.

Xenophon   1.8

ca. 430–355 BCE or after. Author of several works on Socrates, also historical and other non-philosophical works.

Zeno of Citium   1.230, 236, 321, 331, 332, 422, 433; 2.139, 355

334–262 BCE. Founder of the Stoic school.

Zeno of Elea   1.7

Born ca. 490 BCE. Student of Parmenides; devised paradoxical arguments in support of Parmenides' conclusions.

Subject index

References give page number (not book and section number).

apparent items (*see also* plain items) xx,
  xxii, 12, 31, 34, 36, 39, 40–41, 70, 73,
  74, 78, 80, 81, 85, 91, 95, 100, 101,
  117, 119, 123–124, 126, 137, 144,
  146, 147, 150, 158, 160–162, 165,
  167
appearance 9, 14, 31, 34–39, 42–44,
  45–46, 47–52, 53, 68, 70, 73–87, 88,
  92, 99, 101–102, 142, 143, 146, 151,
  168–170
  apprehensive (*kataleptike*) (*see also*
  inapprehensibility) 33, 47, 50–52, 86, 106,
  167–168
  persuasive 14, 39, 79, 86–87
assent xx, 11, 33–34, 36, 39, 46, 48, 49, 50, 52,
  53, 63, 79, 80, 82–84, 88, 98, 113, 120, 149,
  153, 167–168, 182
assertion 62, 66, 77, 88, 93, 95, 100, 102, 136,
  144, 148, 150, 154, 161, 162, 174–175, 176,
  180

body 10, 16, 17, 21–22, 30, 43, 44, 47,
  48, 55, 57–60, 68–69, 101, 109, 119,
  150

conception 31, 46, 48, 53–57, 99–100, 130, 136,
  143, 146, 149–151, 152, 155–156, 165–166,
  178, 179
conclusion (*see also* consequence) 117,
  125, 132–136, 143–144, 147, 148, 149–151,
  158, 162, 170–172, 173,
  175–176
conclusive arguments 113–114, 149–151, 165,
  170–171, 172–173

conditional xvi, xvii, xxvi–xxvii, xxviii, 93,
  111–114, 131, 132–133, 134, 135, 137–139,
  141–142, 145, 147, 149, 154, 170–173, 175,
  176, 177–178, 180–181
conjunction (i.e., proposition of the form
  P & Q) 98, 114, 131, 133, 135, 143–144,
  170–172, 175
consequence (= conclusion) xvi, 101, 113, 131,
  132, 133, 134, 145, 149, 150–151, 154, 158,
  162, 163, 165–166, 172, 173, 174, 175, 177,
  181
contradiction 92, 105, 106–107, 120, 133, 135,
  145, 181, 182
criterion xiii–xiv, xvi–xvii, xviii, xxv, xxvii,
  7–89, 90, 93, 94, 117, 149, 164

definition xxv, 4, 47–49, 54, 84
demonstration xvi, xvii, xxv, 7, 62, 66–67, 78,
  93, 94, 100, 101, 103–104, 114, 117,
  124–125, 131–132, 135–140, 143–144, 146,
  148–183
dialecticians 107, 109, 111, 112, 113, 142
differences among Sextus' works x–xii, xix–xx,
  xxii, xxiv–xxx
  consequences for order of composition
  xxvii–xxx
disagreement xviii, 11, 53, 62, 63, 64, 65, 68,
  69, 73, 75, 85, 90–92, 112, 116, 124–126,
  130, 139, 141, 146, 148, 152–154, 160, 168,
  173
dogmatists xii, xiii, xiv, xvii–xviii, xxii, 3, 7, 8,
  9, 57, 60, 62, 63–64, 71, 73, 77, 88, 90, 94,
  98, 120–121, 122–123, 143, 145–146, 149,
  159, 161, 162, 178, 181, 182

CAMBRIDGE TEXTS IN THE HISTORY OF PHILOSOPHY

Malebranche *Dialogues on Metaphysics and on Religion* (edited by Nicholas Jolley and David Scott)

Malebranche *The Search after Truth* (edited by Thomas M. Lennon and Paul J. Olscamp)

Medieval Islamic Philosophy (edited by Muhammad Ali Khalidi)

Melanchthon *Orations on Philosophy and Education* (edited by Sachiko Kusukawa, translated by Christine Salazar)

Mendelssohn *Philosophical Writings* (edited by Daniel O. Dahlstrom)

Newton *Philosophical Writings* (edited by Andrew Janiak)

Nietzsche *Beyond Good and Evil* (edited by Rolf-Peter Horstmann and Judith Norman)

Nietzsche *The Birth of Tragedy and Other Writings* (edited by Raymond Geuss and Ronald Speirs)

Nietzsche *Daybreak* (edited by Maudemarie Clark and Brian Leiter, translated by R. J. Hollingdale)

Nietzsche *The Gay Science* (edited by Bernard Williams, translated by Josefine Nauckhoff)

Nietzsche *Human, All Too Human* (translated by R. J. Hollingdale with an introduction by Richard Schacht)

Nietzsche *Untimely Meditations* (edited by Daniel Breazeale, translated by R. J. Hollingdale)

Nietzsche *Writings from the Late Notebooks* (edited by Rüdiger Bittner, translated by Kate Sturge)

Novalis *Fichte Studies* (edited by Jane Kneller)

Schleiermacher *Hermeneutics and Criticism* (edited by Andrew Bowie)

Schleiermacher *Lectures on Philosophical Ethics* (edited by Robert Louden, translated by Louise Adey Huish)

Schleiermacher *On Religion: Speeches to its Cultured Despisers* (edited by Richard Crouter)

Schopenhauer *Prize Essay on the Freedom of the Will* (edited by Günter Zöller)

Sextus Empiricus *Against the Logicians* (edited by Richard Bett)

Sextus Empiricus *Outlines of Skepticism* (edited by Julia Annas and Jonathan Barnes)

Shaftesbury *Characteristics of Men, Manners, Opinions, Times* (edited by Lawrence Klein)

Adam Smith *The Theory of Moral Sentiments* (edited by Knud Haakonssen)